D0583440

Baseball's Greatest Season

ALSO BY REED BROWNING

Cy Young: A Baseball Life

The War of the Austrian Succession

*Political and Constitutional Ideas
of the Court Whigs*

The Duke of Newcastle

BASEBALL'S GREATEST SEASON

1924

Reed Browning

University of Massachusetts Press

AMHERST AND BOSTON

For Stan the Man —
A baseball fan beyond compare

Reed Browning
October 2003

Copyright © 2003 by University of Massachusetts Press
All rights reserved
Printed in the United States of America

LC 2002152986
ISBN 1-55849-406-5

Designed by Steve Dyer
Set in Bell Semibold by Graphic Composition, Inc.
Printed and bound by Maple-Vail Book Manufacturing Group

LIBRARY OF CONGRESS CATALOGING-IN-PUBLICATION DATA
Browning, Reed.
Baseball's greatest season, 1924 / Reed Browning.
p.   cm.
Includes bibliographical references and index.
ISBN 1-55849-406-5 (cloth : alk. paper)
1.   Baseball—United States—History—20th century.
2.   Washington Nationals (Baseball team)   I. Title.
GV863.A1 B775 2003
796.357′093′09042—dc21
2002152986

British Library Cataloguing in Publication data are available.

All photographs are from the Baseball Hall of Fame Library,
Cooperstown, N.Y., except where otherwise credited.

To Susan

"I repeat, Freddy, are we looking at the zenith of baseball?"

—Commissioner Landis
to Fred Lieb, October 10, 1924

CONTENTS

Illustrations follow page 100.

PREFACE

WHEN THE baseball season of 1923 ended, one question stood uppermost in the minds of observers of the game: What would it take to defeat a New York baseball team? For the third straight year John McGraw's Giants had faced Miller Huggins's Yankees in the World Series. Twice the Giants had won; most recently, the Yankees had prevailed. But in each case the other ten municipalities that hosted and boasted major league baseball clubs had been excluded from postseason play.

When the baseball season of 1924 ended, the question had been answered. The requirements for success surprised no fan: consistent pitching, dependable fielding, reliable hitting, and a measure of timely luck. But the team that displayed these marks was a surprise to virtually everyone. This book tells the story of how, for one memorable and dramatic season, to the admiring excitement of baseball fans across the country, Washington was first in war, first in peace, and first in the national pastime.

Like most people who write about baseball, I have been a fan since childhood. My earliest baseball memory involves looking through a guide prepared for the 1946 season. This present book thus reflects a lifetime of interest. One long-standing aspect of that interest is the belief that there ought to be a written history of each major league season—a book, that is, to which the curious fan might turn to find out how the pennant races that year evolved, why the winners won and the losers didn't, who the outstanding performers of the season were, and what remarkable events made the season memorable. Fortunately, we have some fine representatives of this kind of history. David Anderson's *More Than Merkle*, Frederick Turner's *When the Boys Came Back*, and David Kaiser's *Epic Season* come to mind, along with Mike Sowell's *The Pitch That Killed* and Lawrence Katz's *Baseball in 1939*. But the large majority of seasons remain as yet uncharted. Happily for me, among the campaigns thus far neglected is the remarkable season of 1924. By the time readers finish this book, I hope they agree with me that it was the most exciting season that major league baseball has ever managed to stage.

(All right. I admit it. In *More Than Merkle*, David Anderson makes exactly the same claim for 1908: "the most exciting baseball season in human history"—in fact, it's part of the book's subtitle. If we were concerned only with the pennant races, his assertion would have merit. But after the Cubs and the Tigers clawed their way to the top of their leagues in the closing hours of the remarkable 1908 pennant chases, they contended in a World Series that was dismally anticlimactic, as Chicago's great pitching staff held Detroit hitters to a paltry .203 batting average and lost only once in 5 games against the Tigers. For a season to be the greatest ever, it must be exciting across its stretch and exciting to the end. And that's the treat that 1924 offers.)

Consider the following points. The 1924 season saw the Washington Nationals win their first pennant and only world championship. (A quick note on usage is in order. Though "Senators" had once been and would later again be the club's name, in 1924 they were the "Nationals," and that's the way the D.C. press identified them.) The tightness of the two pennant races throughout the crucial month of September stamps the regular season as one of the four most exciting (in the sense of offering tight races) in baseball history. The subsequent World Series not only went to its seventh game, but then that final game went into extra innings. By a curious juxtaposition of events, the 1924 World Series came to be seen by many fans as a morality play, pitting good (the Washington Nationals) against evil (the New York Giants). And as an analysis of the styles of play indicates, the 1924 World Series was also a confrontation—and in fact the last confrontation—of the older principles of low-scoring "inside baseball" (exemplified by the Nats) against the newer principles of high-scoring "big inning baseball" (exemplified by the Giants). Beyond the team efforts, the season featured some epic individual achievements, both by batters (especially Babe Ruth and Rogers Hornsby) and by pitchers (especially Walter Johnson and Dazzy Vance). It even offered elements of athletic tragedy (Grover Cleveland Alexander and George Sisler). It is a season that calls out for its recorder. With this book I hope to do it justice.

This book represents other intellectual engagements as well. Structurally it is an effort to weave together two strands of baseball studies that all too often exist almost independently of one another. The first strand is represented by yarn-spinners, chroniclers, and most sportswriters. Whether considering a career, a decade, a season, or a single game, they view baseball as an unfolding tale: They provide narratives, commentaries, and reminiscences. Their writings feature heroes and goats, dramatic turns, extraordinary feats, and examples of athletic triumph and tragedy. Their descriptions capture evanescent moments; their analyses reveal unexpected ligatures. The second strand is represented by stats buffs, number-gatherers, and the whole clan of sabermetricians (a wonderful neologism evolved from SABR, the acronym by which the Society for American Baseball Research is usually known). They dissect baseball into its component activities; they seek ways to quantify the outcomes of these activities; and they assess the relative values of various kinds of statistical calculations. When their writings are studded with mathematical formulas, they may offend the eyes and perplex the understanding of the more traditional fans. But their work is important, for when it clicks, it reveals both the enduring consistencies and the subtle long-term changes that have marked the game, it allows cross-generational comparisons, and it provides correctives for overhasty judgments based on anecdotes or press releases.

To the task of combining these two strands I bring the training of a fairly traditional historian. By "fairly traditional" I mean that, from among the historian's various charges, I give primacy of place to getting my information straight and to arranging that information into a coherent story. With respect to accuracy, I can only say that I am dismayed at how much misinformation passes for truth in popularized baseball history; I have tried hard to avoid factual errors, and I expect to be held to that standard by my readers. With respect to arranging my information, I interpret my duty to be the telling of a good story, but I recognize that such a narrative is likely to have a number of structural foundations that can and (for the purposes of the story) should be presented as independent entities. My plan for the book is therefore to divide it into alternating chapters of narrative (the even-numbered ones) and analysis or description (the odd-numbered ones). The odd-numbered chapters treat such topics as the business of baseball in the 1920s, the life of a major league player in the 1920s, and the character of the game in the 1920s. The even-numbered ones tell the story of the greatest season in major league history.

Five introductory points are in order, to get the reader oriented. First, there were only sixteen major league teams in 1924, eight in each league. As a consequence, there were no divisions and no postseason qualifying rounds. Each league produced a winner; these winners fought it out with each other; the victor of this World Series was regarded as the championship team of baseball. Second, organized baseball was a segregated activity, and therefore not a single player of (known) African American descent held a position on a roster. Third, since there are sometimes discrepancies among the published sources of statistical information about the careers of players, it has been necessary to choose a reference of last resort. For me—whether in verifying standard statistics or as a source of data for making my own calculations—the seventh (2001) edition of *Total Baseball* has usually served that function. Fourth, there are a handful of notes to the text, which are not necessary to an enjoyable reading of the book but which contain additional information that readers may be pleased to have access to. Fifth, I have quoted freely, and therefore insert this notice up front: The words ascribed to players and managers in the writings of the 1920s were sometimes ghost-scripted and, even when the core was authentic, were often bowdlerized or in other ways altered to conform to what some editor believed the sensibilities of the public would tolerate. *Caveat lector.*

By 1924, Americans no longer felt that they were living in a postwar era. Instead of the material shortages of the wartime years, the United States was enjoying an affluence unparalleled in the history of the republic. The repudiation of the experiments of the first two decades of the twentieth century—of the efforts, that is, to tame the influence of wealth and to make the wider world safe for democratic values—was virtually complete. Hence, the United States now basked in a sense of American exceptionalism. Republican dominance in presidential elections signaled the electorate's longing for a return to less turbulent days, when a wayward world could not disrupt American life. A presidential election loomed on the November horizon, and most observers expected the electorate to signal its approval of Republican policies by returning the recently elevated Calvin Coolidge to the White House.

This national longing for simpler, earlier days can be detected in the ongoing legitimization of racism, in the creation of novel hurdles to immigration, and in the legislative experiment with the prohibition of the consumption of alcoholic beverages. But even so, the relentless forces of technology and democracy were producing vast changes across the country. An electrification program was altering the rhythms and habits of domestic life, radio broadcasting was making music and news available to millions, and the automobile was transforming patterns of residence and leisure. Meanwhile, the enfranchisement of women and the emergence of an identifiable youth culture were beginning to place their mark upon the country. The United States, in short, was (as always) a country of contradictions. Above all else, however, the mood of the nation in 1924 was a product of its palpable prosperity. And for millions of Americans in 1924, whether sharing in the prosperity or not, baseball was a central element in this happy American way of life.

Anyone who writes about baseball must make a conscious decision about tone. Charles Fountain in *Sportswriter* underlines the importance of tone when he asks us to speculate on the consequences for our understanding of the 1920s if Damon Runyan and Ring Lardner had not abandoned sportswriting—that is, if Runyan's irreverence or Lardner's cynicism had challenged Grantland Rice's compassionate optimism as our lens for the age. As readers familiar with the literature about baseball know, writings about the game range in tone from the gee-whiz school to the hard-ass school. Along the spectrum of styles, one will find the heroic, the mock-heroic, the brash, the chatty, the swashbuckling, the nostalgic, the mawkish, the revelatory, the apocalyptic, the muckraking, and the inspirational. And one will find writers who see baseball as—to cite common examples—a metaphor for life, an icon of American exceptionalism, or a training ground for character. As I have remarked elsewhere, writing about sports is the last haven for the extravagant trope. I want only to say that what I've tried to employ in this book is something I'd call the "dispassionate" style, and what I've tried to avoid is the conceit that baseball represents something bigger than itself.

In writing this book I have benefited from the good work of the staff of the National Baseball Hall of Fame and Museum, the assistance of Cindy Wallace and Carol Marshall of the Olin Library at Kenyon College, the generosity of the microfilm lending library operated by the Society for American Baseball Research, the generosity of Tom Simon (who gave me access to his collection of 1924 press clippings), the encouragement of bemused friends, and the strong support of my wife Susan, my son Stephen, and my daughter-in-law Sara. I thank them all and hope they will enjoy the final result.

Baseball's Greatest Season

Waiting for the Cry,
"Play Ball!"

Spring Training

IN FEBRUARY 1924, sixteen major league baseball teams began gathering at sites stretching across the southern United States from Florida to California. They were launching the eight-week exercise called spring training. The tradition of assembling players in warm climes—whether for drying out, honing skills, or raising money—had begun in the nineteenth century, and its conventions had changed very little since then. The southerly migration officially involved seven hundred to eight hundred people, although unofficial contingents of camp followers swelled these ranks by an indeterminate amount. Among the formal participants were the players themselves, both veterans and aspiring rookies, numbering more than five hundred; the corps of team officials for each club (at least a manager, a club secretary, some coaches, and a trainer); the umpires; and a battery of approximately a hundred sportswriters. Conditions were austere. Players suited up in their hotels and clattered down dusty roads in their spiked shoes to their playing fields. The ballparks themselves were often primitive, scarred by holes, dunes, ridges, or gullies. Since veterans usually viewed newcomers as predators bent on snatching their jobs, they were disinclined to be of assistance to the youngsters and could sometimes be actively discouraging. Only one custom of the era, however, strikes the reader of today as genuinely foreign: Many players chose to ease their annual readjustment to the athletic life of spring by spending time beforehand at Hot Springs, Arkansas, where they could use baths, hiking trails, and recreational facilities to limber up creaky limbs in the company of old pals.[1]

After several weeks of conditioning, drilling, and engagement in what Frederick Lieb called the "horseplay and crude humor of the training camp," teams began playing each other in exhibition games.[2] These contests were an important element in the economics of spring training, for if one purpose of the annual exercise was to give managers a chance to assess talent, another was to make money by selling the spectacle of major league baseball to sections of the country that otherwise never witnessed these games. These contests were often surprisingly informal. One spring day in 1924, for example, when the Giants played the White Sox, no one apparently cared that the scoreboard was miscounting the runs.

Though relatively casual, spring training provided a basis for managers, players, and sportswriters to begin to measure the comparative quality of the various major league teams. In making these annual assessments, the writers had a hallowed duty, for by linking their preseason impressions with their knowledge of what the teams and individual players had done in recent years, they could offer speculation about the upcoming pennant races. This rite of forecasting was a central element in the annual focusing of wider national attention on the question that was paramount for most fans: Which was the best team in baseball?

The New York Giants: The Pick of the National League

As spring training in 1924 moved to its conclusion, most observers of the National League picked the New York Giants to become the first major league team of the twentieth century to win four consecutive pennants. After all, in 1923 they had been the first major league team ever to hold first place from opening day on, and in May 1923 the New York sportswriter Joe Vila had called them "the most powerful baseball team ever put together."[3] Many felt that the Giants' failure in the 1923 World Series had been a fluke. Their infield for 1924 promised to be the best in baseball, featuring the powerful George Kelly (.307 in 1923, with 16 home runs) at first base, the switch-hitting Frank Frisch (.348, with a league-leading 223 hits) at second, the rookie Travis Jackson at shortstop, and the iron-chested Heinie Groh (.290) at third base.[4] Two strong outfielders were also assured of regular assignments: John McGraw's favorite player, Ross Youngs (.336), and Irish Meusel (a league-leading 125 runs batted in). Catching responsibilities would be shared by two men whose major league careers stretched back to pre–World War I days: Frank Snyder (only .256 in 1923, but .332 during 1921–22), and Hank Gowdy (.328 during the portion of 1923 he had spent with New York). Plainly this was a difficult lineup to break into. And yet, in addition to Travis Jackson, McGraw had three other youngsters coming along who might be able to accomplish precisely that feat. There was the hard-hitting Bill Terry, who had distinguished himself by batting .377 at Toledo in 1923. There was the powerful Lewis Wilson (soon to become known as "Hack"), "built close to the ground," Joe Williams said, "like a toadstool."[5] And there was the sharp-fielding Fred Lindstrom, who at eighteen years of age was the youngest player on a major league roster in 1924.

Only on the mound were the pennant winners suspect—and even here the weaknesses were scarcely glaring. Though no hurler had won more than 16 games in 1923, five had won at least 13, and four of these five were back. Art Nehf was past his peak but still, at age thirty-one, useful in clutch games. Jack Bentley, who boasted the most contorted and distracting windup in baseball, was coming off his first good major league season. Hugh McQuillan, though a souse, had led the staff with 15 complete games. Rosy Ryan, pitching both as a starter and a reliever, had posted the team's best winning percentage (16–5, for .762). These pitchers were backed up by the one-eyed Claude Jonnard, whose 45 appearances had led the league in 1923.[6] It was McGraw's readiness to turn to Ryan and Jonnard that made the figure of only 62 complete games in 1923—third lowest in the majors and lowest ever for a championship team—relatively untroubling.

All these capabilities no doubt made the Giants formidable enough as they stood. But the team had yet another weapon—John McGraw, the most respected manager in baseball. McGraw had learned the game in the school of "inside baseball" or "scientific baseball" as a teammate of William Keeler and Hugh Jennings on the great Oriole teams of the 1890s.[7] Famed as a stern disciplinarian with a remarkable memory for the strengths and weaknesses of opposing players, McGraw was also a celebrated motivator of men and, despite reports to the contrary, a flexible tactician. He drilled his players in fundamentals, assessed unproven talent well, paid large sums of the owner's money to acquire promising youngsters, and kept track of his players during their after-hours wanderings. To umpires he was a scourge: "McGraw," said Arlie Latham during his arbitratorial career, "eats gunpowder every morning and washes it down with warm blood."[8] For all of these reasons, McGraw boasted an unparalleled record of managerial success. Since assuming the field reins of the Giants part way through the 1902 season, he had led his team to 9 National League pennants and 3 World Series victories. Three times in that twenty-two-year span he had constructed championship teams virtually from scratch, and his current juggernaut was widely acclaimed as the best of them all. Not surprisingly, then, he shared the general belief that the Giants would win a fourth consecutive pennant, and when asked as the team headed north who would pitch the first game of the World Series, he eschewed mealymouthed sports-babble to reply: "Nehf, I suppose. He generally does."[9]

Forecasting the Rest of the National League

But observers knew that nothing was certain in baseball. And so, if injuries, complacency, or simple bad luck should contrive to give John McGraw's charges a disappointing season, the team deemed likeliest to supplant them atop the National League was the Cincinnati Reds. They were a seasoned club, with the highest median age of any team in baseball. And in Edd Roush they boasted the second-best offensive player in the league. Swinging a remarkably heavy bat, Roush was machinelike in his seasonal consistency (.352 in 1921, .352 in 1922, .351 in 1923). In the three-year period 1917 through 1919, he had been the best hitter in the National League, with two batting championships to his credit, a league-leading batting average for the period of .332, and a league-leading 404 runs produced during those years. After Rogers Hornsby caught fire in 1920, Roush yielded first place to the Cardinal second baseman. But his .347 average for the 1920 through 1923 period was second-highest in the league. Even without a bat in his hand, he was magnificent: John McGraw said that he patrolled center field "with the regal indifference of an alley cat," and Heinie Groh added that he was "far and away the best outfielder I ever saw."[10] Other strengths in the Cincinnati batting order were the veteran first baseman Jake Daubert, a great bunter, who, like Roush, was a two-time league batting champion, and outfielder Silent George Burns, who had led the league in bases on balls in 1923.

Most important of all for a team that aspired to a championship, the Reds possessed the strongest group of "boxmen"—a 1920s term for pitchers—in the league. At the heart of this mound staff was Dolf Luque, baseball's first great Latin player. A light-skinned Cuban—hence able to pass baseball's carefully policed color barrier—the durable Luque had posted a 27–8 record in 1923 and compiled a remarkable earned run average of 1.93.[11] With good control and a sharp, dropping curve, he had pitched 322 innings and completed 28 games while giving up only 2 home runs. Behind Luque in 1923 were two other 20-game winners: Eppa Rixey and Pete Donohue. At the age of thirty-three, the tall and brainy Rixey was a shrewd veteran—a "manipulator" on the mound in teammate Rube Bressler's apt characterization.[12] With speed and control, he established the mark that still stands for allowing the fewest home runs per innings pitched of any post-1920 hurler.[13] Donohue, on the other hand, was a youngster, just coming into his own; his promise appeared immense. And if this trio did not supply enough mound power, the Reds had acquired the four-time 20-game winner Carl Mays during the off-season. Mays was notorious as the hurler whose pitch had killed Ray Chapman in 1920, and his former manager, Miller Huggins, dispatched the submarine pitcher to the Reds with an admonition: "I may be sending you the best pitcher I have, but I warn you that Carl is a troublemaker."[14] Manager Pat Moran's comment, however, was tersely apt: "I have an idea that Mays will win ball games for us."[15]

Unfortunately, Pat Moran was not around to learn how prescient his remark was, for in a stunning blow to his team, he died suddenly on March 7. Moran had led the Reds through five seasons, once winning the pennant and World Series (the famous 1919 series against the Black Sox) and twice finishing in second place. It was an enviable record. His death was a genuine shock to the group of young ballplayers in training camp, many of whom still privately believed that athletic youth was blessed with immortality. Jack Hendricks was appointed to replace Moran, but since he had just arrived as a new coach, he knew little about his charges. Still, Carl Mays predicted a Reds–Yankees World Series (adding that he could handle Babe Ruth), and Dolf Luque was quoted as saying: "Give us any break in the luck of the game, and we ought to come through."[16]

The other team given a real chance for the pennant was the Pittsburgh Pirates, managed by Bill McKechnie. Like the Reds, the Pirates had a talented pitching corps. Johnny Morrison, on the strength of his sharp curve, had enjoyed his best season ever in 1923 (25–13), and

Wilbur Cooper, though he had won only 17 games, was nevertheless a fearsome hurler, having earned 86 victories in the 1920s thus far. For the infield, the Pirates boasted third baseman Pie Traynor, who had come of age as a hitter in 1923 with a .338 batting average, and first baseman Charlie Grimm, who while batting .345 in 1923 had also won a reputation as the best in baseball at initiating a 3–6–3 double play. In the outfield, the Pirates had the fleet Max Carey, who had eight base-stealing titles to his credit and stood only 20 hits shy of becoming the first switch-hitter in the history of the game to collect 2,000 base hits in his career.

But what made the Pirates' prospects particularly tantalizing was the roster of rookies they were preparing to deploy. In Glenn Wright, they had a big shortstop who in 1923 had batted .313 and hit 15 home runs in the American Association. In Ray Kremer, a thirty-year-old right-handed pitcher, they had a hurler who had amassed 25 victories in the Pacific Coast League. Even more promising was Emil Yde (EE-dy), a twenty-four-year-old left-handed pitcher, whose jerky underhanded style had befuddled batters in the Western League. Above all, there was Kiki Cuyler, who, at twenty-four, seemed primed for the majors after batting .340 in the Southern Association.[17] This quartet made the future of the Pirates look bright, and with a measure of luck, that bright future might also be a prompt future.

The Chicago Cubs were deemed to have enough talent to hold their own in the middle of the pack. In Grover Cleveland Alexander, a 22-game winner in 1923, they had one of the game's most gifted pitchers. At the age of thirty-seven, he was past his prime and disguising his epilepsy with alcohol, but he still possessed the best control and the widest array of pitches of any hurler in the league. The Cubs also had un-rivaled depth behind the plate, with veteran Bob O'Farrell backed up by the youngster Gabby Hartnett. The big question for the Cubs was the health of shortstop Charlie Hollocher. A .340 hitter in 1922, Hollocher had left the Cubs part way through the 1923 season, disabled by a mys-terious stomach ailment. After the Cubs had spent thousands to support his return to health (tests never identified his problem), he quarreled with them about back pay that he believed was coming to him for his in-complete season. He was thus at odds with the team, and whether he would play in 1924 was unresolved when spring training ended.[18] The

Cub manager was Bill Killefer, a former catcher who believed that aggressive baserunning was a central ingredient in a team's success.

The St. Louis Cardinals were likely to be fun to watch, for, in Rogers Hornsby, they had the National League's most famous embodiment of the game's new slugging style. Hornsby was the circuit's best player, the winner of every league batting title since 1920. He also hit with power, having won the home run title in 1922 with 42. Although he was only twenty-eight, most observers were prepared to adjudge him the greatest right-handed hitter in the history of the game. And he intended to improve on that reputation, declaring shortly before spring training, "I want to have the best year in baseball I have ever had."[19] Thoughtful about his batting, Hornsby stood tall at the back of the batter's box, strode into the pitch with a level swing, and lashed out line drives and stinging grounders in all directions. Contemporaries held him in awe. Ty Cobb called him the greatest hitter he had ever seen, Branch Rickey doubted that he had ever had a slump, and he was the only batter in the league who regularly attracted a knot of curious ball-playing observers during batting practice. Hornsby was a single-minded man who lived only for baseball (and horse racing), and his candor alienated most who came in contact with him. He was, said Burleigh Grimes, "blunt as hell, but he never gave you any bullshit."[20] He would proudly have accepted those words as his epitaph.

Hornsby's supporting cast at St. Louis was not distinguished, but young Jim Bottomley was a first baseman who had never failed to hit .300 in the majors, and Jesse Haines was an improving veteran pitcher coming off his first 20-victory season. The manager of the Cardinals was Branch Rickey. A devout and crafty Christian, Rickey refused to manage on Sundays, leaving his charges to the Sabbath guidance of Burt Shotton. Although he was a repository of baseball knowledge, he had not proved to be a successful manager, and people were beginning to suspect that he was, in Hornsby's words, "too smart . . . for the ballplayers. He talked over their heads."[21] The Cardinals were a long shot in contention for the pennant in 1924, but they promised to keep things interesting for the fans.

Two teams even less likely to offer a pennant challenge were the Boston Braves and the Philadelphia Phillies. During the winter the Braves had acquired the smooth-fielding Dave Bancroft from the Giants to serve as shortstop and manager. He inherited, however, a difficult assignment. The team's strongest hitter in 1923, Billy Southworth, had been traded away; its third baseman Tony Boeckel, team leader in home runs, had been killed by an automobile during the off-season; its catcher Earl Smith was notoriously undisciplined—"a goddammed anarchist" in John McGraw's pithy formulation;[22] and the only addition to its strength was another famous free spirit, Casey Stengel. The team's owner, Judge Emil Fuchs, claimed that "the Braves of 1924 will be fighting it out . . . for the highest honors of the game,"[23] but few observers held this remark to be anything more than the blather of an owner trying to sell tickets. The Phillies' situation was no better. Art Fletcher was a good manager, but he had only one genuinely talented batter on the entire team, Cy Williams. A dead-pull hitter, Williams's skills were tailor-made for the shrunken dimensions of Baker Bowl. He was coming off an extraordinary season in which he tied Babe Ruth for the major league lead in home runs with 41–and in considerably fewer games. The Phillies also had, in Jimmy Ring, a single talented pitcher. But behind Ring the staff was so thin that the team's earned run average in 1923 had been the worst in the majors and a full run above the next highest. "McGraw says it is hard to manage a ball club in the lead," Fletcher chuckled, but "I would like to trade jobs with him."[24] Nevertheless, Fletcher predicted at least a fifth-place finish for his team.

Finally there were the puzzling Brooklyn Dodgers—also widely called the "Robins" (after manager Wilbert Robinson) or the "Superbas" (once their official name). The Dodgers had finished a miserable sixth in 1923, despite having two of the ablest pitchers and two of the sharpest batters in the league. The hurlers were Burleigh Grimes and Dazzy Vance. While winning 21 games, the wily Grimes, one of the seventeen major league pitchers permitted to continue using the spitball after its banning in 1920, had led the National League in complete games and innings pitched. Though a frequent preseason holdout, he was always ready when the season opened.[25] The speedballing Vance, who did not win his first major league game until he was thirty-one years old, had given the Dodgers 18 further victories and led the league in strikeouts. The two hitters were Zack Wheat and Jack Fournier. Though injured for part of the 1923 season, Wheat had still batted .375 to reinforce his claim as the most popular Dodger with the fans. And Fournier had complemented Wheat's success, batting .351 and, with his 22 home runs, trailing (though by a significant distance) only Cy Williams for the league lead.

To account for the Dodgers' failure to present a challenge for the pennant despite their strengths at the plate and on the mound, most observers looked first to their defensive work. Not only had the Dodgers turned the lowest number of double plays in the National League in 1923 and committed 61 more errors than any other team in baseball, they were reputed to have the slowest infield in the game. But there was another possible source of difficulty—the manager himself. Though nursed on the same Baltimore brew that had inflamed John McGraw, Wilbert Robinson was a far less driven, less irascible, and—to be blunt—less intelligent manager than McGraw. When the Dodgers performed poorly in spring training in 1924, he was quoted as saying, "There is no need to worry. . . . I'm certain that when the season begins, we will be in there."[26] His casual attitude toward discipline was legendary. When asked how Robinson handled players, Grimes later commented: "Well, I think they handled him more than he handled them."[27] Robinson himself knew very well what people thought of him and laughed it off. He could claim the respectable record of two pennants over his decade of managing. His philosophy was simple and succinct: "Give me pitchin' and some stren'th at the plate and let the other guy be smart."[28]

The New York Yankees: The Pick of the American League

When writers turned their attention to the imminent American League race, they identified a wider field of authentic contenders, but they gave the inside track to Miller Huggins's New York Yankees. The only doubt that arose about them was that, although virtually intact from their world championship season of 1923, they had not taken significant steps to strengthen themselves through trades. Still, even standing pat, they were impressively formidable. They boasted what almost all observers saw as the richest pitching depth of any contender—five hurlers with at least 16 victories and the lowest team earned run average in the league in 1923. Sam Jones had used patience and control to win 21 games. Herb Pennock, the only southpaw on the staff, had won 19 on the strength of excellent control and his sharp-dropping curve. Joe Bush, an early exponent of the forkball, had capitalized on a reputation for wildness to keep batters nervous and to win another 19. The roistering Waite Hoyt had experimented with a three-fingered pitch and was rewarded with 17 victories and the team's lowest earned run average. Curve-balling Bob Shawkey had rounded out the starting staff with 16 wins. The fact that all five had played for the penurious Red Sox or Athletics before coming to the Yankees only underscored the fear among observers of the game that rich teams were increasingly able to buy perpetual success.

The lineup of daily players was marked by strength, too. In the field the 1923 Yankees had been the only major league team to average less than one error a game. First base was patrolled by the veteran Wally Pipp, Aaron Ward was at second, the shortstop was the durable Everett Scott, and Joe Dugan handled third. In Bob Meusel, the left fielder (and brother of the Giants' Irish Meusel), the Yankees had the most powerful outfield arm in baseball, and in Whitey Witt, the center fielder, they had a .314 hitter who had gotten on base almost 40 percent of his times at bat in 1923. Should Witt turn out to be losing a step or two to age, the Yankees also had rookie Earle Combs, who had batted .380 for Louisville in 1923.

But so far I have been describing *Othello* without the Moor. For, in addition to all of the foregoing strengths, the Yankees had the greatest player in baseball, Babe Ruth. Bouncing back from his difficulties of 1922 to play in every game of the 1923 season, Ruth had arguably had his greatest year yet, winning the League Award as the most valuable player in the circuit.[29] Certainly his batting average reached a new height (.393–second-best in the league), and his home run total (41), while lower than in the days when all alone he hit more home runs than any *team* in the league but his own, still exceeded the total of his closest rival by 12. He and Tris Speaker tied for the runs batted in championship with 130. But it is in the less flashy statistics that one finds the most striking evidence of Ruth's dominance. He had been walked 170 times in 1923, a figure that stood unequaled until the twenty-first century.[30] When these 170 passes are added to his 205 base hits, it works out that Ruth had reached base on 55 percent of his plate appearances during the season. And then, in October, he had begun amassing his remarkable list of postseason exploits by becoming the first player in history to hit 3 home runs in a World Series. During spring training in 1924, Ruth declared that he had two personal goals for the coming season: to win a batting championship and to hit 60 home runs.[31] The first goal shows that Ruth bought into the conventional wisdom of the day, now deemed somewhat suspect, which held that the clearest indicator of batting primacy was winning a batting championship. The second goal—an eerie prefiguring of what he would finally do in 1927—shows that he was rankled that his vault to fame had stopped with 59 home runs in 1921. Contemplating the genuine plausibility of Ruth's fulfilling these prospects, Jacob Ruppert, the owner of the Yankees, predicted that "our boys will win their fourth straight pennant as sure as the sun rises and sets."[32]

Forecasting Other American League Teams

The Yankees were not viewed as invulnerable, however, with most observers concurring with American League President Ban Johnson's judgment that "the days of top-heavy pennant races in the American League are over."[33] Foremost among the Yankees' challengers was the Detroit Tigers, managed from center field by the still formidable Ty Cobb, who was coming into the 1924 season with a lifetime batting average of .371 and who, as recently as 1922, had batted .401. The Tigers had improved each year since Cobb had assumed managerial responsibility in 1921. No detail was too small for the man who, in Eddie Collins's words, "saw, decided, and acted all at once."[34] The Tigers' batting strength extended beyond Cobb. The American League batting champion in 1923 had been Cobb's greatest pupil, Harry Heilmann. Chopping at pitches from a right-handed crouch, Heilmann had won his second batting championship in 1923 with a .403 average.[35] Then there was Heinie Manush, probably (on the basis of his .334 batting average) the best American League rookie in 1923. The Tigers were so deep in hitting strength among outfielders that Bobby Veach, a .321 hitter, had been traded away, and Fats Fothergill, who could have broken into almost any other outfield in the league, had frequently sat on the bench despite a .318 batting average since coming up to the Tigers in 1922. Waite Hoyt spoke for many pitchers when he said, with the engaging hyperbole that makes sports-speak so enjoyable, that hurling against the Tigers was "murder. You'd go into Detroit for a series in August and find that the entire Tiger outfield was hitting .400."[36] Even though the Tiger infield was only average and the team's pitching mediocre at best, Cobb harbored hopes: "As it is right now," he told a sportswriter during the off-season, "both New York teams are unbeatable. [But] if the Yanks are beaten out," he added, "I believe we are the club that should pass them."[37] The coming season would be Cobb's twentieth in the majors, and he said during the spring that he might retire when it was over: How sweet it would be to go out with a bang!

The Cleveland Indians figured to be another challenger of New York's ambitions. Under the leadership of player–manager Tris Speaker, the Indians in 1923 had posted the highest team batting average (.301) in the league and featured, in George Uhle, the league's best pitcher. Uhle's performance in 1923 had been, in some ways, even more remarkable than Dolf Luque's. On the strength of a quick curve ball, the laconic pitcher had led the American League in victories with 26, in innings pitched with 357⅔, and in complete games with 29. Including starts, relief efforts, and pinch-hitting assignments (he batted .361), he had appeared in more than one-third of the Indian games. Not surprisingly nicknamed "the Bull," Uhle had been improving for three consecutive years, and Speaker had great confidence in him.[38] The team's other stars were Speaker himself, a .380 hitter at the age of thirty-five, and the remarkable Joe Sewell, the shortstop who in 1923 had batted .353 and struck out only 12 times.[39] To help his team turn potential into reality, Speaker was one of the few managers to use the Hot Springs conclave to organize formal training for his players.

Of all the teams in the league, the St. Louis Browns presented forecasters with their most perplexing task. In 1922 the Browns had challenged the Yankees throughout the season, missing the championship by the margin of only 1 game. Led in that memorable year by George Sisler, who had won the batting championship with a .420 average, the highest in the American League since Napoleon Lajoie's .426 in its first year of existence,[40] the Browns had posted a remarkable team average of .313. Sisler had received the League Award. But then the nationally popular Sisler had contracted a sinus infection that blurred his vision; he had sat out the entire 1923 season while recuperating, and the Browns had slipped to fifth place while attendance plummeted. The Browns had still had some thunder in their lineup, especially Ken Williams, who had batted .357 and hit 29 home runs. They also had had a good pitching staff, featuring Urban Shocker, a quarrelsome man whose injury-bent finger created a curve ball that had led him to four consecutive 20-victory seasons. But the 1923 season had shown that, without Sisler, the Browns were only an average team.

George Sisler was returning in 1924, bearing the new and additional responsibility of managing the team, and observers were excited at what they hoped he could do. To understand the basis for that excitement it is necessary to look at his record before he became ill. In the five-year period from 1918 through 1922, Sisler had stroked out 1,053 base hits, 70 more than Hornsby and 150 more than Cobb. His five-year average of .3812 was fractionally higher than Cobb's .3808 and significantly higher than Speaker's .368 and Hornsby's .359. He had stolen 201 bases, almost 100 more than Cobb and almost 150 more than Hornsby. He was, moreover, regarded as the smoothest-fielding first baseman in the game. Blessed with a beautiful batting stroke, speed afoot, and a keen instinct for doing the right thing, Sisler was, in John McGraw's words, "one of the marvels of baseball. If he has a weakness nobody, so far as I know, has ever located it."[41] Sisler encouraged his fans to be optimistic about the coming season. "I am feeling fine," he reported as spring training began, "and see no reason now why I should not be as good as ever."[42] Good news for the Browns, bad news for the Yankees.[43]

A number of sportswriters believed that 1924 would see the renaissance of the Philadelphia Athletics. Managed (as they had been since their founding in 1901) by Connie Mack, the Athletics had been a magnificent team a decade earlier when they had won four pennants in the five-year span of 1910 through 1914. But want of money had led the widely respected Mack to sell his stars, and the Athletics became the denizens of the American League cellar for seven consecutive years. Only in 1922 had they begun to crawl back up, and with the 1924 season about to commence, Mack was talking as if this might be the year for reclaiming the heights. In Eddie Rommel the Athletics had baseball's first outstanding knuckleball pitcher, who had appeared even more often than George Uhle in 1923 and had won 18 games. In Joe Hauser— "Unser Choe," as his German-speaking Milwaukee fans called him— they had a batter of immense power, who had batted .307 in 1923.[44] Mack was also counting on strong assistance from two rookies with wonderful minor league credentials, Paul Strand (who had pounded out an incredible 325 hits in the extended Pacific Coast League season of 1923) and Al Simmons. Mack said early in 1924 that he needed only "one good dependable pitcher to make my team real."[45] While it was not clear who that pitcher might be, the claim struck many observers as credible.

No reasonable person gave either the Chicago White Sox or the

Boston Red Sox much of a chance for the pennant. The once mighty White Sox team, pennant winners in 1917 and 1919, had evaporated with the disclosure late in the 1920 season that such stars as Eddie Cicotte and Joe Jackson had accepted money to lose the 1919 World Series. After the 1923 season, which saw the club finish 30 games behind the league leader, even its durable manager Kid Gleason had had enough, and the assignment of guiding the White Sox in 1924 was entrusted to John Evers. The team was not without talent. The remarkable Eddie Collins, thirty-six in 1923, had still been able to bat .360 and lead the league in stolen bases with 49. Ray Schalk, whom Ty Cobb later called "one of the two or three greatest catchers who ever lived," gave the White Sox dependable defense behind the plate.[46] The young Bibb Falk was improving with each season.[47] And Chicago expected grand things from the speedy rookie Maurice Archdeacon, who had batted .357 in the International League. But White Sox pitching in 1923 had been wretched, and it was difficult to see a pennant contender in this aggregation of relics and novices. The Red Sox could also muse on a fall from recent glory. Winners of four World Series between 1912 and 1918, they had subsequently sold off their talented players (most famous among them, Babe Ruth) to allow owner Harry Frazee to meet debt obligations, and although the new owner Robert Quinn was trying to turn the team's fortunes around, the ground to be recovered was vast. It was a mark of new manager Lee Fohl's difficulties that his second-most effective hurler was Jack Quinn, forty years old as the season began and playing under his twenty-fourth manager since launching his baseball career.

The Washington Nationals

It may at first seem puzzling that virtually no one placed the Washington Nationals among the contenders during preseason analyses. The Nationals had, after all, finished fourth in 1923 and lost their season's series only to New York and Philadelphia. In part, the pessimism was grounded in the fact that no Washington team—whether in the American League, the National League, the American Association, or the Union Association—had ever won a pennant. More empirically, it was rooted in the perception that the Nationals had not strengthened themselves over the winter and the knowledge that they had in recent years chewed up managers at an annual rate—and were, when calendar year 1924 dawned, the only major league team not to have named a manager for the coming season. Above all, the pessimism was plausible because of the conviction that Walter Johnson, the greatest pitcher the American League had ever nourished, "can not go much farther"—that he was a "great, heroic, pathetic figure."[48] Despite his 354 lifetime victories, Johnson was thirty-six years old, his legs had become gimpy, and his once-unrivaled fastball had lost a touch of its zip. More to the point, even though the Nationals kept the pitching mound deliberately low to enhance the effectiveness of Johnson's sidearm deliveries,[49] the "Big Train" had not won 20 games since the 1919 season. It was even a moot question whether he was still the best pitcher on the National staff, since, in both 1921 and 1922, George Mogridge had posted more victories than "Old Barney." Most observers believed that the Nationals would slip lower.

Still, the Washington team that gathered at Tampa in February had a number of capable players.[50] Whether as manager (1912–20) or as majority owner (since 1920), Clark Griffith had been working to convert the perennial also-rans into champions. Through insightful trades and purchases he had acquired the rights to Sam Rice (1915), Joe Judge (1915), Bucky Harris (1919), Goose Goslin (1921), Ossie Bluege (1921), George Mogridge (1921), Roger Peckinpaugh (1922), and Muddy Ruel (1923). Members of the Nationals had not often figured prominently among the league's offensive leaders (though Goslin and Rice had a propensity for hitting triples), but it was a squad that featured high defensive skills: Rice was acknowledged to be one of the game's premier outfielders, Ruel had established himself as the league's finest catcher, and the combination of Peckinpaugh at shortstop and Harris at second base was the best in the league at turning double plays.

In his playing days, Griffith had been both a starting pitcher and a relief pitcher. Among baseball men only he and John McGraw realized that a strong relief corps, far from being a frippery, was becoming an essential component of success. This general argument acquired added point when applied to Washington's situation, because a good bullpen might allow the Nationals to extend the careers of Walter Johnson and George Mogridge. Griffith had thus brought Allan Russell to the Nationals in 1923, and Washington sportswriters soon called him "the king of finishers."[51] (Calculations made decades later show that Russell promptly led the league in saves with 9.) Griffith was also counting on Firpo Marberry, who had compiled a 4–0 record during a brief stint with the team in 1923, to help out in the bullpen.[52] If very few others could see the potential in this squad, Griffith saw it, and to assure that his team was prepared for a summer of baseball in the torrid District of Columbia, Griffith was the earliest among owners to gather his team in spring training camp in 1924.

Griffith never lost an opportunity to energize fan interest in the Nationals. That was why he left Donie Bush's successor as manager unnamed in the early winter; so as long as the job was unfilled, there would be extensive newspaper speculation about the opening. But he dared not delay so long as to compromise the new manager's ability to develop the team, and so, in January 1924, Griffith startled fandom with the announcement that the position of field manager was to be held by Bucky Harris. At twenty-seven, Harris was one of the younger members of the team and would be the youngest major league manager in 1924.[53] According to one account (a story that's probably too good to be true), Harris responded to Griffith's written invitation with a brief telegram: "I'll take that job and win Washington's first American League pennant."[54] The press put more circumspect words in Harris's mouth: "I figure that our team has a chance to slip in there because the Yankees, Tigers, and Indians will be fighting one another tooth and nail."[55] The youthful Harris needed to prove that he was really the boss in spring training, and he chose the public disciplining of the bumptious Goose Goslin as a way to send the message to his squad that he meant to be obeyed.[56] But, in general, he was pleased with what he saw in camp. He drilled one group of players in the morning, another in the afternoon. Walter Johnson reported to camp in the best shape in years; his legs had relished his hikes through the Arkansas hills. He promised 20 victories.[57] "Walter looks better to me right now," Bucky Harris declared in March, "than he has any spring since I have been with the Washington team."[58] Goslin, Judge, and Rice also batted well during the spring. And in a preseason series of 6 games with the St. Louis Browns, the Nationals prevailed 5 times. There were not many believers yet—Norman Baxter, for example, used his column in the *Washington Post* to predict a second-division finish for the Nationals—but Clark Griffith was able to hope that the additional seats that he had put into Griffith Stadium over the winter would frequently be filled in 1924.

From Opening Day to Memorial Day

Launching the New Season

THE 1924 SEASON opened on April 15 with all sixteen major league teams in action. In the American League, the Yankees, scoring 2 unearned runs in the ninth inning off luckless Howard Ehmke, launched their campaign for a fourth consecutive pennant with a 2–1 victory over the Red Sox in Boston. Characteristically, Babe Ruth was involved in the success, contributing a single to the rally and stealing a base. In the National League, the Giants were less successful in their parallel ambition. The visiting Dodgers scored early off Rosy Ryan, while Dutch Ruether held the Giants to 7 hits, and Brooklyn won 3–2. The forty-five thousand fans—an unprecedented opening-day crowd— also noted that for the first time in his long career John McGraw began the season in civvies. Washington's American League season began auspiciously, as twenty-six thousand—the largest opening-day crowd in the Nats' history—saw Walter Johnson pitch the Senators to a 4–0 victory over the Philadelphia Athletics. In allowing only 4 hits, recording the 101st shutout of his career, and winning his first season-opener since 1919, the Big Train gave baseball's youngest manager a triumph over the game's oldest. In St. Louis, Rogers Hornsby served notice that he would not tamely surrender his National League batting championship by hitting safely twice. Meanwhile, the other great hitter from St. Louis, George Sisler, began his bid to reclaim the title he had won in 1922 by collecting his own brace of hits. To the delight of the baseball-loving public, the pennant chases were under way.

The Opening Weeks in the National League

After their opening-day loss, the Giants took charge in the National League. First they defeated in succession the mainstays of the Dodger pitching staff, Burleigh Grimes and Dazzy Vance. Then they swept a 3-game set from the visiting Braves. Finally, vaulting the East River, they won the first game of a series in Ebbets Field. Dazzy Vance briefly broke their 6-game streak with a performance that invited comparison to "Christy Mathewson or old Cy Young," but they then regained their form, reeling off 5 victories in a row against the Phillies and the Braves.[1] It is true that neither Philadelphia nor Boston was a powerhouse, but by the evening of May 7, when the Giants had a day off so that the team could travel west for the first intersectional encounters of the year, they sat in first place in the National League with a record of 14 wins and only 5 losses. Giant pitching was solid, but the great strength of the team, as foreseen, lay in its hitting. George Kelly, Frankie Frisch, and Frank Snyder were all batting above .350, and the team in aggregate was hovering around the .300 mark. At times their power could be crushing: On May 4, for example, the Giants humbled the Phillies in a doubleheader by a 2-game score of 25–6.

The two teams that stayed closest to them in the early weeks of the chase were western squads, the Cincinnati Reds and the Chicago Cubs. The Reds' strong start was unsurprising. On April 25, buoyed by a 5-game winning streak, Cincinnati even briefly seized the league lead. Dolf Luque, the hero of 1923, looked as sharp as ever. Carl Mays, facing hitters unfamiliar with his submarine style, was mystifying the opposition every fifth game. And so even though Rube Benton dropped out of the rotation with a broken hand and an injured Eppa Rixey was unable to pitch, the Reds were showing the mound strength that had been expected of them. Their batting, however, was not exciting, in part because Edd Roush and Bubbles Hargrave had also sustained early-season injuries. Still, various lesser lights provided enough punch to allow Cincinnati to forge a 13–6 record before the teams from the east arrived. The only ominous note, puzzled over by a statistically inclined sportswriter, was that the Reds were being oddly inefficient at converting base hits into runs.[2]

The early success of the Cubs, on the other hand, was unexpected. At the break for intersectional travel, the Cubs stood at 12–10, good enough for third place; on April 19 they had even briefly held first place. The pitching hero of the charge was Grover Cleveland Alexander, who combined his extraordinary command with an unnerving determination to deliver the next pitch almost as soon as the catcher had returned the ball to his hands. George Grantham and Ray Grimes supplied hitting punch. Grantham, in particular, Chicago's young second baseman, launched his season in grand style, catching attention on April 20 by contributing a double, a triple, and the first home run ever hit into the right field bleachers at Crosley Field, to the Cubs' victory over the Reds. As promised, the Cubs were aggressive on the base paths, averaging better than 1 stolen base per game.

The Brooklyn Dodgers suffered from a highly visible flaw in the opening weeks of the season: Though formidable against every other team in the east, they rolled over almost every time they faced the New York Giants, losing 5 of 7 encounters. Still, they went into the first stage of intersectional play with a record of 10 victories and 9 losses. Zack Wheat was in fine form, challenging Rogers Hornsby for batting leadership in the National League, and Jack Fournier, crediting a new power-enhancing swing, seized the league lead in home runs by striking them in braces—on April 27, on May 5, and on May 15. The addition of veteran Milt Stock to the lineup on April 30 brought steadiness to Brooklyn's defense at third and a boost to the team's offensive power. At the same time Brooklyn featured the league's outstanding early-season pitcher in Dazzy Vance, who, after losing his first outing of the year (to the Giants, of course), pitched approximately every fifth day and spun off 6 consecutive victories. Deliberately garbing his pitching arm with a fluttering shirt sleeve, Vance struck batters out at a pace not seen in the National League since Christy Mathewson's youthful days two decades earlier.

The Opening Weeks in the American League

The opening three weeks of the American League race featured the play of the Yankees, the Tigers, the Red Sox, and the Browns. The Yankee success was founded on strong pitching. After a set of uncertain engagements against Boston and Washington, the New York staff found the groove: Waite Hoyt, Herb Pennock, Bob Shawkey, and Joe Bush won 8 straight games before Walter Johnson finally checked the Yankee surge. On the eve of intersectional play in the second week of May, Babe Ruth, although weakened by a persistent lung ailment and struggling to raise his batting average, even to the .250 level, had collected a major league–leading 6 home runs and was on track for another season of unexampled power. For greater consistency at the plate, Miller Huggins was relying on Joe Dugan, Bob Meusel, and Whitey Witt. As a consequence of good pitching and timely hitting, the Yankees won 16 of their first 22 games, a record good enough for first place in the league on the eve of the visit from the western clubs. It seemed reasonable to assume that, once Ruth began to perform as he was expected to perform, the team would only get tougher.

The Detroit Tigers were the Yankees' closest challenger, occupying first place from the opening of the season until an early-May stumble. As predicted, Detroit featured magnificent power at the plate and inconsistency on the mound. Three weeks into the season, Ty Cobb was batting .385, and as if to show that his legs were still springy at thirty-seven, he stole home on April 27. Harry Heilmann was even better. Bidding for a repeat as league batting champion, Heilmann led the major leagues in both hits (34) and batting average (.493) on the eve of intersectional play, and in a 2-game set against the White Sox he terrorized the Chicago staff by going 8-for-9, including a home run and 2 doubles. Pitching, on the other hand, was a different story. Only the inexperienced Lil Stoner was dependable. As for the others, Hooks Dauss was regularly given a turn on the mound and almost as regularly shelled, and Bert Cole and Earl Whitehill could manage no more than alternating good outings with poor ones. Three weeks into the season, with a record of 11 wins and 8 losses, Manager Cobb knew that the club needed pitching help if it was to remain a contender through the rigors of summer.

The biggest surprise of the early season was Lee Fohl's Boston club. The Red Sox stood at 10 wins and 8 losses when intersectional play began. With 2 shutouts to his credit, Howard Ehmke was the leading hurler of the squad. Jack Quinn and Alex Ferguson also pitched well. But even more startling than the consistency of the hurling was the force of Red Sox hitting. The team was winning contests by large margins—among their victories were games with scores of 13–0, 15–6, 11–0, 14–4—and during a 6-game winning streak they averaged over 10 runs a game. Bobby Veach, the erstwhile Tiger, was batting .362; Ira Flagstead, another exile from the outfield wealth of Detroit, was hitting .313; Steve O'Neill, late of the Indians, added a .314 average. To these hitting accomplishments of proven refugees from elsewhere, the achievements of two unheralded players were added: Young outfielder Ike Boone, in his first year of regular play, was batting .316; and veteran first baseman Joe Harris, out of major league baseball for three years until rehabilitated by the Red Sox in 1922, was actually among the league's batting leaders with an average of .417. Few observers believed that the Red Sox could continue for long to run in fast company, but their early-season successes seized the imagination of many fans.

The followers of the St. Louis Browns were just becoming excited by the time intersectional play began. After losing 8 of their first 10 games, critics had written them off. But then, invigorated by the return to action of Ken Williams, the Browns took up arms against the Indians and Tigers, winning 9 of 11 contests and moving out of last place and above .500. In 1921, Williams had been among the first batters to adopt a stance designed specifically to enhance power. When he was hitting well, as he was upon his return, Williams was almost as dangerous as Babe Ruth. He hit safely in his first 10 games, on May 3 he stroked out 5 hits against the Tigers, and three weeks into the season he was batting over .400. Moreover, Williams was not alone. George Sisler, though not hitting with the uncanny skill he had evinced in 1922, continued to have more good days than bad, and Baby Doll Jacobson was almost as successful as the manager. The Browns' pitching, however, remained uncertain. Spitballing Urban Shocker was angry with management and undisguisedly interested in being traded to a team that would, he supposed, better appreciate his talents, and his pitching in this period of embitterment showed the strain.[3] Shocker's ineffectiveness forced Sisler to place reliance on such uncertain pillars as Dave Danforth, a veteran who had spent most of his career as a relief hurler, and Ernie Wingard, who was in his first month of major league competition. Fortunately for the Browns, these two provided at least consistent competence on the mound and thus regularly offered the promise that, if the Browns could hustle up 5 runs, they were likely to win.

Early-Season Disappointments

The early-season performances of the remaining eight major league teams were, in varying degrees, disappointing. The most distressed fans were those who followed the Cleveland Indians and the Pittsburgh

Pirates, since each of these presumed contenders was wallowing in sub-.500 territory at the opening of intersectional play. The Indians' record of 7 wins and 11 losses and their brief residence in the cellar of the American League testified chiefly to the wretchedness of the pitching available to Tris Speaker, though injuries to key players, including the manager himself, also damaged Cleveland's performance. Certainly the Cleveland batting order, when healthy, was not wanting in punch. Tioga George Burns ran off an 18-game hitting streak in the first five weeks of the season, and Charlie Jamieson contributed a 15-game streak. The entire team was batting about .300. But Speaker did not have a single reliable hurler: George Uhle, the star of 1923, set a miserable example of fatuous flinging, and Stan Coveleskie was only sporadically better. The Pirates were also stumbling, mustering a record of only 10 victories and 11 defeats at the end of three weeks of play. Almost every aspect of Pittsburgh's game was inconsistent. Rookie Ray Kremer, for example, would pitch well in one outing and poorly in the next; hitting was inexplicably disabled; and meanwhile manager Bill McKechnie was distracted from other concerns by the need to find a leadoff batter able to launch rallies for the struggling Pirates. When asked if his decision of early May to increase the number of practices might not tire the Pirates, McKechnie snapped, "We can't be much worse overdoing them than underdoing them."[4]

Five other teams that had been seen only as long shots seemed bent on justifying the forecasts. The St. Louis Cardinals boasted the strong hitting of Rogers Hornsby and little else. In fact, the second baseman was so central to Cardinal chances on the field and success at the box office that, when a dislocated thumb briefly sidelined him early in May, the team's management, descrying "threatening weather" amid the sunbeams, postponed 3 contests with the Reds. "Three successive games," the Cincinnati sportswriter Jack Ryder wrote, "have now been called off due to cold feet."[5] The Boston Braves were so beset with illnesses (including a peculiar run of appendicitis, which, after felling two others, finally claimed playing manager Dave Bancroft) that their outstanding hitter was Casey Stengel, who barely topped .300. The Philadelphia Phillies, the National League's third contender for last place, had only the hitting of Cy Williams to brag about.

Over in the American League, the Chicago White Sox, after winning 4 of their first 5 games, collided with reality and sank rapidly, weighed down by lackluster pitching. But the feeblest team of all was the Philadelphia Athletics. Joe Hauser was showing the power that made him a fan favorite. But the much-touted Paul Strand could not decipher major league pitching, Eddie Rommel led a staff of mound flounderers, and when intersectional play began, the Athletics were well into a 12-game losing streak that would give them unchallenged possession of the cellar. Connie Mack still professed to be hopeful: "A lot can happen between now and the last of September."[6] Maybe. But any predicted rebirth in Philadelphia was invisible in early May.

About the great venture that Clark Griffith had launched in Washington, doubts were proliferating. No manager experimented more imaginatively, sought additional talent more vigorously, or juggled lineups more frequently than Bucky Harris. But three weeks into the season Washington's record was a disappointing 9 victories and 11 defeats. Moreover, Harris was still learning. For all of his baseball savvy and cockiness (even in spring training, for example, he was prepared to pronounce upon the proper way for pitchers to deal with Babe Ruth), Harris had much to learn, especially about the handling of pitchers. But at least made sure that his players learned, too. He experimented with Doc Prothro at third base, hopeful that Prothro's lively bat could compensate for his fielding deficiencies. And he tested a number of players, Lance Richbourg, Carr Smith, Carl East, Showboat Fisher, Wid Matthews, and Nemo Leibold, in the role of third outfielder, to complement his duo of future Hall of Famers, Goose Goslin and Sam Rice.

Nevertheless, whatever Harris did in the early weeks of the season to hone himself and his team, the Nationals were unable to gain momentum. The hitting was disappointing, with only Joe Judge consistently able to get on base. Sam Rice spent time on the bench nursing a sore knee, the still-ailing Goose Goslin was struggling at the plate, and Roger Peckinpaugh was batting only .154 after 13 games. Relief pitching was no better, for Allan Russell was recuperating from an arm injury sustained in Florida, Firpo Marberry was slow at working himself into playing shape, and Slim McGrew, By Speece, and Ted Wingfield were unreliable.

Only one star shone in the Nats' firmament: the rejuvenated Walter Johnson. Though his fastball was a shade slower than it had been when he was in his prime, it was still an awesome pitch. Thrown with an easy sidearm motion by an inordinately long right arm, the fastball was devastating because it appeared to rise and break. It was Johnson's basic delivery and his only good offering.[7] It was, batters often said, the only fastball in baseball that one could actually *hear*—"swoosh" or "swish" were frequently used descriptors.[8] Johnson served notice on the league that he had the stuff of old by beating the world champion Yankees twice in the first three weeks of the season; the victory of May 1 was notable for being the first game of the year in which Firpo Marberry made a finish-for-Johnson appearance. Johnson made another statement on May 23, when he threw one of the great games of his career, a 1-hit shutout of the White Sox in which he struck out 14 batters, including 6 in succession. Nevertheless, Bucky Harris could use Walter Johnson only every fourth or fifth day. As late as May 22, with the first visit from the western clubs nearing completion, the Nationals were lodged in seventh place, laid low by poor hitting and uncertain pitching and saved from the ignominy of the cellar only by the miserable play of the Philadelphia Athletics. Clark Griffith continued to display confidence in his manager, and he used waivers to secure Curly Ogden from the Athletics to add another starter to the staff. But such was the strength of the Yankees and Tigers that, even though the 1924 season was scarcely three weeks old, the Washington Nationals were in danger of being irredeemably lost if they could not quickly discover a formula for consistent winning.

The First Round of Intersectional Play

With the opening of intersectional play on May 9, weather suddenly became a significant factor in the progress of the season. As the country endured one of the rainiest springs in memory, more than forty postponements interrupted the baseball schedule. The major rescheduling effect of the rain-outs was to increase the number of doubleheaders that teams could anticipate in the heat of summer; and the major strategic effect of this proliferation of doubleheaders was to advantage teams that had pitching depth. In the National League, that augured well for New York, Brooklyn, and Cincinnati (if the Reds could get their mound staff back to health). In the American League, New York, Washington, and Cleveland (if the Indians could prod their pitchers into replicating past effectiveness) seemed the likeliest beneficiaries of the bunching of contests to come.

The chief surprise of the season, as east met west for the first time in each league, continued to be the Boston Red Sox. Visited at Fenway

Park in turn by the Browns, the White Sox, the Tigers (including a quick trip by both teams to play a Sunday game in Detroit), and the Indians, the Red Sox won 9 of 12 games. This streak was part of a longer one in which they won 16 of 20 games. Manager Lee Fohl ascribed the success to his decision to manage from the dugout rather than the baseline: "There are a lot of things that I missed when I was coaching from third base."[9] No doubt. But that does not explain the individual performances of his players. For a while, in fact, the Red Sox could scarcely do wrong. They won with power (10–9, over the Indians on May 26) and with cunning (a successful hidden-ball trick against the White Sox on May 17). They benefited from strong pitching performances from Howard Ehmke and Jack Quinn and from an infield built upon strength up the middle in the persons of Bill Wambsganss and Dud Lee. Above all—and this was the biggest of the surprises—they enjoyed the happiness of good hitting. Ike Boone soared to join Joe Harris in challenging the .400 mark, and Bobby Veach batted safely about one-third of the time. On May 25, when the Yankees lost while the Red Sox were idle, Boston moved into a tie with New York for first place. An exultant James Curley, mayor of Boston, sent the team a congratulatory telegram that concluded with an exhortation: "There is no better place for the World's Series pennant than at Fenway Park."[10]

The Browns and the Tigers used their trips through eastern ballparks to mount their own challenges for the league lead. The St. Louis charge came first, being a continuation of the surge they had begun while playing in the west. By beating Boston on May 13 the Browns reached second place. Behind strong pitching from Urban Shocker (who finally realized that if he wanted to be traded, he needed to be tradable) and Ernie Wingard, they then won 2 straight from the Yankees, spoiling "Babe Ruth Day" at Yankee Stadium in the process, and climbed on May 15 to within half a game of first place. Though they lost their final contest with the Yankees, they then took the only 2 games of a rain-shortened series with the Washington Nationals. But just when they seemed on the edge of success, their offense evaporated, and they lost 3 in a row to the anemic Athletics, managing but 2 runs in 26 innings. Meanwhile, George Sisler's performance at bat remained so uneven— he was batting over .300 but was patently troubled by some pitchers— that on May 24 he took the unprecedented step of sending in a pinch hitter for himself.

As the Browns lost momentum during the fourth week of May, the Tigers made their charge. In fact, it was by beating the Browns on May 27 that Detroit took over third place from St. Louis, a team to which they had lost 4 straight earlier in the month. Harry Heilmann and Ty Cobb continued to pace the Tiger attack; during their May series in Yankee Stadium each had a 4-hit game. Cobb was encouraged that Bert Cole was beginning to flash the form that had earned him 13 victories the previous year. On May 26 the team even showed that it could be briskly efficient, dispatching the Athletics in a 9-inning game that lasted only seventy-two minutes.[11] But pitching problems continued to haunt the Tigers, leading Cobb to cast his eye on a former Tiger, Dutch Leonard, whose suspension from organized baseball for playing in the nonrecognized Imperial Valley League was soon to expire.[12] Leonard and Cobb heartily disliked each other, but if they could be mutually serviceable in a run for the pennant, past enmity could be overlooked.

Though others nipped at their heels, the Yankees sat atop the American League throughout the final three weeks of May. Sometimes they shared the position with the Red Sox, but they never slipped out of first place. Bob Meusel and Joe Dugan sustained the hitting pace they had established earlier, and Dugan was also sensational in the field (even securing 2 putouts in a 5–3 triple play on May 28). But the chief element in the team's steady success was the return to health of Babe Ruth. It had been an embarrassment to Ruth that, after declaring his intention to win the league batting championship, he had wallowed for several weeks around the .250 level. But as the western teams came through Yankee Stadium, he began to complement his long blows with timely singles, thereby pushing his average over .300. On May 13 and again on May 23 he collected 3 base hits in a game. On May 26 he hit his eleventh home run of the season. In almost every game he received at least one base on balls, most of which were quasi-intentional. The word was spreading around the league: Babe Ruth was warming up as the weather heated up.

Over in the National League intersectional play brought the Giants their first shock of the season, as the hitherto-feeble Cardinals took them in 4 straight games. In the first 2 contests the outcomes were not entirely surprising, since John McGraw chose the occasion to test out marginal starters. But even when he turned to Wayland Dean and Jack Bentley to stop the hemorrhage, the Cardinals continued their assault, inspired in part by the return to the lineup of Rogers Hornsby, who delivered 7 base hits during the series. Consequently, when the Giants left St. Louis after losing on May 13, they had yielded their position atop the National League to the Cincinnati Reds. To complicate John McGraw's world further, the Giants' next opponent was the charging Chicago Cubs team, which had profited from the Giants' distress to close the gap between them to half a game. In the first contest of the series, Charlie Hollocher made his long-awaited return to the Cubs, collecting 3 hits, including a home run, and showing the agility of old in the field.[13] But the Giants won, as George Kelly drove in four runs and Bill Terry began to establish his reputation as a gifted pinch hitter. The next day the Cubs won, with Grover Cleveland Alexander, who had recently pitched 29 consecutive innings without walking a batter, turning in another strong performance. The teams split the 2 remaining games as well, and because the Reds had stumbled against the Braves, the Giants were able to reclaim first place on May 16. They did not, however, hold it for long, ceding it back to the Reds on May 19. The tight race assumed yet another shape on May 21, when the Chicago Cubs, relying again on Alexander, defeated Philadelphia to slip by Cincinnati into first place and drive the Giants down into third (albeit only by percentage points). Only half a game separated the top three teams in this tight and tangled race.

But at this point the Giants showed why they were the defending league champions. Beginning on May 23, they won 3 of 4 encounters with Cincinnati, benefiting from the Reds' mounting hospital list and from Dolf Luque's sudden inability to get past the first few innings of any game he started. It was a typical Giant series: No one starred—or rather, everyone took a turn at starring. Then, when the Giants returned home on May 28, they promptly won a doubleheader from the Dodgers, once again beating Dazzy Vance in the process. John McGraw, though hobbling on crutches from a knee injury sustained away from the ballpark in Chicago, was delighted that his team, by winning 6 of 7 games, had dramatically proved that their slump was over. The Cubs, meanwhile, hung in. Grover Cleveland Alexander was outstanding on the mound, while other starters, though not overwhelming, could usually be relied on to keep the Cubs in the game. George Grantham and Denver Grigsby continued to hit well, and the team's baserunning threat, increased still further by the return of Charlie Hollocher, meant that defensive lapses by the opposition were likely to be quickly punished.

For the Reds, however, the bad news had now begun. They lost 6 of

10 games. The ranks of their injured grew to proportions that seemed unprecedented, encompassing Edd Roush (muscle pains), Bubbles Hargrave (broken hand), Jake Daubert (dizziness brought on by a beaning), Lew Fonseca (dislocated shoulder), Ike Caveney (strained leg), Sam Bohne (strained muscle), and Pat Duncan (lameness). The total collapse of Dolf Luque—he quickly gathered 6 losses, 2 short of his total for the entire season of 1923—left the still-tender Eppa Rixey and Carl Mays standing alone as reliable hurlers. Unless Jack Hendricks could find a formula for overcoming weakness at bat and on the mound, the Reds were fated to become a team of middling capability and middling success.

The Memorial Day Doubleheaders

The first quarter of the season came to its traditional close with a full array of morning–afternoon doubleheaders on May 30, the Memorial Day holiday, which was then also called Decoration Day. In the American League, only the Tigers profited from the opportunity: While six other teams in the league split their twin bills, Detroit pummeled the Indians twice, moving to within a game and a half of first place and driving Cleveland down into seventh place. The Yankees and the Red Sox, sharing the league lead when the day began, remained tied when the day ended. The story of the Yankee–Athletic doubleheader was supplied by Babe Ruth, who became the first player in baseball history to hit 250 home runs. The story at Fenway Park was the crowd—more than twenty thousand, the largest in years, coming out to applaud the unexpectedly competitive Red Sox. Although Boston split the twin bill, the fans had much to cheer about. In the first game Ike Boone hit a grand-slam home run, and in the second, the Red Sox pulled a 4-3-2 triple play. The astonishing Red Sox had won 18 of their last 24 games.

In the National League, the doubleheaders had a major impact on the race. The Chicago Cubs, half a game behind when the day began and playing at home before forty thousand partisan fans, lost 2 games to the Cincinnati Reds. Meanwhile, the Giants swept a doubleheader from the Phillies. As a result, the New Yorkers opened a lead of 2½ games over Chicago, while Cincinnati held its own at yet another game off the pace. The double loss was not a catastrophe for the Cubs, for the season was still relatively young. However, since the range for possible change on May 30 was 4 games, and since the Cubs had sustained the maximum loss allowable within the range, it is understandable that their disappointment was keen. The Giants, on the other hand, were happy: Every player (barring pitchers) who had come to bat in the doubleheader had gotten at least 1 hit. John McGraw had always preached that solid team play wins games, and the 1924 Giants were emerging as exemplars of his maxim.

Standings at the End of Play, Memorial Day, May 30

AMERICAN LEAGUE

Team	Won	Lost	Pctg.	Games Behind
New York Yankees	21	13	.618	—
Boston Red Sox	21	13	.618	—
Detroit Tigers	22	17	.564	1.5
St. Louis Browns	18	18	.500	4.0
Washington Nationals	16	19	.457	5.5
Chicago White Sox	15	19	.441	6.0
Cleveland Indians	14	20	.412	7.0
Philadelphia Athletics	13	21	.382	8.0

NATIONAL LEAGUE

Team	Won	Lost	Pctg.	Games Behind
New York Giants	24	14	.632	—
Chicago Cubs	23	18	.561	2.5
Cincinnati Reds	21	18	.538	3.5
Brooklyn Dodgers	19	17	.528	4.0
Pittsburgh Pirates	18	20	.474	6.0
Boston Braves	16	18	.471	6.0
St. Louis Cardinals	17	21	.447	7.0
Philadelphia Phillies	11	23	.324	10.5

The Business of Baseball

THROUGHOUT *its entire existence, organized baseball has been a branch of the entertainment business.* By pulling that sentence apart and identifying the implications of each of its three key terms for the 1920s, we can understand the relationship of the general statement to the circumstances of the 1924 season. The key terms are *organized, entertainment,* and *business,* and I'll approach them in reverse order.

Baseball as a Business

The men who owned baseball clubs in 1924 expected to make money from them. "In the baseball business," Barney Dreyfuss, the Pirates owner, had explained several years earlier, "An owner must act quickly and secretly. . . . He must act on the jump and talk afterward."[1] The chief expense item for every major league baseball club was the payroll line: preeminently the salaries for players, but also the salaries for a field manager, a club secretary, several coaches, a trainer, a property manager, two to six scouts ("ivory hunters," in the jargon of the day), and several office personnel (including at least an accountant and a public relations representative).[2] Team travel by Pullman car was also a major cost, especially for clubs that played in cities where games were still prohibited on Sunday.[3] Then there were such items as the purchase of equipment, the maintenance of the playing facility, the staging of spring training, the acquisition of new players,[4] and insurance premiums. Finally, since many teams had built new stadiums in the fifteen years prior to 1924, some owners were still paying debt service.

How large were these costs? Although major league teams were not obliged to open their books to public scrutiny, happy accident provides us with occasional glimpses into their finances. We know, for example, that in 1925 the payroll of the free-spending New York Yankees came to $370,000, tops in the majors, while at the other end of the scale, the payroll of the St. Louis Browns barely exceeded $100,000. As a proportion of costs, payrolls probably constituted between 35 percent and 40 percent of total expenses in 1924. Spring training amounted to almost 10 percent of the expenditures on an average team. The compensation and travel costs of scouts accounted for approximately the same proportion. Even the balls that the game was played with rose to visibility as an expense item, costing each team over $3,000 per year.[5] All of this is very rough, but we can venture the tentative conclusion that the total expenses of a team in 1924 amounted on average to $550,000, give or take $200,000.[6]

The money to pay for these expenses came preponderantly from gate receipts. Television did not exist in 1924, and although the first radio broadcast of a baseball game had occurred in 1921, no club had yet sold the right to transmit descriptions of games. Clubs had a few other standard ways to make money: concession sales (food, drink, scorecards),[7] exhibition games, rentals of facilities (during road trips), and parking fees. But with ticket sales accounting for over 85 percent of the revenues of the average club, it is clear that these other areas of income-production, though worth cultivating and expanding, were not make-or-break categories of revenue.[8] Nevertheless, because major league attendance rose to unprecedented levels in the early 1920s, reaching 9.5 million for the exciting 1924 season, gate revenues sufficed for most owners, with profits for most clubs ranging from 10 percent to 25 percent of gross operating income.[9] These were strong returns, and although perhaps only Charles Comiskey of the Chicago White Sox and Frank Navin of the Detroit Tigers actually got rich from baseball, only two clubs—the Boston Red Sox, owned by Harry Frazee and then by Robert Quinn, and the Philadelphia Phillies, owned by William Baker—stood outside the general prosperity of the era.

With gate receipts looming so large, much attention was given to identifying the factors that encouraged and sustained strong ticket sales. Two unsurprising considerations were paramount: the quality of the playing of a team and the size of the population pool from which a team could draw support. It is, of course, simple common sense to note that a good team outdraws a poor team. But the effect on receipts of changes in quality of play could be dramatic and quick. The Yankees, for example, had their worst attendance of the decade in 1925, when they plummeted to seventh place. The Pirates, on the other hand, enjoyed their greatest attendance success in the same year, when they won the World Series. This recognition of team quality as an important source of box office success provided owners with a straightforward strategy for improving revenues: strengthen the team.

Unfortunately for ownership, the population factor was not susceptible to adjustment. These variations in demographic pools thus constituted a major and ineradicable source of financial inequality. New York City, for example, had three teams drawing on a metropolitan population of 7.9 million, or over 2.5 million people for each team. Washington, D.C., on the other hand, had one team drawing on a metropolitan district of just over a half-million people. And even worse was the situation in St. Louis, where two teams, drawing on a pool of less than a million, had fewer than half a million each.[10] In these data lies one of the explanations for the fact that the New York Yankees accounted for 22 percent of all ticket purchases in the 1920s, with the New York Giants just behind at 20 percent, and the Brooklyn Dodgers—exceeded only by the Chicago Cubs (18 percent) and the Detroit Tigers (16 percent)— falling into fifth place (at 15 percent) among the sixteen franchises. These demographic differentials were also the chief explanation for the fact that, as the 1924 season began, only three major league teams had not won pennants in the twentieth century—the Washington Senators, the St. Louis Cardinals, and the St. Louis Browns.

In considering baseball as a business we cannot confine our attention to the owners, since for the players, too, baseball was an attractive way to make money. The average major league salary in 1924 approached $6,000, and strong performers—for example, Burleigh Grimes and Dolf Luque—made at least twice that amount. "Superstars" (and the term was already in use in 1924) might receive even more. Babe Ruth, naturally enough, topped the list, at $52,000, but Edd Roush commanded $19,000, Rogers Hornsby pulled in $18,500, and Frankie Frisch, in only his sixth year in the major leagues, was paid $18,000. Walter Johnson, on the other hand, playing for the tight Clark Griffith, earned only $12,000.[11] By the standards of the free-agency era, these are paltry amounts, of course, and they may lead readers of our day to scoff at the remark of Yankee owner Jacob Ruppert that "the salaries offered to our men are extremely liberal."[12] Still, the claim had at least this kernel of truth: For the large majority of players, major league salaries represented at least five times the income that they might reasonably have expected for their labors in any other likely occupation, and their pay levels put them in the top 5 percent of American wage earners.[13]

Moreover, because the span of the baseball season left four or five months free, many players held off-season jobs that allowed them to capitalize on their celebrity to earn additional income. Jack Fournier, Harry Heilmann, Joe Judge, and Eppa Rixey sold insurance. Ray Schalk and Aaron Ward dealt in real estate. Kiki Cuyler supervised sporting activities. Muddy Ruel was a lawyer and Art Nehf a bank director. And let's not forget Thomas Griffith, a professional songwriter, or Nick Altrock, a professional comedian. Other players, preferring to trade time in the present for money in the future, used the winter months to prepare themselves for postbaseball careers: Ossie Bluege for example, took courses to become a certified public accountant, while Bibb Falk studied civil engineering.

To say all this is not, of course, to say that the players thought themselves adequately compensated. This deficiency is one reason players, rather than resenting Babe Ruth for commanding such a large salary, applauded him. "We depend upon men like Ruth," one explained, "to increase our salaries all along the line."[14] The history of labor–management relations in professional baseball has always been rocky. As one player said, the owners "will see that this is a business with me as well as with the club."[15] Still, the reader should remember that, if players were truly dissatisfied, they could choose alternative careers. Few did. And while his words must be understood as tainted by the hyperbole of nostalgia, Lefty O'Doul provided an explanation for why the exodus was so limited: "If I had to do it all over again I'd be a ballplayer again without pay. . . . I loved it."[16]

Baseball as Entertainment

Although baseball was a business, its purpose was not to produce items that could be purchased in stores but to present spectacles that people would pay to see. In the prosperous 1920s, a variety of entertainments—

theater, films, books, amusement parks, horse racing, and the like—vied for the public's support. It was incumbent on the baseball industry to devise strategies to lure people with money to spend into the ballparks.

This ambition had been the basis for the stadium-building vogue that marked the years prior to World War I, when over half the major league teams moved into new homes. These arenas were more conveniently located than their predecessors, more readily accessible by public transportation, with more ample seating for the spectators and parking for their automobiles, and they were less vulnerable to fire. As a consequence of this building frenzy, with all its upgradings major league baseball was well situated to accommodate the surge in spectator interest that followed the end of World War I. To make the experience of attending games less boisterous—and hence (it was believed) more attractive to women—clubs took steps to reduce rowdiness, drunkenness, and profanity among the fans. The national experiment with Prohibition assisted the ballpark magnates in achieving this goal. Game times were set to suit the convenience of prospective fans, most notably in Washington, D.C., where a 4:00 P.M. starting time gave government workers a chance to take in a game before going home.

But these impresarios also believed in the utility of actively courting fans. They knew that most American boys, and many American girls, had played and followed baseball while growing up. Appeals to the past were already part of baseball's armory of self-promotion in the 1920s; and the names of legendary nineteenth-century figures such as Cap Anson, Dan Brouthers, and John Clarkson were used with a frequency that suggests that fandom's memory spanned at least forty years. Then there were the "Days" that were set aside to allow fans to bestow gifts on particular favorites. The custom of the era decreed that the honoring ceremony, rather than preceding the contest, should interrupt the game whenever the hero first appeared at the plate. On occasion the directors of the game even changed its rules in order to promote attendance; the banning of "doctored" pitches in 1920 was the most recent example of the magnates' belief that fans preferred offense to defense.

It is in the context of the campaign to win fans that the enforcement of baseball's color line must be understood. Knowledgeable major leaguers knew very well that black baseball boasted performers as good as the best the majors could display. Jimmy Cooney, for example, after playing winter league ball in Cuba, reported that Oscar Charleston was "a great ball player, who reminds you for all the world of Tris Speaker when Tris was at the top of his game."[17] But the owners worried that the appearance of black players on major league teams would turn fans away, and so they continued their informal conspiracy to exclude men of African ancestry.

In one important way baseball was extraordinarily fortunate in its efforts to promote itself. Because nineteenth-century newspapers had discovered that information about baseball sold dailies, big-city papers offered their readers diamond coverage. They provided accounts of games, box scores, and anecdotage about players, reported the team standings, and often listed the batting leaders. Player interviews were still uncommon, but the personalization of the game was fostered by the verbal identification of teams with their managers; thus, Ty Cobb's Tigers sometimes became the "Cobblers," George Sisler's Browns were the "Sizzlers," and Wilbert Robinson's Brooklyn squad was more often styled "Robins" than Dodgers. Nicknames tended to be vivid: To millions who had seen only his photograph, it made perfect sense, for example, to call Connie Mack the "lean leader." Finally, and above all other publicity resources, baseball had Babe Ruth. The press could not get enough of the strange man–child who was almost single-handedly forcing a rearrangement of baseball strategy. The total cost of journalistic coverage probably came to about $1 million annually.[18] Very few other businesses in the United States could rely on external interests to provide and pay for a regular and positive presentation of their product to a potential audience.

Still, in the long run, advertising needs a good product if it is to succeed. And it is in this context that the oddest of baseball's various oddities emerges. If an owner was to be able consistently to present attractive contests, he needed to be confident of at least three factors: that competition would regularly be strong enough to make the contests interesting, that his own team had players of demonstrable skill, and that the outcomes of the contests were not "fixed." And so, although baseball owners, like all businessmen, viewed their competitors as their foes, they also needed to view them as invaluable allies, on the principle that none could prosper if the owners could not collectively present an attractive product. On that principle rested the elaborate governance structure that organized baseball relied upon.

Organized Baseball

Professional baseball was Organized Baseball. And we can best comprehend the character of that organization if we understand how the owners defined the problems that threatened to undercut their collective enterprise.

The first problem was the need to keep the level of competition reasonably well balanced despite the inherent revenue inequalities of the clubs. As Branch Rickey, speaking for the financially strapped St. Louis Cardinals, said at the meeting of major league owners in 1921, "We want rules that will have a tendency to equalize the strength of the teams and minimize the powers of money-making clubs."[19] Over the course of decades baseball owners had developed several tools to accomplish that goal. The first was the convention of territorial rights, which—allowing for exceptions in the case of very large metropolitan areas—granted each major league team the exclusive right to offer major league baseball in its home city. The point of the convention was to assure each licensed team access to a ticket-buying populace large enough to assure an unchallengeable and dependable foundation of local support. The exceptions were, of course, significant: New York City had proved itself large enough to support three teams, and Chicago was readily handling two. But the marginal situations of some of the clubs in Philadelphia, St. Louis, and Boston suggested that even demographic centers with as many potential fans as these were not broad enough to support more than one competitive team. The principle of territorial rights was so central to Organized Baseball that occasions of its violation were ipso facto occasions of baseball warfare. The last successful challenge to that principle, in 1901, had been an aspect of the American League's campaign to win recognition as a major league.

But if the convention of territorial rights provided each team with a financial floor, it did not suffice to guarantee even an approximation of revenue equality. And so other devices had been adopted over the years to restrain the buying power of the richest teams. Home teams were obliged to share their gate receipts with visiting clubs. Interlocking ownerships—"syndicates" in the parlance of the day—were prohibited. Rosters were limited in size. Trading deadlines were imposed. All of these steps were designed either to diminish inequalities of wealth among the owners or to inhibit the power of wealth to secure and stockpile talent.

The most dramatic tool of quality-equalization, however, remains to be noted: the notorious reserve rule. Designed to address the concern that wealthy teams might lure talent away from poorer teams through higher salaries, the reserve rule specified via a clause in each player's contract that he could not sell his services to another club. His only recourse, if he was unhappy about his salary or his playing conditions, was to leave the game entirely and find employment in some other sphere of activity. The effect of the reserve rule was to make it impossible for a player, once he had signed his first contract, ever again to auction his baseball-playing skills to the highest bidder. To put the matter in the starkest terms, there was no such thing as a free agent in baseball in 1924.[20] John McGraw pronounced the view of management on the reserve rule: "All baseball men know that it is really the backbone of the game."[21]

The second problem that the owners had to deal with was establishing assurances that the best ball-playing talent would be available to major league clubs. This task really had two aspects. First, it was important that talent be developed—that is, that a structure of lesser leagues should exist in which aspiring professional ballplayers could hone their skills. Second, it was also important that developed talent should then rise to the top—that is, that those who showed the most ability in these preparatory arenas should then play in the major leagues. The chief vehicle for such development was the hierarchy of minor leagues. In 1924 the minors fell into five categories—from AA down to D—in accordance with the levels of competition they fostered. At the start of the 1924 season, there were 28 minor leagues and 183 minor league teams in organized baseball. A draft system allowed talented players to be pulled up to higher-level teams, even if local minor league owners did not want to lose them.

The third problem confronting the owners proved the most intractable: How were both the image and the reality of baseball competition to be protected from the gamblers who sought to corrupt the game by bribing players? It was a difficult problem to deal with, because any owner who learned that his players had behaved so as to shade the outcome of a game and who then acted to punish corruption among his own players would hurt himself first and foremost. Why? First, by publicizing the fact of graft, he raised doubts about the credibility of the product he was offering to the public. Second, by banning a player on the take, he was probably depriving himself of a person whose talents, when he was honest, were considerable. That's why indirect responses were preferred. If the player involved was a journeyman, the owner was likely to drop him without comment at the earliest convenience, thereby protecting his own reputation but leaving the corruptible athlete still at large to damage other teams. And if the player involved was a star, then the owner might even be reluctant to release him at all, on the principle that an occasional slip from grace was not too high a price to pay for ballplaying excellence. The notorious Hal Chase was the most striking example of a player who had continued to enjoy the privileges of major league status despite a reputation for crookedness. But he was not the only one. And to the extent that Organized Baseball failed to find a way to deal with corruption among the ranks of its players, it was courting a genuine business disaster.

The New Order

It was, in fact, the need to come to terms with this last problem that accounted for the recent revolutionary restructuring of the governance of Organized Baseball. For when the owners learned, in September 1920, that the outcome of the previous year's World Series had apparently been bought, and when they reflected on the consequences for their investment if the fans turned away from a tainted game, they abandoned a long-standing reliance on franchise autonomy. They turned in desperation to the remedy of autocracy, entrusting authority over major league baseball to a single person, whose impartiality was to be assured by virtue of his having pursued a career in some calling other than baseball. This "czar"—a term widely used at the time—was given the power to investigate any person or activity "suspected to be detrimental to the best interests of the national game of baseball." If he found wrongdoing, he could impose any punishment he deemed appropriate, from reprimands and small fines to lifetime banishment. And no entity in Organized Baseball—neither a club nor a league nor a player nor an owner—could claim exemption from this punitive power. The czar was also to be the final arbiter of all disputes involving the leagues, the owners, or the players. The most striking evidence of the owners' sense of desperation was their agreement to waive their right to appeal the czar's decisions to the courts; instead, they agreed to honor all decisions, "even when we believe them mistaken."[22]

In defining the powers of this office, the owners knew whom they wanted. He was the strikingly named Kenesaw Mountain Landis—a federal judge with populist tendencies, known for his implacable hostility toward labor unions and his fervent love of baseball.[23] To secure his services they extended him a seven-year contract and $50,000 per year. Looking for all the world like an Old Testament prophet, Judge Landis was a godsend from central casting. He chose the title of Commissioner of Baseball for himself. Then, with a deliberate flair for the dramatic gesture, he set about facing down the great men of the game in order to establish his own absolute dominance. He took on baseball's most famous manager, refusing to allow John McGraw to acquire Heinie Groh in 1921 and depriving him of Shufflin' Phil Douglas in 1922. He slammed its most famous player, suspending Babe Ruth from play at the start of the 1922 season for barnstorming. He tormented various owners, compelling Charles Stoneham of the Giants to rid himself of horse-racing interests and resisting Samuel Breadon's efforts to create a St. Louis Cardinal farm system. And throughout this campaign he ostentatiously ignored the man who for two decades had been the most powerful figure in baseball, American League President Ban Johnson, reducing him to the status of a lobbyist for his association. Sometimes Landis's decisions seemed designed more *pour encourager les autres* than to distribute justice, but an occasional dash of high-handedness only enhanced the aura of fearsomeness he sought to surround himself with.

Above all else, he cast himself as the foe of corruption. His most famous action occurred in his first year in office when, despite the failure of the courts to find any legal fault with the eight Chicago White Sox players implicated in the throwing of the 1919 World Series, he banned them from organized baseball for life. "Baseball," he explained to Hugh Fullerton, "is something more than a game to an American boy; it is his training field for life work."[24] Others who consorted with gamblers or criminals soon felt his wrath. He seemed intent in his early years in office to establish the principle that—whatever may have been tolerated prior to 1920—under the new order, any player who conspired to influence the outcome of a game, who appeared to conspire to influence the outcome of a game, or who knew of such conspiratorial actions and failed to report them would be swiftly expelled from baseball. Within a few years, events would force him to soften his stand, but, in 1924, fifty-three players were on the commissioner's ineligible list, either for a specified period of time or for life. Judge Landis was not yet a national institution, but, after using a threat of resignation during the owners' meeting in December 1923 to reaffirm his authority over magnates who were beginning to chafe under his arbitrariness, he was more firmly ensconced than ever in his seat of unprecedented power.

One last element was needed for the new regime to become firmly established. The reader will have noted that two of the conventions that Organized Baseball had embraced as fundamental to its survival—the reserve rule and territorial rights—were practices that, when engaged in by oil companies or automobile manufacturers, were found by the courts to be in violation of the Sherman Anti-Trust Act of 1890. The capacity of baseball to continue using these tools therefore depended upon its continued success at remaining outside the scope of that act. It is thus centrally germane to this story that, in 1922, the Supreme Court of the United States, in a judgment (*Federal Baseball Club of Baltimore v. National League et al.*) that continues to puzzle many observers, held that Organized Baseball was not subject to the Sherman Act. By this decision the court set the new commissioner free to enforce the reserve rule and territorial rights, and hence Judge Landis became more truly a czar than ever. It was he who supplied the assurance of integrity in baseball, Babe Ruth and his emulators who supplied its prospect of excitement, and postwar prosperity that supplied the financial underpinnings for the game. By 1924, baseball was thriving as a branch of the entertainment business.

From Memorial Day to Independence Day

The Giants Finally Take Charge

THE OPENING WEEKS of June found National League fans focusing their attention on the continuing challenge that the upstart Cubs were mounting against the talent-rich Giants. The contest pitted New York hitting against Chicago pitching—Frank Snyder, George Kelly, Frankie Frisch, and Ross Youngs against Vic Keen, Vic Aldridge, Tony Kaufmann, and above all, Grover Cleveland Alexander. Although both clubs had their bad days—the Giants, for example, committed 7 errors on June 1, and the Cubs blew a lead and a game in the bottom of the ninth on June 9—each team was winning more often than it was losing. When they faced one another for 2 games at the Polo Grounds in the first week of June, the Cubs swept the short series. In the encounter on June 5, the Cubs' triumph included a ninth-inning steal of home by Cliff Heathcote. After a day of rain, Grover Cleveland Alexander held the New Yorkers to 6 hits as the Cubs won again. It was Alexander's seventh consecutive victory of the season, and the twin successes pulled the Cubs to within a single game of the league-leading Giants. "He is still," acknowledged the account in the *New York Times*, "Alexander the Great."[1]

Though driven from the dugout by his leg injury, John McGraw retained control of his charges from behind the scene, sometimes using binoculars to follow the games and the telephone to pass on instructions. He was understandably anxious about the unevenness of the club's performance, for even though Art Nehf finally contrived to pitch a full game on June 3, Giant hurling in general remained spotty; and while Hack Wilson was proving a hard-hitting and fine-fielding rookie, the protracted slump of Irish Meusel left McGraw no choice but to drop the left fielder from fourth to fifth in the batting order. McGraw's Chicago counterpart, Bill Killefer, was less frantic in these June weeks, basking in the celebrity that attends unexpected success and reposing faith in the skills that had served the team well thus far—speed on the base paths and strength on the mound. It was characteristic of the team that they registered 5 stolen bases on June 9 and 3 more on June 12. And with reassuring regularity the Cubs' effective pitching rotation brought the marvelous Alexander back to the mound; his victory on June 11, his ninth of the young season, made him the winningest pitcher in baseball. On June 13, when the Chicago team beat Boston 5–1 and the Giants lost to Cincinnati 4–1, the Cubs took a half-game lead over their New York rivals.

The next day, the Giants received their wake-up call, as George Kelly mounted an offensive performance that for leadership of teammates, was unsurpassed for more than seventy years. Kelly collected 4 hits, and since 3 of them were home runs (and since Kelly had stroked out 3 home runs in 1 game in 1923), he became the first player in major league history to hit 3 round-trippers a game on two occasions. Even more devastatingly, by driving in every single Giant run in the 8–6 victory, he participated in the setting of a major league record for—and this is complicated to express—the 9-inning game that boasts the highest score recorded by a team when only one player drives all the runs in.[2]

In keeping with the drama of the day, his final plate appearance was his most memorable. With the score tied at 6–6 in the bottom of the ninth and a runner on first, Kelly, already the hero of the game, drove the ball into the left-field stands for the third time. Having touched first base, he broke off from his circuit of the diamond and headed for the dugout to avoid the crowd that was spilling onto the field to hail him. That action had the effect of pointing up a hitherto unnoticed inconsistency between the *playing* rules of the day and the *scoring* rules. By the former, Kelly rated only a triple, because the game was effectively won when the base runner ahead of him touched home plate and because Kelly had chosen not to exercise his right to touch all four bases. By the latter, however, he deserved a home run, since the ball had left the playing field and had made the circling of the bases supererogatory. Discretion about a matter thus controverted lay in the official scorer's hands, and in conformity with a reasoning that seems natural today, the scorer awarded Kelly his third home run of the game.[3]

Kelly's performance ignited the Giants. The victory on June 14 was followed by a succession of triumphs over the Cardinals, the Braves, and the Dodgers. Irish Meusel recovered his batting eye, and each day offered a new hero—Ross Youngs, or Frankie Frisch, or Heinie Groh, or Travis Jackson, or Hack Wilson. The streak extended to 10 games before Brooklyn, benefiting from a convenient thunderstorm that wiped out a tying Giant run in the top of the eighth inning, defeated the New Yorkers 3–2 in 7 innings. But treating this loss as a mere blip, the Giants resumed their surge, winning 5 of their next 7 games. Even the team's pitching improved, with Jack Bentley hurling the Giants' first complete-game shutout of the year on July 1. Going into the Independence Day doubleheaders, the Giants had won 15 out of 18 games, and while Wilbert Robinson might mutter about their being "the luckiest guys in the world," most observers believed that talent was the foundation for New York's undeniable good fortune.[4]

For a while the Cubs kept the race tight. Although they fell back into second place on June 15, they hung just off the pace for another ten days. But then the descent began. Moving into Pittsburgh only 2½ games behind the Giants (and only 1 behind in the loss column), they dropped 4 straight engagements to the Pirates and staggered out of Forbes Field 5 games behind the leader. Their batting punch suddenly gone, they went scoreless in the final 25 innings of the series. Their fielding became erratic. And their pitching, though strong in 2 of the 4 games, failed at crucial moments. Worst of all, in the first game of the series, a disastrous contest which the Cubs managed to lose 8–7 after taking the lead in the top of the fourteenth inning, Grover Cleveland Alexander suffered a broken wrist when hit by a batted ball.

It would be difficult to exaggerate the significance of this accident, for by it Chicago lost the services of a pitcher regarded by many as being "as good as or better than any pitcher who ever lived."[5] Although the Cubs steadied themselves after leaving Pittsburgh and, powered by the strong hitting of Denver Grigsby, won consecutive victories over the Reds on the first three days of July, they were finally—with their star hurler sidelined for an indefinite period of time and the Giants on fire—looking baseball reality in the face. They were not playing poorly; indeed, they won 18 of 27 games between Memorial Day and July 4. But they were finding that contending against one of the most devastating lineups ever placed upon a baseball field was a frustrating activity.

The Other National League Challengers Sputter

If a .667 pace was inadequate to keep the Cubs in step with the Giants, it is easy to imagine what a .429 pace did to the Cincinnati Reds. Only 3½ games out of first place on Memorial Day, the Reds fell to 13 games out by the eve of the Independence Day doubleheaders. Their formidable injury list remained a drag on their performance. But Jack Hendricks did not focus attention on the vagaries of fortune. "Hard luck," he remarked, "can't last forever."[6] Moreover, even in these difficult weeks the Reds were not without happy omens. Veteran outfielder Rube Bressler, savoring a career year, was hitting well above .300, and Babe Pinelli was finally fulfilling his promise. When available, Edd Roush was as reliable as ever. The problem lay with the pitching corps. Rated by preseason forecasts as one of baseball's finest staffs, Cincinnati's squad of hurlers was turning out to be one of baseball's least consistent. Take Eppa Rixey. Formidably good when his control was sharp, he was easy pickings when he could not command his curve. That's why he defeated the mighty Giants 4–1 on June 13 and retired the first 23 Pirate batters he faced on June 24 but failed to last even an inning against the Cubs on July 2. Then there was Dolf Luque. He was not exactly bad. But although he had yielded only 2 runs a game in 1923, he was averaging about twice that number in 1924. Carl Mays was suddenly floundering. And although Tom Sheehan, back for his third try at pitching in the majors, had begun the season well, he faltered after winning his sixth game on June 4. The Reds' long summer of misery had begun.

Had the Dodgers been allowed to play a schedule that ignored the Giants, they would have sat atop the National League on the eve of the July Fourth holiday. Against the six teams that did not call New York City their home, Brooklyn boasted a record of 34 wins and 19 losses, for a winning percentage of .642. Against the Giants, they were a woeful 3 and 11. Consequently they were in third place, 7½ games behind the leader. Jack Fournier and Zack Wheat led their attack, Fournier ("the Babe Ruth of Flatbush") by hammering home runs at a pace scarcely exceeded by the Bambino himself (he had 16 as July began), and Wheat by challenging Rogers Hornsby for the league batting-average lead. Above all, there was the sandy-haired, high-kicking Dazzy Vance, who was staking his claim to be the best pitcher in baseball. On June 13 he struck Rogers Hornsby out 3 consecutive times.[7] On June 19 he became the first hurler in either circuit to win 10 games. By early July he had 12 victories to his credit. But against the Giants even Vance faltered. In fact, Vance at midseason owed all 3 of his losses to the cross-city rivals.[8] Looking ahead, Wilbert Robinson knew that if he could figure out how to beat his old friend John McGraw, the Dodgers might still get back into the race, and with that goal in mind Brooklyn signed the veteran spitballer Bill Doak in June. But the corollary to that premise was clear: There was no hope for Brooklyn if the team continued to play the role of doormat for New York.

In Pittsburgh, Bill McKechnie, having settled upon Max Carey as his leadoff batter, used June to experiment successfully with various combinations of youth and experience lower down in the order, and the Pirates, though unable to match the bracing pace set by the Giants, won 16 of their first 27 post–Memorial Day games and moved into fourth place on June 21. The Pirates' talented clutch of rookies was leading the team's charge. Emil Yde and Ray Kremer, for example, joined with veteran Wilbur Cooper to give Pittsburgh a consistent pitching staff. Yde broke in with a shutout victory on May 31 and was the winning pitcher in a 10-inning relief appearance in the 14-inning game with the Cubs that sent Grover Cleveland Alexander to the sidelines. Kremer had good control and an almost matchless pickoff move to first; he strutted his stuff in shutting out the Cubs on June 28, thereby completing the devastating sweep of Chicago in that important series.[9] The two other rookie standouts, Kiki Cuyler in right field and Glenn Wright at shortstop, added both defensive leavening and offensive might—Cuyler in fact was batting in regions defined by Rogers Hornsby and Zack Wheat—to the character of the team. Had the veterans been doing the jobs expected of them, the Pirates might have managed to challenge the Giants in June, but Carson Bigbee and Charlie Grimm faltered, and Pie Traynor, slowed down by illness, played so raggedly that McKechnie benched him for a while. Nevertheless, by winning 7 of their final 8 games in June, Pittsburgh sent a signal to the rest of the league that it still meant to make a mark on the pennant race.

No such signal came out of Boston, Philadelphia, or St. Louis. The problem for the Braves was that the heart of their offense was composed of three players in their midthirties—Dave Bancroft, Stuffy McInnis, and Casey Stengel. Their play bespoke their age. The Phillies were even more distressed, having only Cy Williams to boast of in their batting order. At times their play could be embarrassing: On June 17, for example, they outhit the Cubs 13 to 4 but lost the game 6–5 when their defense committed 5 errors and their pitching yielded 8 bases on balls. Still, the title of worst in the league thus far in 1924 went neither to Boston nor to Philadelphia, but to the St. Louis Cardinals. In this company, Rogers Hornsby stood out like Gulliver in Lilliput. Despite his injury in May, Hornsby was threatening to repeat as a supra .400 batter. When he tripled on July 2, he became the first National League player to reach 100 base hits in 1924—despite his being so frequently walked. But it was a mark of the Cardinals' problem that their pitching was the worst in the league, and their team batting average, despite Hornsby's contribution, challenged for that honor. Going into Independence Day they had lost 22 of their last 30 games. It was months such as June of 1924 that led Branch Rickey, many years later (and in characteristically mellifluous cadences), to tell a congressional committee, "It is not a joy continuously to experience the emotions of defeat."[10]

The American League: A Bevy of Contenders

In the American League during June, fans were offered a richer array of exciting developments. For if the National League seemed threatened with yet another variation in the succession of annual victory parades by the relentless New York Giants, the American League boasted seven teams that appeared to have a crack at the pennant. Team after team lunged forward—the Red Sox, the Yankees, the Tigers, the Indians, the White Sox, the Browns, the Nationals—only to falter. At some point during June, four of them secured sole possession of first place. As a result, the gap from first place to seventh place in the American League, as play began on the morning of July 4, was narrower than the gap from first place to third place in the National League. As Red Sox Manager Lee Fohl said, "This is a corking fine race."[11] It was no wonder that attendance in the American League was exceeding attendance in the National League.

The Yankees and the Red Sox were coleaders of the American League as May passed into June, but neither team was playing well. That the Red Sox found the atmosphere of first place too heady surprised no one; they had, after all, been performing beyond everyone's expectations. And in fact, aided by the inconsistencies of the Yankees and the strong pitching of Howard Ehmke, the Red Sox shared first place as late as

level in batting at midseason and hitting home runs at a pace that would have elicited comment in any league not occupied by Babe Ruth. Gene Robertson, enjoying the best season of his career, and Baby Doll Jacobson, who hit 2 home runs against the Tigers on June 24, were batting around .320. As for George Sisler, though it was clear by midseason that his batting eye of old had not returned, it was also clear that he was still a force to be taken seriously. In speculating about Sisler's batting problems, people wondered whether the strains and distractions of managing were hurting his playing, especially after intemperate words from the ordinarily calm first baseman got him ejected from a game by umpire Ducky Holmes on June 21 and subsequently suspended by president Ban Johnson.[18] The key point, however, is that the Browns were not out of contention and, with a few breaks, could plausibly still make a run for the flag.

The same evaluation could be applied to the Chicago White Sox—and surprisingly, with even greater force. It was true that Chicago's pitching in the first half of the season was poor, but the team had sounder hopes than most that the work of its mound staff might improve. After all, the effectiveness of both Red Faber and Charlie Robertson had thus far been limited by surgeries to remove elbow chips; with both hurlers now on the mend, they might reasonably be expected to make larger contributions to the play of the team in the second half of the season. Meanwhile, the team already had a dominant pitcher in Sloppy Thurston, who, although only in his second major league season, became the league's first 12-game winner on July 3 with a victory over Detroit. Scarcely remembered today, Thurston was not an overpowering hurler. He did, however, command a good screwball and possessed fine control. The chief offensive power of the White Sox was provided by two other youngsters, Bibb Falk and Maurice Archdeacon, both of whom were hitting above .350. The speedy Archdeacon was sensational, and after the games of July 4 he had the highest batting average in the league (.378). He and the fleet Eddie Collins, who at thirty-seven was on the way to his fifth base-stealing title, gave Chicago the league's most fearsome pair of base runners. If the rookie-of-the year award had existed in 1924, and if the vote had been taken at midseason, Archdeacon would have swept the balloting.

The Cleveland Indians played wonderful ball in June and climbed back into the race. As late as June 6, when they lost to Philadelphia, they were still stuck in the cellar. But then Tris Speaker's charges turned their play around. Over the next four weeks they won almost twice as often as they lost, taking every game of a 4-game series with the Washington Nationals, 3 out of 4 from the New York Yankees, and 3 out of 5 from the Detroit Tigers. Finally, with a victory over the St. Louis Browns on July 1, the Indians reached the first division. The basis of their success was their offense: On Independence Day, Cleveland boasted the highest team batting average in the league. Charlie Jamieson was hitting above .370, and just before July 4, while on his way to the best year of his career, he became the second player in the American League to reach 100 base hits. Joe Sewell, Homer Summa, and Pat McNulty (who stepped in for the injured Tris Speaker) were batting around .330. Riggs Stephenson, Glenn Myatt, Tioga George Burns, and Speaker himself were batting above .300. Injuries sometimes benched one or two of these batters. But this was a team that was capable of pummeling opponents by scores of 11–3 (against Washington, on June 8), 10–2 (against New York, on June 15), 16–5 (against Detroit, on June 18), and 11–9 (against Detroit again, on June 20). The fact that the Indian could occasionally score in double figures and still lose, as they did, 16–10, against the Browns on July 3, pointed up their chief problem in the longer run: Their pitching was vulnerable. But during June even the two chief disappointments of the staff, the balding George Uhle and the spit-balling Stan Coveleskie, usually held their opponents to fewer than 5 runs, while Joe Shaute (SHAY-ute) emerged as one of the league's premier pitchers. Cleveland's fans had expected the Indians to provide a challenge for the pennant in 1924: The team's performance over the month prior to Independence Day reinforced that expectation.

The Surge of the Washington Nationals

For the generation of excitement in June, however, no team could touch the Washington Nationals. In a reversal of fortune as stunning as it was unexpected, the Nationals exploded out of sixth place, vaulted past five rivals, and captured first place. The swiftness of their success testified, to be sure, to the tightness of the pack in the American League pennant chase. But it also meant that the patient labors of Clark Griffith to create a sound team, and of Bucky Harris to find an effective combination of talents, were finally paying off. Two lineup changes coincided with the charge. First, after much experimenting with various candidates for center field, Harris finally declared Wid Matthews—"Matty" to his legions of local fans—as his choice. "There isn't a better hustler in the American League," Al Schacht commented, "than little Wid."[19] Then Harris replaced Doc Prothro with Ossie Bluege (bloo-ghee) as his third baseman, giving up greater success at the plate to gain wider range in the infield.[20] Both changes paid off. Though Matthews would later fade, he hit around .350 for the month of June, and the installation of Bluege gave Washington the sharpest defensive infield in the league.

The Nationals' rebirth—halting at first—began with a 12–1 pasting of St. Louis on June 11. Paul Zahniser returned to the mound that day for the first time in a month, Goose Goslin homered, and Roger Peckinpaugh collected 3 hits. After a rain-out, the Nationals took fourth place on June 13 with a 6–4 win over St. Louis. The next day they won their third straight game from the Browns, Goslin stroking out 4 hits. The team then moved on to Chicago for a 4-game series. Despite Goslin's continued success at bat—he managed 11 hits in 17 official at-bats—the Nationals lost the first 2 games, on June 15 and June 16, by scores of 6–4 and 9–8 and fell back into sixth place. But on June 17, Tom Zachary broke the short losing streak with a 13–6 victory.

Then, in the game on June 18, the Nationals showed for the first time that they could play like thoroughbreds. Coming into the ninth inning trailing 4–3, they combined a single by Bucky Harris, a walk to Muddy Ruel, a fielder's choice, and a single by Peckinpaugh to take a 5–4 lead after 2 outs. Then, in the bottom of the ninth, the White Sox having loaded the bases with only 1 out, Firpo Marberry came to the mound and put Chicago down without allowing a run. After a scheduled day off, the team went to Philadelphia, where, on June 20, they won 3–2 in 12 innings and went over .500. Wid Matthews saved the game in the eighth with a spectacular, inning-ending catch with the bases loaded; Peckinpaugh doubled for the winning run in the top of the twelfth inning; and Marberry again came in to get the final outs. An 11–3 victory over Philadelphia on June 21 placed the Nationals in third place, and a 5–4 victory on June 22, featuring a bases-loaded triple by Sam Rice and a superb 5-inning relief effort by Oyster Joe Martina, set the stage for Washington's trip to New York, where the Nationals would play the defending-champion Yankees in the first critical series of the year.

The doubleheader on June 23 provided all the evidence needed to show that Washington was an authentic challenger. George Mogridge won the first game, 5–2, and Paul Zahniser won the second game, 4–2. Goose Goslin and Joe Judge each collected 4 hits on the day, and one of Goslin's was a home run. With these two victories, Washington moved into a virtual tie for second place with the Yankees, only half a game behind the league-leading Tigers. The game on June 24 featured new strokes of good fortune for the Nationals. In the first inning, a Yankee error gave Washington an unearned run. In the top of the fourth inning, Yankee first baseman Wally Pipp and catcher Wally Schang collided while pursuing an easy foul pop fly off the bat of Peckinpaugh. Given a second opportunity against Herb Pennock, the National shortstop hit a home run. "What the Yanks needed," a *Times* reporter quipped, "was a traffic cop."[21] These runs allowed the game to go into extra innings, and the Nationals, kept in the contest by 6 innings of shut-out pitching from Allan Russell, took the lead, 4–3, in the top of the tenth. The game ended with a sensational, run-saving catch by Goslin. With this victory the Nationals swept past both the Yankees and the Tigers to seize an exclusive hold on first place. "The mountain," the *Washington Post* declared, "has come to Mohammed."[22]

The next day, although they could muster only 5 hits in a rain-shortened game, Washington completed its rout of New York by a score of 3–2, with Firpo Marberry pitching (and stalling) the entire game. It was the first time the Yankees had been swept in a 4-game series in Yankee Stadium. That evening, traveling back to Washington by train, the Nationals could reflect on the deeply satisfying results of the past two weeks: Having won 9 straight games and 12 out of their last 14, Washington was in possession of first place at a later date than in any previous season in the club's history. "We're happy and we're tough to beat," Bucky Harris rejoiced.[23]

Their return to the nation's capital scarcely slowed their momentum. With President Calvin Coolidge and the Navy Band present to celebrate their success, they played a doubleheader against Philadelphia on June 26. In the first game, Walter Johnson shut out the visitors to give Washington its tenth consecutive victory; and while the second game—a 1–0 loss to knuckleballing Eddie Rommel—finally ended the team's winning streak, the loss seemed only to reenergize the Nationals. In the succeeding days they strengthened their grasp on first place, winning 2 more from the Athletics and 5 of 6 from the Red Sox before the schedule gave them another day of rest on July 3. Going into Independence Day, they led the second-place Tigers by 3½ games and the third-place Yankees by 4. "We are going to win Washington's first pennant," Clark Griffith declared: "The Senators are coming while the Yankees are going."[24]

Altogether, the Nationals had sustained an astonishing pace. Between June 11 and July 3 they had played 24 games and won 20 of them. Throughout that period their fielding had been exemplary; in the 4-game series against the Yankees, for example, they had committed only 1 error. In the early part of the surge, the batters led the way. Goose Goslin ran off a 19-game hitting streak; Wid Matthews, Joe Judge, and Sam Rice joined him in hitting well above .300; and on three occasions between June 11 and June 21, the team scored in double-digit numbers. But in the latter part of the surge, the credit for success shifted dramatically to the pitching staff. In the 14 games between June 23 and July 3, the Nationals' hurlers were astonishing: They held their opponents to an average of scarcely more than a run a game and only once allowed them to score as many as 3.[25] Walter Johnson, George Mogridge, Curly Ogden, and Paul Zahniser all threw shutouts. Moreover, even though Walter Johnson pitched well during the 24-game period and had 10 victories on the eve of Independence Day, he scarcely qualified as the pitching star of the surge, since his wife's appendicitis had pulled him away from the team for the entire New York series. Instead, it was Zahniser and Oyster Joe Martina, each of whom twice held opponents to a single run, who won the laurels. Finally, it's important to note that the pitchers accomplished this collective feat in the face of a schedule—5 doubleheaders (and no days off) in nine calendar days—that seemed expressly designed to expose weaknesses in pitching depth. It was very gratifying to Bucky Harris to see that his club possessed exactly the kind of hurling resilience he had worked to cultivate.

The Independence Day Doubleheaders

In the years before an All-Star game provided a scheduled interruption to the daily flow of baseball, the Fourth of July was the traditional mid-season milepost.[26] And on that day in 1924 the law of the attraction of the mean suddenly reasserted itself in the American League, as the league-leading Washington Nationals lost 2 games to the New York Yankees while the cellar-dwelling Philadelphia Athletics won 2 games from the Boston Red Sox. In other action in the American League, the St. Louis Browns ruined the Detroit Tigers' opportunity to advance on the Nationals by sweeping the morning–afternoon doubleheader, while the Chicago White Sox and the Cleveland Indians split their twin bill. In the National League, the activity of Independence Day brought delight to Cincinnati, as the Reds shut down the Pittsburgh Pirates both before and after lunch, and disappointment to Brooklyn, as the Boston Braves kept the Dodgers' formidable batting order confined and won 2 games. The other doubleheaders in the National League ended in splits between the Cubs and the Cardinals and the Giants and the Phillies.

The double loss to the Yankees before a home crowd was a sobering disappointment for the Nationals. But when the day was over, Washington still held first place in the American League—to the pleased astonishment of fans almost everywhere in the country. The National League standings were less startling: The league-leading Giants had, after all, been almost everyone's pick for the pennant. But the tenacity of the Cubs lent a measure of excitement to this chase, and the strength of the Dodgers and the Pirates meant that they could not be totally discounted. And so, with summer beginning, followers of the game had ample grounds for believing that this might be a year in which the temperature of the pennant races would match the temperature of the season.

Standings at the End of Play, Independence Day, July 4

AMERICAN LEAGUE

Team	Won	Lost	Pctg.	Games Behind
Washington Nationals	41	30	.577	—
New York Yankees	38	31	.551	2.0
Detroit Tigers	39	35	.527	3.5
St. Louis Browns	35	33	.515	4.5
Chicago White Sox	34	35	.493	6.0
Cleveland Indians	34	36	.486	6.5
Boston Red Sox	32	37	.464	8.0
Philadelphia Athletics	27	43	.386	13.5

National League

Team	Won	Lost	Pctg.	Games Behind
New York Giants	46	24	.657	—
Chicago Cubs	41	27	.603	4.0
Brooklyn Dodgers	37	32	.536	8.5
Pittsburgh Pirates	34	33	.507	10.5
Cincinnati Reds	36	38	.486	12.0
Boston Braves	29	40	.420	16.5
Philadelphia Phillies	28	39	.418	16.5
St. Louis Cardinals	26	44	.371	20.0

CHAPTER FIVE

◦◦◦

The Players

Who Were These Major Leaguers?

DURING THE 1924 season more than five hundred men—from Adams (Babe) to Zahniser (Paul)—played in a major league baseball game. Almost 90 percent of them came from British, German, or Irish stock; none was of known African descent.[1] The youngest was the Giants' rookie third baseman, Freddy Lindstrom, who batted .253 at the age of eighteen; the oldest to play regularly was Jack Quinn, the extraordinarily durable Red Sox spitballer, who, although turning forty-one in July, pitched 228⅔ innings with an earned run average a full point lower than the league's.[2] These men came from all over the country. Illinois, Pennsylvania, and Missouri produced forty or more each. Texas, Ohio, and California produced thirty or more. New York, Massachusetts, and Indiana produced twenty or more. Though no traditional southern state appeared on the list until Tennessee broke through (the tenth highest, with fifteen), the South (even without Texas) supplied 109 players to the majors, second only to the 187 born in the Midwest. Only five sparsely populated western states, Idaho, Nevada, North Dakota, South Dakota, and Wyoming, had no representatives in the major leagues.

By today's standards these players were not big men. The Washington Nationals, to take a dramatic example, had no regular player who was 6 feet tall, and none who weighed more than 185 pounds. Ty Cobb, whom we often think of as small, was in fact a big man, standing 6 feet, 1 inch. Babe Ruth was bigger still, at 6 feet, 2 inches. The tallest player in the majors was Cincinnati pitcher Eppa Rixey at 6 feet, 5 inches; the shortest was Pirate second baseman, Rabbit Maranville, who stood 5 feet, 5 inches. An estimate from 1925 declared that about one-third of major leaguers grew up on farms.[3] But contrary to a popular image of the major league player as a hayseed, this was an educated group of men, with perhaps one in four having attended college.[4] Harry Hooper, the veteran White Sox outfielder, later remarked: "I think it's pretty clear we had *more* than our share of college men in baseball. And it's also pretty clear that the usual picture you get of the old-time ballplayer as an illiterate rowdy contains an awful lot more fiction than it does fact."[5]

Because of the premium it placed on the reflexes of youth, playing major league baseball was not a lifetime career prospect for any man. Still, it is startling how brief such careers could be. A study from the first decade of the twentieth century showed that the turnover of players in the ranks of the major leagues approximated 90 percent each decade, and of the more than five hundred major leaguers playing in 1924, only thirteen, or 2.5 percent, had played in the majors in 1910.[6]

It is likely that the Great War (1917–18) produced a decline in the quality of the personnel who played in the majors in the immediate post-war years. Although I know of no analysis of these matters, several lines of reasoning are suggestive nevertheless. For example, many major leaguers joined the armed forces or at least transferred out of ballplaying careers in 1917 and 1918. For some, in an era of nonstratospheric baseball salaries, this disruption probably meant the effective end of a career. Then, there was the war's effect on the recruitment of new talent. The virtual demise of the minor leagues in 1918 obliterated the chief channel for training and winnowing talent, and it is likely that, as a result of the war, one brief generation of talent was underrepresented in the majors in the succeeding years.[7] I find it suggestive, for example, that, rich as the 1920s would turn out to be in future Hall of Famers, only one of them entered the majors in 1919 and only two in 1920 and 1921.[8]

Still, I don't mean to suggest that the major leagues in 1924 were peculiarly shorn of talent. Even if we believe that the decade is overrepresented in the Hall of Fame,[9] it is undeniable that at least five of the game's absolutely greatest players—Grover Cleveland Alexander, Ty Cobb, Rogers Hornsby, Walter Johnson, and Babe Ruth—were performing in 1924. Thus, I think that the effect of the war, at least in the early years of the decade, was to widen the spread between the most talented and the least talented beyond the range of variation that ordinarily obtained in the majors. Close observers provided anecdotal corroboration. "They don't seem to teach them anything in the Minors," John

McGraw complained.[10] "I don't think pitching is as good as it was . . . when I first came into the league," Rogers Hornsby noted.[11] It follows that one reason for the extraordinary quality of some of the accomplishments of the superstars in the early 1920s is that the skills of the average player had not yet quite returned to prewar levels.

The Life of a Major Leaguer

Major leaguers led a life that most of them found enchanting. "We were all tickled to death playing ball in those days," George Kelly reported at the distance of half a century.[12] Ballplayers were in the enviable position of being paid to engage in an activity that for most of them offered the satisfaction of extending childhood; they knew that their job was gainful employment, "but somehow, way deep down,"—the words are Bob O'Farrell's—"it's still play."[13] In their home cities they were celebrities, enjoying the adoration of children and the perks that lighten a life: special treatment from the police, opportunities to meet screen and stage stars, unsolicited gifts, and exemption from the frustration of standing in queues. "The major league player," Hugh Fullerton wrote, from many years of observation, "is the most pampered, best cared for and conditioned live stock in the world."[14] When players were on the road, they stayed in good hotels, dined well, and traveled to and from the ballpark in taxis. For those to whom the fragility of this privileged style of life was a constant vexation and who never ceased hearing the panting of younger men seeking to displace them, baseball was—in the famous words of Stan Coveleskie—"a worrying thing."[15] But for the majority, more inclined to let the future take care of itself, the judgment of Rube Marquard that "every single day I spent in the Big Leagues was . . . like a dream come true" was closer to the mark.[16]

The reality of psychic satisfactions, however, did not mean that major league ballplayers lived without pressure, fatigue, worry, boredom, and pain. During the season, baseball was a daily activity; it required physical exertion and involved a margin of risk. Even when a team was not scheduled to play an official opponent, it often used the occasion to make money by playing an exhibition game against a minor league club.[17] As with almost all jobs, there was a monotony to the daily routine. When the team was at home, a player's schedule consisted of travel to the ballpark (most players lived close by), morning practice, a break for lunch, afternoon warm-up, the game, postgame washing up, and travel back to home. When the team was on the road, hotels replaced the home (two men to a room), and morning practice was less likely to occur. But the biggest change in life for a team on the road was the amount of free time that players had on their hands. Responsibilities at the ballpark took scarcely more than four hours. The rest of the day and night was the player's time, spent variously in such placid activities as writing letters and visiting libraries and in such livelier activities as gambling, prowling speakeasies, and cruising the red-light districts.

On those days when a team moved on to the next city, packing and travel suddenly became significant consumers of time. Although a property manager bore responsibility for transporting team equipment, players were expected to do their own packing and to carry their own bags. Teams used the railroad between cities, and, to choose the longest likely example, the rail trip from Chicago to Boston took twenty-six hours.[18] Goose Goslin's reminiscing cadences reflected the drone of life on the road: "hotel . . . taxi . . . train . . . taxi . . . hotel . . . train."[19] Rail travel was not without risks: A train carrying both the Cincinnati Reds and the Pittsburgh Pirates suffered an accident on June 21, 1924, and the Philadelphia Phillies were forty-five minutes late for a game on August 21, 1924, because their train hit an obstacle, crushing its engineer and badly burning its fireman. But it was a sense of discomfort rather than of danger that train travel most readily evoked. Midsummer rail trips in pre–climate-control days could be thoroughly unpleasant, blighted by the smell of smoke drifting through open windows, the obligation to wear suits by day, the confinement of sleeping berths by night, and a prevailing atmosphere of hot and sweaty griminess.[20] It is true that the men and women of the 1920s expected nothing else of the season. But we should not forget just how exhausting an environment of sticky heat and sodden clothes—flannel uniforms were washed but once a week—could be for those who made their living through vigorous outdoor activity.

With few days set aside for rest and recuperation, men who sustained sprains and bruises were often forced to ignore them. "Players," Willie Kamm recalled, "were expected to play with injuries."[21] Many commentators believed that the 1924 season was peculiarly beset with injuries, and while I do not have the information that would allow that judgment to be tested, it is worth noting that such notables as Grover Cleveland Alexander, Rogers Hornsby, Edd Roush, and Ken Williams were kept out of their lineups for significant portions of the season by injuries sustained on the field.[22] The care that an injured player received from his team was not intensive. Each club had a trainer, who nursed the sprains and aches of the players—and especially of pitchers—with massages and lotions. But the trainer was not a physician, and his chief remedy was rubbing alcohol.[23] And so if the hurt did not quickly heal, it was customary for a player to leave his team for a short while (usually at his own expense) to seek the help of one of a small number of medical men, usually called "bonesetters," who had gained celebrity as healers of the sore limbs of athletes. Bonesetter Knight lived in Rochester, Bonesetter Sweet practiced out of Battle Creek, and the most famous of all, Bonesetter Reese, hung out his shingle in Youngstown, Ohio.[24] Players frequently visited these sites, for they knew that their ability to continue to command a decent salary depended upon their ability to continue to perform at a certain level.

Baseball life was an all-male activity. In locker rooms and dugouts, in hotels and trains, men interacted with men. They ate with men, showered with men, shared rooms and bathrooms with men, and passed much of their spare time with men. A baseball team was like an exotic boys' club, with all the undercurrents of bravado, cooperative competition, childish pranksterism, uninhibited profanity, and masked homoeroticism that one often associates with army life and men's colleges. In choosing a word to capture the fraternal essence of a team, John McGraw spoke of "the gang"; Christy Mathewson called the Giants his "home"; Goose Goslin reported that being traded from the Senators in 1930 "broke my heart"; and Edd Roush called the Reds of his era—1916 through 1926—"one of the nicest bunch of fellows ever gathered together."[25] Even allowing for the capacity of nostalgia to blur memory, these affective terms are significant cues to warm recollections of male bonding.

Still, I do not want to exaggerate the accuracy of memory. Many players from the era have gone on record about how they "talked baseball all day and night."[26] That's just nonsense. When away from the ballpark, most players wanted to get away from the game as well. It is clear, following a boys-will-be-boys principle, that rowdyism, drinking, and sex played major roles in the lives of many ballplayers when they were on the road. When the Boston Braves visited Cincinnati in July of 1924, one of their nightlong parties led to broken furniture, bruised players, and press commentary. Although less usual than it had once been, this kind of behavior was not considered uncommon. Such rowdyism was often precipitated by drinking, for despite the Volstead Act, alcoholic beverages were available to almost anyone visiting any city; and while many players from the era later stated that the extent of drunken boisterousness at the time has been exaggerated,[27] it is clear that several beers a night was considered natural for most and hard liquor was deemed necessary by many. Indeed, according to Ty Cobb and Hans Lobert, the advent of Prohibition, rather than curtailing indulgence by ballplayers, actually increased it.[28]

Some years ago Pete Rose remarked that sex was one of the fringe benefits of being a major leaguer, and he was not the first ballplayer to have reached that conclusion.[29] In the 1920s a cordon of silence protected major leaguers from direct public scrutiny of their private lives, and even after the code crumbled in later decades, few players from the earlier days discussed their escapades for writers. But the protective screen was not inviolate. There was always the vehicle of innuendo, as when *Collier's* noted in a piece about women and baseball that "the big, guileless Babe in the Wood" had been forced to pay hush money to companions.[30] And there was the cartoon—one of society's sanctioned ways to explore what could not otherwise be discussed. A *Sporting News* cartoon from March 1924 presented a player who was jubilant that his manager was not allowing wives at spring training: "He has the interest of the ball players at heart—especially the married ones!" In another from a June issue, a manager fumed: "No wonder my pitchers haven't got any control!! out with wild women every night." An August cartoon explained that conversations on the mound often concerned "apple sauce": The catcher depicted told the pitcher that "th' two swell dames sittin' in the box!!—they're goin' to wait for us after the game!!" And in a November cartoon one player sought advice from another about the "brand of apple sauce" he used "to land the wrens."[31]

In *My Thirty Years in Baseball*, John McGraw discussed whether ballplayers should be married. Acknowledging that it was a subject that he did not wish to say too much about, he nevertheless advanced the view that sweethearts and wives were liabilities to a team. Without a doubt, he noted, the young man from a small town was vulnerable to the entrapments of city women who hung out in the lobbies of hotels. But permission for wives to travel with the team—none of the big-league clubs permitted conjugal travel in 1924, though some have been more permissive in recent years—would not be a solution, both because many players were unmarried and because the wives themselves, aside from being fomenters of gossip, were a more enduring distraction.[32] Moreover, some players had established semipermanent ties with female companions in various cities around the league. In light of management's point of view, which strikes us today as antediluvian, it is not surprising that baseball teams were often pursued by "baseball Sadies" and "diamond Daisies"—women whom David Voigt has likened to "camp followers."[33]

In sex, as in much else, the gargantuan Babe Ruth was the man whose prowess most staggered his peers. "He'd stick his thing into anything that had hair on it," one teammate bluntly opined.[34] It was said that he knew the prostitutes' quarters in every city of the league's circuit, and it was reported that he was often seen off by women when leaving a town. In light of all of this not-very-startling testimony and inference about the 1920s, we can appreciate the full dimensions of Casey Stengel's remark to his high-spirited Yankee teams of the 1950s that he knew all of the tricks they might try from his own playing days. And, in fact, it was Stengel himself who provided the most amusing example of the fascination with the interplay of sex and baseball that the 1924 season produced. In mid-August, at the age of thirty-four, he got married, and on his first day back on the diamond after the wedding, he drove in 5 of the 7 Brave runs in a doubleheader sweep of the Cubs. The sporting press was not slow to suggest appropriately raunchy explanations for Stengel's power explosion.

From Independence Day to Labor Day

The Giants' Juggernaut Stalls

THE PHASE of the baseball season that stretched from Independence Day to Labor Day—the great backstretch of summer—was the game's annual test of physical endurance. In any major league city, daytime temperatures might rise into the 90s, and thermometers sometimes broke the 100-degree mark in St. Louis, Chicago, and Washington. In such weather, the daily grind of playing out in the sun, with no weekends off, gnawed at the resilience of even the strongest of men. Against the ravages of summertime heat and humidity, a ball club's only good protections were bench strength and pitching depth.

Of all the National League clubs, the New York Giants seemed the best endowed with these advantages, and as if to demonstrate the point, they cruised easily through the opening days of the backstretch, enduring their first shutout of the year on July 6 but in general looking comfortable and impressive. The Giants made a major statement when they swept through Chicago in mid-July, shattering whatever hopes the Cubs might still have nourished in 4 devastating games. They took the first contest, 14–3; George Kelly hit 2 home runs, while Irish Meusel, Frank Snyder, and Hack Wilson added round-trippers of their own. The next day, propelled by more home runs from Kelly and Wilson, the Giants pounded the Cubs 9–6. In the third game Kelly and Snyder hit round-trippers, and Virgil Barnes, who had emerged as McGraw's fourth starter after Rosy Ryan continued to disappoint, allowed only one Chicago runner to get as far as second base. The Giants won 7–0. In the final game, another Giant victory (9–4), Kelly hit his fifth home run of the series. Irving Vaughan reflected the spirit of the moment in Chicago when he wrote, "The undertaker backed his cart up to the front door of the Cubs' residence last week and took away the remains of little Pennant Hope."[1] Before Kelly's one-man blitz was over he had stroked out 7 home runs in six days. Meanwhile, on July 16, by defeating the Pirates, the Giants extended their lead to 10½ games over the second-place Cubs, 11½ over the third-place Dodgers, and 12 over the Pirates. They had won 55 of their first 81 games, playing at an impressive .679 pace. "The all conquering Giants," Joe Vila wrote, "have turned the National League race into a top heavy farce."[2]

But then the mighty Giants fell to earth. They split back-to-back 4-game series against the Pirates and the Reds and took only 3 out of 5 from the seventh-place Cardinals. These teams, it is true, were improving, especially on the mound. Wilbur Cooper of the Pirates, for example, belatedly hitting his stride, marched up to third place in victories among league pitchers during July, and the two outstanding Pirate rookies, Ray Kremer and Emil Yde, were the talk of the league. For the Reds, the advent of summer had brought with it Eppa Rixey's traditional hot-season form, allowing the tall left-hander to spin off 31 consecutive scoreless innings in early July. Meanwhile, his teammate Carl Mays launched a winning streak of 9 games. As for the Cardinals, their ordinarily unimpressive pitching garnered headlines on two occasions in the third week in July. First, on July 17, Jesse Haines baffled the Boston Braves with the first no-hitter in Cardinal history and the only 9-inning no-hitter in the majors in 1924. Then, two days later, Herman Bell pitched and won both contests on a twin bill, dropping the Braves into the cellar; his feat marks the last time in National League history that a pitcher threw 2 complete-game victories in a doubleheader. But even when all of these achievements by their opponents are allowed, there is no denying that the Giants, although still leading the Cubs by 7 games after play on July 29, were off their customary stride in the second half of the month. In retrospect, we note that Ross Youngs was out of the lineup during this period in order to receive medical attention for symptoms that were the first manifestation of the intractable infection that would kill him three years later at the age of thirty.

The Pirates' Surge

The fact that the Giants were struggling was driven home when the Pirates, led by Kiki Cuyler, roared through New York at the very end of July to win 3 out of 4 from the league leaders. A fortnight earlier the hard-hitting rookie had first caught New York's attention by stroking out 10 hits against Giant pitching, including 2 doubles and 3 triples. Now Cuyler resumed his mischief-making, collecting 7 more hits, including a double and a triple. He also lost a home run in the second game when rain forced the umpires to wipe the blow from the books. The veteran Wilbur Cooper was the winning pitcher in the first game; the rookie Ray Kremer, ordinarily a starter, saved the fourth game. When the Pirates left New York after the game of August 2, they had won 11 of their last 12 contests and had advanced to within 8 games of the Giants.

At that point the New Yorkers steadied themselves. John McGraw had resumed his regular managerial duties at the end of July, and the club benefited from a schedule that served up the Chicago Cubs as their next visitor. Even though the Cubs played well against the rest of the league (and hence were still hanging around in second place, 7 games off the pace), they were almost helpless against the Giants. That pattern held, as they lost all but 1 of the 6 contests. Encouragingly for the New Yorkers, it was not Giant batting power but Giant pitching skills that led them to their victories. Only in the single game that Chicago won did the visitors score more than 3 runs. Art Nehf, finally showing the finesse that had made him a mainstay of the staff during four consecutive seasons, pitched complete-game victories in both the first and the last games of the series. The Reds followed the Cubs into the Polo Grounds, and although the Giants lost 2 of the 5 contests, they had the satisfaction of ending Carl Mays's winning streak at 9 and seeing Hack Wilson break out of a horrendous 0-for-23 slump with a triple that drove in 3 runs. Next on the schedule, however, was a trip to Pittsburgh. And even though the Giants had performed at a crisp pace since being roughed up by the Pirates in July, Pittsburgh had played even sharper ball. Coming off successive doubleheader sweeps of the Phillies, and aided by a remarkable 6-for-6 performance by Kiki Cuyler in one of those games, the Pirates stood only 7 games off the pace—not yet close enough to provoke panic, perhaps, but impressive for a team that had launched its season so calamitously.

In the first game, played on August 13, Lee Meadows of the Pirates outpitched Virgil Barnes to win 4–2. Ross Youngs was back in the leadoff position in the New York lineup, and he delivered a hit, helping the Giants to score first. But the offensive star of the game was Kiki Cuyler, who continued to punish the Giants by stroking out 3 hits and stealing a base. The second game was also well pitched. The Giants scored a run in the first inning, but thereafter Wilbur Cooper held them scoreless. Meanwhile, the Pirates got to Hugh McQuillan for single runs in each of the three middle innings and won 3–1. Cuyler sat this game out. The third contest was played on August 15, and although Cuyler got only 1 hit, it was a 3-run round-tripper off Art Nehf that provided the winning margin in a 6–4 Pirate win. Again Giant pitching had proved unable to hold on to an early lead.

For the final game, thirty-five thousand fans crowded into Forbes Field. They saw the most exciting contest of the series. With Jack Bentley and Emil Yde in good form, it was scoreless until the sixth inning, when the Giants finally broke through with 3 runs. Going into the bottom of the eighth the New Yorkers led 4–1. But Bentley then allowed the Pirates to tie the game, thereby becoming the fourth consecutive starter unable to hold a lead for John McGraw. The score remained knotted until the bottom of the twelfth inning, when, with 2 out, Carson Bigbee, Kiki Cuyler, and Glenn Wright got consecutive singles to secure the winning run. The victory gave the Pirates their fourth straight win over the reeling New Yorkers, their ninth straight win against National League teams, and their thirtieth victory in the 41 games they had played since Independence Day. With 5 hits in the final game, including a triple, Cuyler could count 9 more blows (in just 3 games) in his most recent encounter with New York. By stroking out 31 hits in his last 60 at-bats against McGraw's staff, the marvelous rookie had established himself as an authentic Giant-killer. A grateful swarm of Pirate fans carried him off the field after the final game. More important, the Pirates, who as late as July 23 had been 12 games out of first place, on the evening of August 16 stood just 3 games off the pace.

"The Brooklyn Rising"

The next team scheduled for a visit to the Pirates' lair was the Brooklyn Dodgers. Thus far in the 1924 season, the Dodgers had been uneven performers. Since July 25 they had been resident in fourth place, but, assisted by the addition of Bill Doak to the pitching staff in June, they were beginning to win more consistently. When they arrived in Pittsburgh, they were 8 games off the pace (5 behind the Pirates), having won 9 of their last 11 contests. Their batting strength continued to reside in Jack Fournier, who led the National League in home runs, and Zack Wheat, who was consistently good and occasionally—as when he stroked out 5 hits on July 23—sensational. Their pitching strength continued to rest on the strong right arms of Burleigh Grimes, who came into the series with 16 victories to his credit, and Dazzy Vance, who had just become the major leagues' first 20-game winner. Writers who enjoyed Brooklynese liked to say that when Grimes was on his game, "Boiley is boining them."[3] And Vance was even better, prompting fans to chant the mantra of "Vance and Victory." On August 1, Vance had pitched his first shutout of the year and in the process struck out 14 Chicago Cubs, tying his own league record (set in 1923) for the most strikeouts in a game. At one point he fanned 7 Cubs in succession and was as close to unhittable as a pitcher is ever likely to become. Vance and Grimes had been the last two pitchers to defeat the Pirates before Pittsburgh had launched its current winning streak. Since both men nursed ill feelings toward a club that had once—in 1915 for Vance and after 1917 for Grimes—traded them away, they did not disguise their hopes to shackle the Pirates once again.

Billed as a collision between two surging teams, the 3-game series opened on August 18 with a spectacular show of Burleigh Grimes's multiple talents. Not only did the spitballer hold the Pirates to 4 runs, enough to assure a 7–4 victory for Brooklyn, he also contributed 4 singles to the Dodgers' offense and even stole a base. The game on the next day pitted the leading hurler of each team, Wilbur Cooper and Dazzy Vance, against each other. Both were good, but Vance prevailed, winning his twenty-first game (and ninth straight) when Eddie Brown's 2-run homer in the top of the eighth inning gave Brooklyn a 4–3 triumph. The third game was tighter still, as Brooklyn's other spitballer, Bill Doak, and Pittsburgh's fine rookie, Ray Kremer, shut down the offenses on both teams. Pittsburgh scored twice in the first inning and never again. Two Robin runs came off a bases-empty home run by Jack Fournier in the second inning and a run-scoring triple by Zack Taylor in the ninth. Then, in the top of the tenth, Eddie Brown emerged as hero for the second consecutive day when he doubled to get on base and subsequently scored as a consequence of a sacrifice and a fielder's choice. The Dodgers' sweep of the series legitimized their claim to be authentic contenders as the season moved into its final six weeks. When Dazzy Vance was asked after his victory if he was pleased with having now won 10 consecutive games from the Pirates over the course of two years, his reply betrayed his intensity: "Yes, and that isn't half enough."[4]

In the eight days following the games of August 20 there were no head-to-head matches between any of the three National League contenders. Instead, each team used the respite from the sharpest competition to try to eke out an advantage over its competitors. During this stretch the Giants won 5 out of 8 against the Cardinals and the Cubs; this record served to stabilize their lead. In the same span, the Dodgers won 4 out of 7 against the Cubs and the Cardinals; in one of the victories over the Cubs Dazzy Vance set a new National League single-game strikeout record by fanning 15 opponents.[5] The Pirates used successive series against the Braves and Phillies to seek to rediscover the formula for winning; but even though they prevailed in 5 of their 9 contests, the embarrassment that two of their losses were by a single run showed that they had not yet mastered the knack of seizing opportunities.

The schedule decreed that the Giants and Dodgers should begin a 3-game series on August 29; a final 2-game encounter between the cross-river rivals loomed beyond Labor Day on September 7 and 8. These 5 contests afforded a grand opportunity for both clubs. And if Brooklyn could remain hot, each victory would bring the Dodgers a game closer to the lead. Pittsburgh, meanwhile, knowing that it would not have another head-to-head crack at its two eastern rivals until the last two weeks of September, was compelled to root for Brooklyn, since any victory for the third-place Dodgers was also a triumph for the second-place Pirates.

In the game of August 29, Dazzy Vance and Virgil Barnes dueled well, but Vance had the edge, winning his twenty-third game of the season and his eleventh straight. In the first inning his pitching hand was hit by a batted ball, but, given five minutes to shake off the pain, he stayed in to strike out 8 Giants and push his season strikeout total over two hundred. Zack Wheat contributed 2 doubles to the 3–1 Dodger victory. In the game of August 30 the Giants moved out to a big lead off Bill Doak. But with 5 runs in the seventh inning off Hugh McQuillan and another 2 in the eighth off Walter Huntzinger, the Dodgers stormed back to win by a score of 8–5. On August 31, Burleigh Grimes and Art Nehf gave the spectators a well-pitched game, but again the Dodger hurler was better. In winning the game with a 3–2 score, the Dodgers swept the series and moved to within 4 games of the suddenly punchless Giants. "The Brooklyn rising," wrote the *Times* reporter, "is still on in all its fury."[6] The Pirates, meanwhile, had used the 3 Dodger victories to full advantage, winning 2 games from the Reds and a 2-hit shutout by Emil Yde from the Cubs. As a consequence, on the eve of the Labor Day doubleheaders Pittsburgh stood between New York and Brooklyn, only 2 games off the pace. Not since the end of May had there been such congestion at the top of the National League.

Rogers Hornsby's Rampage

The tightening race was not the only focus of attention for National League fans in the final eleven days of August, as 4-time batting champion Rogers Hornsby, who for almost two months had been hitting with mounting success, used the fourth week of the month to launch a batting spree that served as an unexampled showcase of his batting prowess.[7] Ever since the second game of a doubleheader way back on June 28, Hornsby had been on a tear. When the schedule offered St. Louis a day off on August 19, the baseball world confronted the remarkable fact that over the previous seven weeks Hornsby had been batting at a .438 clip.

What followed, however, suggested that that pace had only been a warm-up. In a doubleheader on August 20, the Cardinal second baseman quickened his pace by batting out 6 hits, including 3 doubles. On August 21, during the course of another doubleheader, he gathered 7 hits, including 2 home runs. On August 22, he singled and homered. On August 23, he stroked out 2 hits, one of them a double. On August 24, he got only 1 hit, but it was a home run in the bottom of the ninth inning to give St. Louis a 1-run victory. On August 25, he singled and homered. On August 26 he collected a home run and 3 doubles. On August 27, he hit a single and a double. In a doubleheader on August 28, he collected 4 hits, including a double and a home run. Not until August 29 did the fantastic run of plate success end, when Hornsby, injuring his back while running out a single in his first at-bat, was forced to leave the lineup— an absence that would last for nine days.[8]

The aggregate achievement of the 12 games in this streak was staggering: In 51 official at-bats, Hornsby collected 34 hits for an average of .667; he pounded out 16 singles, 10 doubles, 1 triple, and 7 home runs for a total of 67 bases; at one point he hit safely in 9 consecutive trips to the plate. Already batting over .400 when his streak began, Hornsby left the lineup with a .434 average for the season and—get this!—a .489 average for the span of games from June 28 through August 29. This "rampage" is unparalleled: No player in major league history has batted with such consistency over a period of two months. It is understandable that National League President John Heydler chose the final full week of August to declare that, with all due respect to Babe Ruth and Ty Cobb, "Hornsby is the greatest batsman of all time."[9]

A Three-Way Race for the American League Crown

The two pennant races caught public attention during the summer of 1924 for different reasons. In the early weeks after Independence Day the chase in the senior circuit aroused interest chiefly because, in the New York Giants, it featured a team that might be not only John McGraw's greatest—after all, it boasted George Kelly, Frankie Frisch, and Ross Youngs—but perhaps one of the most formidable baseball assemblages of all time. Then, as the heat of late July and August wilted the New Yorkers and their pretensions to historical singularity, interest was seized by the startling and successive surges of the Pittsburgh Pirates and the Brooklyn Dodgers. The American League offered its followers different attractions. Its great surge—the Washington Nationals' unexpected leap to the top of the standings—was already over when the post–Independence Day season began, as fans would quickly learn in the early weeks of July. Instead, the junior circuit featured a twisting and hard-fought race among three teams, a brief and rousing challenge from a fourth, numerous changes in league leadership, and a margin between first and second place that on only one summer day exceeded 2 games in size. Not since 1908 had the major leagues seen a pennant race as close as the one that the American League presented in 1924. That's why Miller Huggins predicted that the pennant race was "more than likely to be won by a club with a percentage lower than .600."[10]

The week following Independence Day demonstrated that Washington's collapse on the Fourth of July was not an isolated setback. The Nats split a doubleheader with New York on July 5, as a good Walter Johnson lost to an even better Herb Pennock in the first game; and then, in a single game on July 6, they blew a 4–2 lead, as the Yankees scored 5 runs in the last two innings. During one 22-inning stretch, the Nats failed to register a single tally. Even though he had been knocked senseless by running into the right-field fence the previous day, Babe Ruth led the Yankee attack on July 6 by stroking out his twenty-second home run and 2 doubles. Matters did not improve for the Nationals when, after a two-day break, they hosted the Tigers. After splitting a doubleheader with Detroit on July 9, Washington lost the single games on July 10 and July 11. On July 10 the teams actually played two engagements, but because the first game of the twin bill lasted 13 innings and more than four hours—an eternity in this era of no-nonsense baseball—before Detroit prevailed 12–10, the second contest was launched near dusk and ended in a 3–3 tie after 5 innings amid gathering darkness. Walter Johnson started the slugfest for Washington but couldn't survive the fifth inning. Not exhausted by such a relatively short outing, he returned to the mound to open the single game on July 11. On this occasion he was in much better form, holding the Tigers to 2 hits until late in the game. But he buckled in the eighth inning, and the Nationals, though outhitting the Tigers, lost 4–3. With 3 losses in the series, they fell into second place, a game behind a Yankee team that was using the period to club the White Sox. After the game, and for the first time all year, Bucky Harris vented his frustrations in public. The Tigers, meanwhile, as a consequence of their successes against the Nationals, stood only 2 games off the pace.

During the following week the Yankees strengthened their hold on first place. With Babe Ruth using the full range of his talents—bunting for a single on July 12, leading the team in putouts on July 13, and hitting a brace of home runs on July 14—the Yankees took 4 of 5 games from the Browns and 4 of 6 from the Indians. Herb Pennock led a pitching staff that appeared to be rounding into predicted form. And in one game against the Indians, Babe Ruth hit a ball with such force that—if reports can be trusted—even though it grazed the pitcher's glove, it sailed over Tris Speaker's head, bounced off the fence in straightaway center field, and allowed Ruth to run out an inside-the-park home run. The Tigers were almost as successful during this week, pummeling opponents by scores of 11–9, 11–2, 15–1, and 9–7 and winning 7 of 8 games. On both

July 17 and July 20, they swept doubleheaders from the plummeting Boston Red Sox. Almost everyone in the lineup was contributing to the parade of Tiger hits, but the star of the week, offensively and defensively, was Heinie Manush, the "Tuscumbia Thumper."[11] On July 16 he collected 3 hits, on July 18 he made a game-saving catch and then scored the winning tally, and on July 19 he hit a grand-slam home run.

The third mid-July contender, the Nationals, used a visit from the impoverished Indians mound staff to recover their batting eyes. Scoring 16 runs in one game, 12 in another, and 9 in a still another, and, turning to Walter Johnson for a 5-hitter when their bats suddenly fell silent, they won 4 of 5 games from Cleveland. Joe Judge led the batting assault. But when St. Louis came to town, the Nats stumbled, losing 3 games out of 5, including a 16-inning struggle that turned out to be the longest American League game of the season. Their inability to sustain momentum—one of the losses was a consequence of an error by Roger Peckinpaugh with 2 out in the ninth inning—cost them another place in the standings, and after play on July 20, Washington stood 2½ games behind New York and 1 game behind Detroit.

At that point, with the schedule assigning a visit to first-place New York as the next stop for second-place Detroit, the American League season offered its second critical series of the year. Ty Cobb sent his outstanding rookie Earl Whitehill to the mound in the first game, and although he was far from his top form, Detroit's slugging power gave him his eleventh victory of the year and pulled the team to within a half-game of first place. Johnny Bassler collected 5 of the Tigers' 18 hits; Waite Hoyt and Joe Bush shared the indignity of the pasting. The next day, behind the solid pitching of Ed Wells, another rookie, the Tigers won their eighth straight game, 3–1, beating Herb Pennock and taking over first place from New York. Wells held Ruth hitless.

For the third game of the series, Detroit turned to Rip Collins, and he, too, delivered a fine performance. But despite home runs by Bassler and Heinie Manush, the Yankees prevailed in 11 innings, winning 4–3 and reclaiming first place on Babe Ruth's twenty-ninth home run of the year. It was a contest rich in exciting moments. In the eighth inning, Bob Shawkey closed a Tiger threat by picking Ty Cobb off at second base with the bases loaded. In the ninth inning, Wally Schang scored the tying run for New York by knocking the ball loose from Johnny Bassler's hands in a collision at the plate. In the top of the eleventh inning, Yankee relief pitcher Milt Gaston fanned Heinie Manush with the bases loaded and 2 men out. And finally, in the bottom of the eleventh, in his second misjudgment of the day, Cobb chose to bring Hooks Dauss to the mound precisely when Ruth was due at the plate, even though the Bambino had logged 13 lifetime home runs against Dauss. A delighted crowd immediately clogged the base paths for their hero, obliging Ruth to move people aside as he made his way from third base to home.

For the final game of the series, Cobb returned Whitehill to the mound as Al Mamaux started for New York. Neither was around when Detroit scored in the top of the eighth (and final) inning to win 5–4 and again dislodge the world's champions from first place. In a decision that turned out to be ill judged, the game was shortened not by weather but at the request of the Yankees, who needed to catch a train—today this strikes us as an incomprehensible miscalculation—to play an exhibition game. The *Times* writer noted that if the truncation had cost the Yankees a victory in the 1924 race, "They may be sorry for it."[12] Very prescient. The Tigers, however, were quite happy to accept the win and thus complete a triumphal swing through the east that netted them 13 victories in 16 games and lodged them in first place.

This series between Washington's two closest rivals offered the Nationals a fine opportunity to gain ground, and they did not miss the chance. Hosting the White Sox for 5 games, they lost only 1 contest in the series, to the remarkable Sloppy Thurston, who shut them out for his sixteenth win of the year. Washington's victories in the 4 other games were the result of consistent pitching from George Mogridge, Firpo Marberry, Walter Johnson, and Curly Ogden, and opportune hitting from Goose Goslin, Sam Rice, and Nemo Leibold. The consequence of all of this tugging and pulling was the kind of delight that baseball fans dream of: On the evening of July 24, with all teams looking forward to a day off on the morrow, the Tigers held a half-game lead over both the Yankees and the Nationals. The race could scarcely have been tighter.

The Browns Make Their Move

Although each of the three contenders came out of the late-July break with hopes for pulling away from the pack, in fact the competition of the following two weeks only increased the congestion near the top of the standings by adding another contestant. The St. Louis Browns, who thus far had alternated dashes of success with gulfs of distress in putting together a .500 record, used a midsummer home stand to contrive a formula for complementing their formidable batting order with consistent pitching. In one dazzling sprint, they caught the attention of observers everywhere. It began on July 27, when George Sisler's eighth-inning home run gave the Browns a victory over the Red Sox. Then, after a peculiar loss on July 28 that Ban Johnson later invalidated,[13] Sisler homered again on July 29 and drove in all 3 runs in a shutout triumph for Dixie Davis.

The Red Sox were, of course, already dropping like lead in the standings, and so the Browns could expect stiffer competition from their next two opponents, the Yankees and the Nationals. But they showed the same strengths against the two eastern powerhouses. On July 31, St. Louis swept a doubleheader from New York, 2–1 and 5–4, as Ernie Wingard and Dave Danforth held the Yankees to only 11 hits—4 of them (including his thirty-third home run) by Babe Ruth. The next day, with tempers lashing out, St. Louis lost 3–2. But on August 2, powered by the bats of George Sisler, Baby Doll Jacobson, and Gene Robertson, the Browns returned to the attack, pounding the Yankees 12–8. Over the course of 2 games Robertson had collected 6 straight base hits.

As the Yankees left town, their momentum a casualty of the just-concluded series, the Nationals arrived, fresh from a successful 4-game series against the Tigers. But the Nats were no more a match for the surging Browns than the Yankees had been. On August 3, Dixie Davis outpitched Curly Ogden, 3–1. On the fourth, Ernie Wingard, aided by 4 hits from Gene Robertson's bat, won 5–1. On the fifth, St. Louis took both games of a doubleheader from the baffled Nationals, Urban Shocker prevailing 2–0 and Dave Danforth following with a 4–2 triumph. The Browns completed their sweep of the 5-game series on August 6 with a 6–5 victory, with Ernie Wingard appearing in relief in the ninth inning to save the win for Dixie Davis.[14] Thus the Browns had won 10 of their last 12 games (and the protested loss would soon disappear from their record) and—since New York and Detroit had spent the period of the Washington series splitting their own 4-game series—had moved from 8 games off the pace to 3½ games off and only half a game behind the shaken third-place Nationals. Having developed a pitching staff that could compete with the best that the east had to offer, Sisler's charges really had become the St. Louis "Sizzlers."

Washington Stabilizes Itself

August 7 was a central moment in this season of wonders. For on that day two trajectories—Washington's wilt and St. Louis's surge—were reversed. For Washington, the success on the seventh was no less than the turning point of the season. Staggering out of St. Louis, where they had scored only 4 runs in their first 4 games, they appeared in disarray, with their pennant hopes blasted. Their 6 straight losses had taken them from second place, half a game from the top, to third place, 3 games out. Even in this moment of distress, however, Bucky Harris contemplated only one adjustment to the lineup he had so carefully crafted. With Wid Matthews's batting fading and Nemo Leibold's uncertain, he was delighted when Clark Griffith spent $35,000 to purchase the contract of Earl McNeely from Sacramento in order to supply outfield assistance for the closing months of the season.[15] To halt the losing streak Harris turned to Walter Johnson, who had not hurled in St. Louis. Johnson was in good form on the seventh, but so was the White Sox's Charlie Robertson, and so the critical game went into extra innings. And in the top of the tenth, Fortuna kissed Washington. With Nationals on all the bases, the White Sox played an infield grounder for a force at home—and catcher Buck Crouse neglected to touch the plate! An instant later, Crouse compounded his mistake by throwing the ball into center field, allowing 2 more runs to score. Saved by this stroke of fortune, the Nationals won 6–3, ending their descent and, as it turned out, saving their season.

On the same afternoon, the soaring Browns dropped suddenly to earth. Matched against the Athletics, they lost both games of a doubleheader. The Athletics, it is true, were no longer the pushovers they had been earlier in the year. Al Simmons was beginning to solve big league pitching, and Joe Hauser, by hitting 3 home runs and a double on August 2, was serving notice that the Athletic batting order could strike with great power. But the double loss was a sharp blow to George Sisler's ambitions—and its severity was only exacerbated by the fact that the manager himself went 0-for-7. Less than a week later the Browns again lost a doubleheader, this time to the Yankees. In subsequent weeks St. Louis would show that it was still able to win a fair number of its games, and as a consequence the team hung around in the pennant chase, generally 5 or 6 games off the pace. But hindsight shows that the Browns had reached their high-water mark on August 6.

Babe Ruth's Storm

On August 10 the Cleveland Indians' Joe Shaute defeated the New York Yankees and dropped them into second place, only percentage points behind the Detroit Tigers. In winning his league-leading eighteenth game, Shaute held Babe Ruth hitless, ending the Bambino's 18-game hitting streak. Shaute's success also brought to a close one of the most extraordinary demonstrations of sustained thunder in the history of baseball. In the 48 games that Ruth played from June 30 through August 9, the Bambino posted 173 official at-bats and collected 83 base hits, for a mind-numbing average of .480. Mired around .250 in early May, Ruth was now batting over .400 for the season. And as one might expect from a slugger of his renown, the hits were not dinky. He supplemented his 45 singles with 14 doubles, 4 triples, and 20 home runs. He hit 14 of these homers in July, thereby surpassing his own major league record of 13, set in June 1921, for the highest number of round-trippers hit in a month. The slugging average that he posted for the 48 games—a staggering .954—makes the point about the fearsomeness of his performance in yet another way. Twice Ruth blasted 2 home runs in a game, and at one point he had 7 consecutive multihit games. His crude on-base percentage for the span of games was .575.[16] But the clearest testimony to Ruth's value to his team is that, of the 5 games in which he was held hitless, the Yankees lost 4.

It is useful to put this storm into perspective. On only two other occasions in major league history has a batter sustained such an extraordinary combination of high power and high average over the course of 48 games. And on both those occasions the batter was . . . Babe Ruth! In 1920—and this must rank as the greatest storm of all—he had a run of 48 games in which he batted .450, stroked out 22 home runs, slugged at a 1.034 pace, and reached base fully 60 percent of the time. In a 48-game period in 1923, he had figures that were not dissimilar: a batting average of .465, with 18 home runs, a slugging average (SA) of .918, and an on-base percentage (OBP) of .590. The storm of 1924 provides the third line of comparison in this chart of batting thunder:

Babe Ruth's 48-Game Rampages

	BA	HR	SA	OBP
1920	.450	22	1.034	.600
1923	.465	18	.918	.590
1924	.480	20	.954	.575

No one—not Rogers Hornsby, Lou Gehrig, Jimmie Foxx, Ted Williams, Mickey Mantle, Willie Mays, Ken Griffey Jr., Mark McGwire, or even Barry Bonds—has combined power and average to the degree that Ruth did.[17]

As if all of this were not enough, during these midsummer weeks of 1924 Ruth was performing as never before in the field, peppering contest after contest with catches or throws that aroused admiring comment. The *New York Times*, whose writers had witnessed the Ruth phenomenon from its Bronx beginnings, may well have been accurate when it stated that—with all due respect to earlier accomplishments—Ruth was "now playing the greatest ball of his career."[18]

Washington Recovers the Lead

For the American League, August 11 was the last day off until late in September—effectively the last day of imposed inactivity before the dash to the end of the season. Each of the three contenders used the break to gather its forces for a closing surge. Ty Cobb's Tigers, elevated into first place the previous day when they had whipped Boston, needed to use the imminent final swing through the eastern cities to hammer the Nationals and the Yankees into quiescence. Against the Red Sox, the Tigers had been impressive. Harry Heilmann, Topper Rigney, and Lu Blue were hitting well. Most impressive of all was Ty Cobb, who, pushing himself to the limit, was flashing again the incomparable style that had marked much of his long career; on August 10, for example, he dazzled fans by scoring 4 runs and collecting 4 stolen bases, including a steal home. Detroit pitching was also looking solider. After a slump,

Earl Whitehill had recovered his early-season form, and Hooks Dauss, disappointing as a starter, was emerging as a reliable relief pitcher. Cobb now had grounds for hoping that the Tigers could finally pull away from the pack.

Miller Huggins's Yankees, only percentage points behind the Tigers on August 11, also looked good. Any team that had Babe Ruth in the lineup was going to score runs, and with Waite Hoyt and Herb Pennock consistently providing well-pitched games, the Yankees were unlikely to fall into a losing streak. Huggins wished his other batters were hitting as well as they had in recent years; only Bob Meusel, lively after his slow start, offered a power complement to Ruth. But in a grinding chase for the pennant, strong pitching was likelier than strong hitting to be the key ingredient for success, and in Pennock, Hoyt, Joe Bush, and Bob Shawkey, New York seemed to have the best foursome in the league.

Bucky Harris's Nationals stood 2 games off the pace. This was remarkable inasmuch as they had won only 7 of 17 games on their recent road trip. Their upcoming encounters with Detroit and then New York were thus central to their hopes for success. Harris remained publicly confident, cheered by the reflection that the team had already exceeded virtually everyone's expectations. He knew that Walter Johnson had recovered from his midseason doldrums, that George Mogridge had snapped a 7-game losing streak with a victory on August 10, and that Sam Rice and Ossie Bluege were regularly getting good wood on the ball. He thought his pitching staff was as strong as New York's and his batting order, if not as powerful as Detroit's, was likely at least to be more consistent, especially with Earl McNeely in center field. He knew that Washington sportswriter John Keller had recently resigned himself to a third-place finish for the Nationals: Harris was determined to prove Keller wrong.

Washington's first visitors were the Indians. In the series opener, played on August 12, Walter Johnson held Cleveland to 5 hits while throwing the 106th shutout of his career. The Indians won next day, however, as Stan Coveleskie held the Nationals to 1 run. Since the Yankees won a doubleheader that day, the New Yorkers reclaimed first place from the Tigers and dropped the Senators to 3 games off the pace. To avoid further erosion in the standings, Bucky Harris turned to George Mogridge for the rubber match on August 14, and the left-hander was dominant, holding Cleveland to 2 hits and no runs. The brilliant performance was needed, for Joe Shaute was in fine form, and the only run of the game came when Harris flew from first to third on a sacrifice bunt and scored on an infield grounder.

The next western team to visit the nation's capital was Detroit, recently expelled from first place but still only half a game off the pace. Ty Cobb was cheered by the success that the reinstated Dutch Leonard had experienced since joining the Tiger staff on August 6, but the more important personnel matter was troubling, since a twisted knee, sustained on August 13, removed Lu Blue from the lineup and left Cobb with the difficult task of replacing his hard-hitting and smooth-fielding first baseman. The opener on August 16 went to Detroit, as Firpo Marberry, donning his starting guise, faded late in the game while Earl Whitehill remained strong throughout. The second contest, on August 17, went to Washington. Walter Johnson was again in top form, allowing only 4 hits in an 8–1 victory. McNeely all by himself matched Detroit's hit output. On the eighteenth it was Joe Judge who assumed the role of batting star, stroking out 3 hits, including 2 doubles, to assist the Nationals in overcoming an early Detroit lead and prevail 6—3 behind Paul Zahniser. But it was the doubleheader of August 19 that made this series significant. Behind another fine effort by George Mogridge and aided by a home run from Goose Goslin, the Nationals took the first game, 4–3. Then, with Allan Russell proving himself a better reliever than Earl Whitehill, the Nationals won the second game, too, by a score of 5–3. On this day, Bucky Harris led by example: He went 4-for-8 at the plate, drove in the winning run in the first game, and stole home in the second. By winning 4 out of 5 games from the Tigers, Washington moved past Detroit into second place and found itself once again just 2 games behind New York.

The stunned Tigers then moved into Yankee Stadium, where they took 2 of 3 games from the Yankees. Neither Joe Bush nor Sam Jones was able to keep Detroit hitting in check, and errant fielding compounded New York's difficulties. In the August 22, game Whitey Witt played a fly ball into a triple, and then in the bottom of the ninth, having loaded the bases with 1 out, the Yankees saw Wally Schang and Mike McNally strike out on 3 pitches each. On August 24, Babe Ruth finally ended his home run drought by hitting his thirty-ninth, but Heinie Manush, with 5 hits, led a successful Tiger assault. Meanwhile, Washington had the good fortune to be hosting the floundering White Sox, from whom they won 3 straight contests. Walter Johnson continued his sensational pitching, winning the first game 2–1. Roger Peckinpaugh figured prominently in all of the scoring, driving in both of the Nationals' runs and erring to allow the White Sox to score their lone tally. In the next contest, George Mogridge won by the same score, defeating the recently luckless Sloppy Thurston. For the third contest, Bucky Harris called upon Tom Zachary, and for the third consecutive game the White Sox were held to 1 run, in large measure because the Washington infield turned 5 double plays. The game was Chicago's twelfth consecutive loss. Throughout the series the Nationals sparkled afield; Sam Rice even pulled off an unassisted double play. But what cheered Washington fans most was the evidence that the team's pitching had returned to its June form: Only twice since August 10 had Nat hurlers allowed their opponents more than 3 runs. Largely as a consequence, on the morning of August 25, with only a single percentage point separating them, the Nationals were in a virtual tie with the Yankees atop the American League.

The Browns were the final western team to come through Washington, and in their first match they ran into Walter Johnson at the peak of his game. In one of the finest outings of his career, the Big Train kept the ball characteristically low and threw a rain-shortened, 7-inning no-hitter, winning by a score of 2–0. An impressed George Sisler declared that Johnson "right now is as good as he ever was,"[19] and that evening, when Johnson and his wife attended the theater, the performers stepped from their roles on the stage to acknowledge his presence, unleashing an explosion of hats and programs from the applauding audience. Nevertheless, Washington lost 2 of the next 3 games, as St. Louis pummeled the offerings of Paul Zahniser and George Mogridge. By doing no better than splitting the 4-game series, Washington allowed New York, which won 2 out of 3 from Cleveland, to take a half-game lead in the pennant race. With these results, the preliminaries for the most important series of the American League season were over, and the Nationals arrived in New York for a 4-game engagement—the third and last of the three crucial series of the season.

The first game of the series, played on August 28, encapsulated the story of the season. The Yankees stormed in front against Tom Zachary, powered by 2 home runs from the bat of Babe Ruth, his forty-first and forty-second. But in the eighth inning, leading 6–1, the New Yorkers collapsed. With Joe Dugan making 2 errors and Whitey Witt misplaying a fly ball from Goose Goslin into a triple, Herb Pennock could not hold the Nats, and before the inning was over Pennock was gone, three pitchers had replaced him in dismal succession, and Washington had scored 8 tallies. That rally was enough to give the Nationals an 11–6 win. Firpo Marberry was superb in relief; Sam Rice collected 5 hits (including 2 doubles) and drove in 5 runs; and Goslin contributed a home run, a double, and a single in addition to his tainted triple. Washington led the league by half a game. Walter Johnson, modestly forgetting his outing on August 7, later called the game "the turning point."[20]

The next day, August 29, Johnson displayed his mastery in a 5–1 Washington win. The game provided a grand scare for the Washington faithful, for in the eighth inning Johnson was hit on the pitching hand by a batted ball. Players from both teams ran to his aid, but he was forced to leave the mound. A postgame examination determined that no bone had been broken, and meanwhile Marberry came in from the dugout to work his relief magic again. A New York writer said that the Yankees had been "outscored, outhit, outfought, and outlucked."[21] Washington led the league by 1½ games.

The third game, played on August 30, showed that the Yankees were not without resources. Though outhit by Washington 11-to-5, New York bunched its blows to eke out a 2–1 win for Waite Hoyt over Curly Ogden. Bob Meusel ended his recent slump and drove in both New York runs. The Washington lead was reduced to half a game. With the league lead thus again at stake, the two teams met for their final game on August 31. Both Sam Jones and George Mogridge were in good form, but Mogridge held a 2–1 lead going into the bottom of the eighth. Then, however, he slipped, almost simultaneously allowing the Yankees to score the tying run and getting himself expelled from the game (in the company of manager Bucky Harris) for protesting a call by umpire Ducky Holmes. For the third time in four days, Firpo Marberry took the mound in relief. And this time he added a victory to his record, for in the top of the tenth inning, Sam Rice doubled with the bases loaded, his ball landing just beyond Bob Meusel's desperate grab, and the Nationals won by a score of 4–2. By taking 3 of 4 from the Yankees, in a series in which possession of first place was the prize on three occasions, the Senators had extended their lead to 1½ games. Goose Goslin had been spectacular, garnering 11 hits and 21 total bases in 16 at-bats.[22] When the Nationals returned to the nation's capital that evening, Union Station was filled with eight thousand screaming fans. Meanwhile, by stumbling badly against the Browns, the Tigers had suddenly taken themselves out of immediate contention and fallen 5 games off the pace.

The Doubleheaders of Labor Day, September 1

In 1924, Labor Day fell on September 1, and not in years had baseball observers known such pennant-race excitement on the season's last great day of doubleheaders. In New York City fans saw the Yankees recover their winning ways by taking both games from the Red Sox. Herb Pennock threw a shutout in the opener. Fans in Washington saw their team yield no ground. Playing the Athletics, the Nationals won the first game on the strength of Tom Zachary's strong pitching and the second game on the strength of a ninth-inning rally, with Earl McNeely driving in the winning run. Detroit fans, on the other hand, received ratification of their fear that the season was spinning awry: Playing in Chicago, the Tigers again fell victim to poor pitching and, by splitting a twin bill with the White Sox, slipped another game behind the leader. As a result of the day's play, the Yankees were still 1½ games behind the Nationals, and the fading Tigers were 6 games out.

Interesting as these American League results were, however, they did not have the effect of reducing the leader's lead. For that kind of exciting outcome, fans needed to turn to the National League. For there, while the Giants split their doubleheader with the Braves, both the Dodgers and the Pirates swept their respective twin bills. In their first game in Boston, the Giants were checked by Jesse Barnes, who savored this crucial victory over the team he had served so well five years earlier. At Pittsburgh, both Pirate victories resulted from late rallies, as Ray Kremer and Lee Meadows teased victories out of tight games. But the biggest story of the day emerged from Philadelphia, where the rampaging Dodgers pounded out their sixth and seventh consecutive victories behind good pitching from Rube Ehrhardt, a recent acquisition from the Florida State League, and Art Decatur. Jack Fournier and Zack Wheat contributed home runs to the cause in the second game. As a consequence of the heroics of the day in the National League, the Giants' once irresistible lead had shrunk to 1 game over the Pirates and 3 games over the Dodgers. As September opened, the clan of McGraw stood in danger of losing their kilts.

Standings at the End of Play, Labor Day, September 1

American League

Team	Won	Lost	Pctg.	Games Behind
Washington Nationals	76	55	.580	—
New York Yankees	73	55	.570	1.5
Detroit Tigers	69	60	.535	6.0
St. Louis Browns	67	62	.519	8.0
Cleveland Indians	61	70	.466	15.0
Boston Red Sox	58	70	.453	16.5
Philadelphia Athletics	58	73	.443	18.0
Chicago White Sox	55	72	.433	19.0

National League

Team	Won	Lost	Pctg.	Games Behind
New York Giants	76	50	.603	—
Pittsburgh Pirates	75	51	.595	1.0
Brooklyn Dodgers	74	54	.578	3.0
Chicago Cubs	68	59	.535	8.5
Cincinnati Reds	69	62	.527	9.5
St. Louis Cardinals	54	76	.415	24.0
Philadelphia Phillies	49	77	.389	27.0
Boston Braves	46	82	.359	31.0

The Game of Baseball
in the 1920s

Take Me Out to the Ball Game

WHAT WAS IT LIKE to attend a major league baseball game in 1924? How were the ballparks different from today's? What about the rules and conventions of the game? The planning and strategizing? The equipment and uniforms? The fans? The assumptions? Now we'll go on a tour, as I identify some of the aspects of viewing a baseball game in 1924 that might strike a fan from the opening of the twenty-first century as peculiar or unexpected. All the reader needs to do is supply visual imagination.

Most of the stadiums used in 1924 were no more than fifteen years old. Built at considerable expense, they stood as mighty monuments to the success and popularity of major league baseball. As I write more than seventy-five years later, the corrosion of time has exacted its inevitable toll: Only three of the arenas used in 1924—Fenway Park, Wrigley Field (then known as Cubs' Park), and Yankee Stadium—still stand, and all three have felt the renovator's touch in the intervening years. But they are sufficient to remind us that one of the characteristics of baseball in the 1920s was that, although infield diamonds were geometrically identical in all ballparks, the circuits of the several major league outfields varied from stadium to stadium and from left field to right field with almost total abandon—a consequence of the owners' need to locate their new arenas on oddly shaped patches of real estate. In fact, only two major league fields were symmetrical, and the average difference in the distance down the two foul lines in the ballparks was 36 feet.[1] Other aspects of these ballparks that would catch the eye of our time-traveler were the absence of warning tracks and padded walls and the presence of bats scattered in front of dugouts and of photographers crouching along the baselines. Moreover, to a much greater degree than spectators of today are accustomed to, attending major league baseball in 1924 could be an intimate experience, with each major league park having its own atmosphere, its own character, and its own quirks.

In some interesting ways baseball games themselves in 1924 were very different from the games of today. First, there's their length. Most contests then concluded in less than two hours, and on September 5, Grover Cleveland Alexander of the Cubs and Pete Donohue of the Reds joined up to complete a 9-inning game in the astonishing time of one hour and ten minutes.[2] Pitchers worked more quickly than modern hurlers normally do, and clubs required less time between innings than teams from an age conditioned to television commercials are inclined to need. As a consequence of their usual brevity, games could start later in the afternoon than they do today—rarely, in fact, before 3:00 P.M. Games were played exclusively in daytime in the 1920s, with night ball being an awkward experiment resorted to only by minor league teams desperate for attendance. The doubleheader was a far more frequent scheduling device in the 1920s than it is now. In fact, certain holidays were regularly filled with twin bills, and when single games were rained out (a common occurrence in the spring of 1924), it was customary to reschedule them as a second game on a day when the two teams were already due to meet. In order not to sacrifice too many paid admissions, the holiday engagements were often staged as entirely discrete events—one game played in the morning, the other in the afternoon—and attended by different ticket-buying crowds.

Spectators sat reasonably close to the action. In many parks they were separated (de facto if not de jure) by race, with African Americans relegated to some section in the cheaper outfield seats. In the absence of a public address system, spectators received information about the game from a man with a megaphone and from a hand-operated scoreboard. In accordance with a very recent innovation, a spectator who recovered a ball batted into the crowd would ordinarily no longer be pressed to return it for further use.[3] The fans' proximity to the field allowed them to hear, and often to contribute to, the barrages of profanity and heckling that all teams used as they sought to unnerve opposing players and umpires alike. Few explicit examples of taunting survive, though we have it on good authority that Ty Cobb, a famous tormenter, regularly called the Athletics' Jimmy Dykes "hot shit."[4] Some commentators of the day occasionally expressed their preference for a softening of the verbal by-play that bench jockeys provided, believing that barroom language was discouraging women from attending games. But the fact that attendance had jumped in the postwar years robbed that argument of credibility. Moreover, like the veteran sportswriter John Sheridan, some people worried that campaigns to curtail profanity would deprive fans of the "Rabelaisian treat" of hearing a player savage a heckler—and might even cause baseball to "degenerate into the status of the 'sissy' English sports."[5] And so, despite the efforts of reformers, a background noise of scatological chatter remained an accompaniment to the game.

A fan from today would find many more small differences in the game of the 1920s. When games likely to draw large crowds were played, management often sold tickets to extra spectators, cordoning them into temporary seating at the edge of the outfield. If a ball then wound up in the midst of the fans, "ground rules"—special regulations for such a situation—were invoked. When rain interrupted a game, the players might assist in rolling out the tarpaulin. Most players except the catcher left their gloves on the playing field when they came into the dugout. By the standards of today these gloves were small, and as a consequence, whenever it was possible, a defensive player (including the catcher) used both of his hands when catching a ball. When managers changed pitchers, they walked to the plate umpire, not to the mound. The coaches who patrolled the boxes adjacent to first and third base and who, when handling this on-field assignment, were called "coachers," sometimes turned their attention from the details of the game to become cheerleaders, exhorting the crowd to get more involved. "Without the noisy support of the fans," John McGraw explained, "it is very difficult to start a rally sometimes."[6] Batting helmets and batting gloves did not exist in the 1920s, though the beaning death of Ray Chapman in 1920 had triggered discussion about the former. The standard uniform of the era was much baggier than the uniforms of today, and that uniform had not yet abandoned buttons nor begun to feature numbers.

In most circumstances a pair of umpires was deemed sufficient to handle a game—one behind the plate and another for the field and especially the base paths.[7] Umpires were the guardians of fairness and decorum. They were likelier then than now to expel an unruly player from a game, although veteran umpire Tom Connally had recently and deliberately softened his philosophy, explaining that "the fans are entitled to see the players. They did not come out to see me dust off home plate."[8] When umpires directed a manager to leave the field, the expellee often took a seat right behind the dugout, or stood just off the field, and continued supervising the work of his team. Despite the general commitment to assuring that regulations were honored, occasionally an incident occurred that bespoke the simpler covenants of an earlier era in baseball. A striking example occurred on May 17, 1924, when Braves third baseman Ernie Padgett, hit in the head by a pitch, was allowed to leave the game for a pinch runner to recover from his grogginess and then to return. The tale is a reminder that baseball was, after all, even when played by rule-loving adults, still a game for children.

Spectators at games in 1924 saw one phenomenon that has become almost nonexistent in recent decades: the playing manager.[9] The American League featured four: Ty Cobb (Tigers), Bucky Harris (Nationals), George Sisler (Browns), and Tris Speaker (Indians). The National League presented only one, Dave Bancroft (Braves). All of them except Harris had already earned reputations as luminaries of the game, and the fact that they had been asked to add managerial responsibility to their portfolios shows a bias toward the (now dubious) presumption that good players make good managers. The mean age of the sixteen managers in service at the opening of the season was just over forty-three years, youthful by today's standards. The median age—which corrects for the presence of the sixty-eight-year-old Connie Mack on the list—was lower still, at just under forty. In general, there was no predisposition to believe that experience at minor league managing or at coaching was a useful preparation for managing in the big leagues.

Strategizing

Managers in 1924 had no choice but to confront the fact that baseball was in the throes of a strategic revolution, as the traditional ways of thinking about the deployment of offensive weapons bumped into the age of Ruth. For what had once been a low-scoring game dominated by pitchers had suddenly and startlingly become a high-scoring game whose heroes were batters.

The most visible sign of the new era of the batter was the emergence of the home run as a significant offensive weapon. From the founding of the National League in 1876 through the 1919 season, an annual figure of 20 home runs by a single batter had been reached or exceeded only eight times. More often than not, entire teams had failed to hit 20 home runs in a season. But beginning in 1920, when Babe Ruth surpassed the old record of 29 by an astonishing additional 25, 20 home runs in a season became commonplace. As early as 1922, the major leagues had four batters who had topped 30 in a single season, while Ruth himself had blasted 59 in 1921. Scarcely less startling was the reappearance of the .400 hitter. In 1920, George Sisler batted .407. In 1922, Sisler batted .420, and Ty Cobb and Rogers Hornsby both batted .401. In 1923, Harry Heilmann batted .403. During the same years, league and team batting averages soared to levels not seen since before the turn of the century. In the years between 1901 and 1919, no league batting average had ever reached .280. After 1920, however, and for the rest of the decade, no league average fell below .280. As a clincher, consider this: When the St. Louis Browns batted .308 in 1920, they became the first team of the twentieth century to bat over .300. Yet by the end of 1923, fourteen teams had reached or surpassed that mark. Clearly something had happened to invigorate the offensive dimension of the game.

Observers were quick to attribute the surge in power to the introduction of a "lively ball." The owners, they said, had directed the manufacturers to "juice up" the ball—to create (in the term of the day) a "rabbit ball." It is now clear that this explanation is wrong. The ball put into play in the 1920s was identical to the ball that had been used in the majors ever since late in 1910. The materials were the same, the specifications the same. What had changed, instead, were various rules that once advantaged pitchers. First, starting in 1920, the spitball had been banned (except for a small and steadily declining set of hurlers, exempted by Organized Baseball lest they be able to claim that the new rule unfairly prevented them from pursuing their chosen careers). This prohibition meant that batters did not need to worry about seeing that notoriously baffling delivery. Second, umpires were directed to keep fresh, unscuffed balls in play. This injunction had two consequences that helped the batter, for it meant that pitchers were less likely to be using a ball that offered them the benefits of scratch marks and less likely to be using a ball that had been softened (and hence deadened) by use.

All batters profited from these changes in the rules, and the rise in batting averages signals as much. But to account for the wave of home runs, we need to add another consideration to the analysis—the presence of Babe Ruth. The Bambino was the first player to recognize the potential advantages in actually *trying* to hit home runs. Whereas batters prior to 1920 had honored the precepts of "inside" (or "scientific") baseball by trying for well-placed singles that would move runners along, Ruth and a growing band of emulators deliberately tried to hit the ball into the stands. The fans were fascinated by the consequent surge in scoring, owners rewarded power hitters with richer contracts, and increasing numbers of batters decided that it made sense to swing for the fences. In light of all these developments, the thinking of the managers was obliged to change.

Here was their calculation. Given that the likelihood had now increased that any particular at-bat would result in a base hit, and given that any base hit was likelier than before to be for extra bases, it no longer made sense in most situations to play for the single run.[10] Upon returning to major league managing after a nine-year absence, Frank Chance reported early in 1924, "I started out on the theory that it was wise to get a run, give my pitchers something to work on, but I early discovered that such a system wouldn't get you very far in the majors these days."[11] Traditionalists like F. C. Lane despised the new order, lamenting that "baseball, in the past few seasons, has become transformed from a scientific pastime to a contest of brute strength."[12] But most managers preferred adjustment to wailing. "Inside baseball is all right," the sage Connie Mack remarked in 1923, "but you gotta have the punch."[13] Moreover, Mack was acting on that principle: He already had Al Simmons and Joe Hauser in his pocket, and he had his eye on Mickey Cochrane and Jimmie Foxx.

This adjustment had two important consequences. First, base stealing declined. As recently as 1913, the number of major league stolen bases had reached its peak figure of 3,402; by the early 1920s, the average annual figure was down to about 1,550, less than half the earlier number. It is easy to understand the managers' thinking. Stealing a base had seemed to make good sense in an era when an advantage of one run early in a game might be sufficient to secure a victory. But attempting to steal a base carried a significant degree of risk, inasmuch as almost as many runners were unsuccessful as were successful in attempting steals.[14]

As the likelihood that a plate appearance would result in a base hit and perhaps even an extra-base hit rose, the marginal utility of an attempted steal declined.[15] Second, reliance on bunts and sacrifice bunts declined. I do not have statistics to demonstrate this point, but observers frequently commented on the change in strategic priorities. Tommy Leach, for example, contrasting baseball in his playing days (1898–1918) with the game in subsequent years, said, "We used to play a running game, a lot of bunting and base stealing."[16] And the flagship of baseball publications, *The Sporting News*, declared in May 1924, "When it became so easy to get hits managers had to change their systems. The change almost eliminated the bunt, the sacrifice bunt, the squeeze play."[17] If base stealing was losing its panache, bunting was in danger of becoming an esoteric art.

In constructing their batting orders, managers also applied newer principles. The reduced utility of bunting meant that one no longer put the best bunter second in the order. Tris Speaker tersely explained his reasoning: "I want a hitter up there."[18] The expansion of rosters allowed managers to experiment with platooning. Tris Speaker, again an innovator, joined John McGraw as an early convert to the practice, and it is worth noting that the manager who later made platooning famous, Casey Stengel, played on McGraw's Giants in the early 1920s. Speaker proposed yet another tactic: alternating left-handed and right-handed batters in a batting order, in an effort to limit the capacity of the opposing manager to neutralize offense with a pitching change. Such practices, to be sure, were far from universal. Bucky Harris, for example, believed that a team did best when it had a settled lineup. Still, the early 1920s must be seen as the era in which managers first had to figure out how to maximize the possibilities opened up by the era of the big inning.

Managers were also changing their thinking about pitching in the early 1920s. There was general agreement among observers that many pitchers of the day could be faulted for not having a wider array of offerings. The majority of hurlers, in fact, commanded only two or three pitches, and the slider, a staple of baseball in the most recent forty years, was thrown by only a handful of men, among whom spitballing Burleigh Grimes was the most successful. For many pitchers, unless they had acted to compensate for the loss, this range represented a reduction in the repertoire they had had access to before the banning of the spitball and other trick pitches. Partly as a consequence of limitations in the capacity of pitchers, by 1924 no team attempted to go into a season with fewer than eight hurlers on its staff. Managers generally hoped to employ four-man rotations and to call on various fifth men as needed to assure that members of the regular quartets got four days of rest. Because it had long been observed that a pitcher had greater success against a hitter who batted from the same side of the plate that the pitcher hurled from, all managers hoped to have at least one good southpaw among their stable of starters, as a possible antidote to left-handed batting poison. But good southpaws were hard to come by, and five of the major league teams in 1924 proceeded through the campaign without a single lefty among their top four pitchers.[19] In the early 1920s it was still reasonable to hope that a pitcher who started a game would finish it, but the hope was no longer an expectation, and in 1923 seven major league clubs had seen starting pitchers complete fewer than half of their games.

In these circumstances, the idea of relief pitching as a separate and legitimate aspect of the game was fitfully emerging. The notion that some pitchers should work solely in relief functions was, it is true, scarcely known: Even as able a reliever as Firpo Marberry of the Senators was sometimes asked to start a game, and conversely as able a starter as Herb Pennock of the Yankees was frequently asked to relieve. Absolutely unknown was the concept of using some pitchers only in what we now understand to be late-inning "closer" situations. Still, with Clark Griffith (guiding both Donie Bush in 1923 and Bucky Harris in 1924) and John McGraw leading the way, teams were testing the possibilities that a starting pitcher's long-term effectiveness might be enhanced if he were replaced late in a game, and that some pitchers might be more adept at relief work than at starting. As with other innovations, relief pitching, too, had its critics. John Sheridan grumped that teams "might get better results sometimes by taking out the manager and leaving the pitcher in."[20] But the Giants and Nationals were not listening. Claude Jonnard of the Giants led the National League in reconstructed saves in both 1922 and 1923, and Allan Russell of the Nationals led the American League in 1923. As the *New York Times* noted editorially, after the Giants claimed their third consecutive pennant in 1923, John McGraw had won "by virtue of the discovery that three three-inning pitchers are numerically equal to one nine-inning pitcher."[21] Though hyperbolic, the statement pointed to a gathering reconceptualization of the role of pitchers.

Baseball in American Life

Looking back on the world of baseball of the 1920s, a fan from the opening of the twenty-first century is perhaps most surprised at how central to the discourse and life of the day the game of baseball was then. Today, we are accustomed to the media attention lavished on such annual sporting extravaganzas as the Super Bowl, the Sweet Sixteen, and the Stanley Cup Playoffs. It is easy for us to forget that in 1924 baseball had no competitors for the spotlight and that the World Series reigned supreme as the central event in the American sporting universe. Even though collegiate football and basketball were emerging as engaging sports, though golf and tennis had their devotees, and though boxing and horse racing appealed to one strand of American machismo, there was nothing to rival baseball. "If the kids in the neighborhood wanted to play a game," Rogers Hornsby recalled, "baseball was the only thing."[22] And for most postadolescent males, whether young men of athletic ability who were thinking about entering upon game-playing as an adult activity or grown-ups who recalled the games of childhood and enjoyed following skilled competition, there were no authentic athletic alternatives to baseball. For those fortunate enough to live in a major league city, it was possible to pay a comparatively small amount of money and see the ablest "boys" and "lads" in the country—the common terminology is suggestive—play baseball. But even for the far vaster majority who never in their lifetimes saw a major league contest, the annual summertime major league competitions held interest. Some of that interest, to be sure, was linked to the attractions of wagering: The gambling industry was an important component of the culture of baseball in the United States. But that ball-loving culture extended far beyond those who obeyed the impulse to place bets and affiliated men and women of all ages and from all regions into the great national order of fandom.

Baseball was thus an activity that spoke to memory, to intellect, and to aspiration; to a love of action, a yearning for simplicity, and a hidden respect for tricksterism; to a need for heroes, a desire for closure, and a hope to find membership in a group of the like-minded. Baseball was successful because there were so many ways in which one could derive pleasure from it. And it united the country. Its heroes hailed from almost every region. California (Harry Heilmann), Texas (Rogers Hornsby), Maryland (Babe Ruth), and Georgia (Ty Cobb) produced its batting stars, while the plains—Kansas (Walter Johnson), Nebraska (Grover Cleveland Alexander), and Iowa (Dazzy Vance)—provided its mound greats. And so, in addition to all else, the institution of baseball was unique in its capacity to bring excellence together. At no era in American history—and I say this despite the glaring fact that Organized Baseball excluded African Americans—has baseball more truly been the national pastime than in the 1920s.

From Labor Day to the End of the Season

The Best Pennant Races in Fifteen Years

NOT SINCE 1908, the year of Merkle's boner, had the baseball public been offered the September spectacle of two transfixing pennant races. In the National League, the once-soaring New York Giants were flailing about, having squandered their mighty lead to the general rejoicing of a national fandom that had grown weary of their success. The Giants were looking for a fortification of pitching that might enable them to withstand two challenges. The first came from the Pittsburgh Pirates. Written off after their dismal opening, the Pirates had solidified around a combination of veterans and rookies and surged to within 1 game of the lead. The second challenge came from the Brooklyn Dodgers, who, led by baseball's finest pitcher, had won 7 consecutive games, including 3 over the Giants, to emerge from the obscurity of the pack to stand 3 games off the pace and to remind a public curious for auguries that presidential election years often produced pennants for Brooklyn.[1] The Giants and the Dodgers were scheduled to meet for 2 more games in September, and then, when the western teams made their last swing through the east, each New York City team would play 3 games with the Pirates. Almost everyone west of Manhattan was rooting against the Giants as September got under way.

In the American League, there was a two-team race, featuring the surprising Washington Nationals, with a youthful manager and an idolized veteran pitcher, against the powerful New York Yankees, with the most feared and crowd-pleasing hitter in the game. The Nationals were almost everyone's favorite team. "It is," the *Sporting News* editorialized, "perhaps the most profound and genuinely sincere sentiment that has been shed for a major league ball club in many seasons."[2] Having just lost 3 of 4 to the Nationals, the Yankees were in the uncomfortable position of being a game and a half out of first place. Their season series with one another now over, these two eastern teams would soon head west, where, in addition to the weaker clubs of the western division, each would play the Detroit Tigers, firmly ensconced in third place and notably dangerous in their own lair. It could be expected that New York and Washington would frequently have their eyes on the scoreboards in September.

The Dodgers on Fire

The story of the opening days of the month belonged to the Brooklyn Dodgers. Having swept their Labor Day twin bill, they returned to the attack on September 2 and again won both games of a doubleheader. But it wasn't easy. Dazzy Vance was terrible in the opener, and Brooklyn quickly spotted Philadelphia a 7–1 lead. The Dodgers fought back, however, tied the game in the ninth, and then won it 12–9 by scoring 3 in the top of the tenth. In the second game Wilbert Robinson gambled on Bonnie Hollingsworth, and the newcomer, in his first mound appearance of the year, secured his only victory of the season, 4–3, in a game shortened by rain. On September 3, the Phillies again hosted them in a doubleheader, and in an eerie imitation of the previous day's opener, the other Dodger ace, Burleigh Grimes, spotted the Phillies an early 5–1 lead; but, once again, a late rally—the winning run was pushed across in the ninth inning—saved the contest for Brooklyn, 7–6. The nightcap found Bill Doak in top form, as he spun a 2-hitter and benefitted from Zack Wheat's 2 home runs to win 7–0. The victory was Doak's seventh straight.

On September 4 the Dodgers changed cities—from Philadelphia to Boston—but faced the challenge of yet another doubleheader.[3] Having scarcely worked up a sweat during his brief and painful pounding in the earlier opening game, Dazzy Vance opened the first game. He was in his finest form, allowing only 3 hits, striking out 11, and winning his twelfth consecutive decision, 5–1. Dutch Ruether dominated the second game, holding Boston to 4 hits, the same number that he himself stroked out, while winning 9–1. The Dodgers were afire: They had swept 4 doubleheaders in as many days, could boast of 13 consecutive victories, and had sped past the Pittsburgh Pirates into a virtual tie with the Giants, only

3 percentage points out of first. A single-game victory over the Braves on September 5, behind Rube Ehrhardt's pitching, gave Brooklyn its fourteenth consecutive win. As a mark of how extraordinary Brooklyn's achievement was, consider this: No team, either before 1924 or since, has equaled their record of winning 8 games in four consecutive days, and only one team—the 1906 New York Highlanders (Yankees)—had matched their dazzling total of 11 victories in the course of a calendar week.[4] The baseball world was agog.

It is not surprising that a rush of such intensity should close the gap between the Dodgers and the Giants. That it did not catapult Brooklyn past New York is testimony to the fact that the Giants were also playing well in the opening days of September. Swapping opponents with the Dodgers, the Giants sometimes treated the Phillies and Braves as rudely as their interborough rival had. In one game they pounded Boston 10–2; in another they blasted Philadelphia 15–3. In the Philadelphia contest both George Kelly and Travis Jackson hit grand-slam home runs. But the Giants were not always successful. In the first game of a twin bill against the Braves on September 2, they collected 12 hits and 4 walks and still scored only 3 runs in a losing effort. In the first game of a twin bill against the Phillies on September 4, they squandered a 4–0 lead and lost 10–6 on a grand slam by Cy Williams in the bottom of the tenth inning. Thus, despite winning 4 of their first 6 games after Labor Day, the Giants held only a half-game lead over the Dodgers on the evening of September 5. And the Pirates, though their schedule had been blighted by rain, had managed to play twice in the interval and stood only 1½ games off the pace.

The doubleheaders of the following day, September 6, showed just how close the race was. In the morning game at Boston, the Dodgers won their fifteenth consecutive engagement, beating the Braves, 1–0, behind Bill Doak's second straight 2-hit shutout. Meanwhile, in the morning game at Philadelphia, the Giants struggled from behind to score the tying run on a George Kelly home run in the ninth inning and to take the lead in the tenth, only to lose when the Phillies mounted their own rally in the bottom of the tenth. Claude Jonnard and Ernie Maun were ineffective in relief. Since both Braves Field and the Baker Bowl had scoreboards, everyone knew when the afternoon games began that the Dodgers had finally dislodged the Giants from first place, taking a lead of half a game over their intracity rivals.

For the second contest at Boston, Wilbert Robinson, managing his fifth doubleheader in six days, turned to Tiny Osborne. It was a tight contest, tied 3–3 after 9 innings. In the top of the tenth the Robins scored the potentially winning run, but in the bottom of the inning their luck finally ran dry. Charged with holding the lead, Art Decatur fielded a grounder and, trying to force a runner at second, threw the ball into left field. Their chances kept alive by this error, the Braves went on to score 2 runs, ending the Robin streak at 15.[5] Meanwhile, in the second game at Philadelphia, the bats were booming. Travis Jackson hit another grand-slam home run, and going into the bottom of the ninth the Giants held a 16–14 lead, while McGraw's fifth pitcher, Art Nehf, was trying to check Phillie power. At first, it appeared he would fail, for Philadelphia quickly put 2 runners on base. But the game ended even more abruptly when Frankie Frisch grabbed a sharp line drive, stepped on second, and threw to Kelly at first to snap off a triple play. "It may just turn out," James Isaminger noted, "that Frisch was the lifesaver of the Giants in 1924."[6] This victory, coupled with the Dodgers' loss, put the Giants back in first place. The real winner of the day was Pittsburgh. With consistent hitting from Kiki Cuyler, Rabbit Maranville, and Charlie Grimm, the Pirates won 2 games from the still Hornsby-less Cardinals and took over second place, a single percentage point ahead of the Dodgers. The race was so tight that Brooklyn had begun the day in second place, seized the top position by noon, and slipped to third place by nightfall.

These doings of September 6 set the stage for the much-awaited 2-game showdown between the Giants and the Dodgers scheduled for September 7 at Ebbets Field and September 8 at the Polo Grounds. John McGraw picked Jack Bentley and Art Nehf as his starters; Wilbert Robinson countered with—who else?—Burleigh Grimes and Dazzy Vance. The game in Ebbets Field became one of the most celebrated in the history of that venerable ball park, both for its on-the-field drama and for its off-the-field turbulence. Interest in the game was so great that droves of fans were sold permission to gather around the edges of the outfield. They came richly armed with straw hats, the favored throwaway artifact of the fans of this era. The thousands who failed to get tickets milled so thickly in the streets around the ballpark that the umpires needed police escorts to enter the building. Many in the throng, frustrated at their exclusion, decided to force an entry and used crowbars and telephone poles to knock down a section of the outfield fence.[7]

Forty patrolmen were assigned to duty prior to the game; before the afternoon was over almost two hundred were in service, and a number of fans had been carried away in ambulances. One play encapsulated the oddness of the occasion: In the third inning Zack Wheat raced into the crowd of spectators to make a sensational but virtually invisible catch off a long fly by Hack Wilson; the Giant base runners, Ross Youngs and Bill Terry, uncertain about what was happening amid the swarm in the outfield, both wound up on second base, permitting the Dodgers to complete a very peculiar double play.

Under these bizarre circumstances a ball game was played. The Dodgers moved to an early lead, only to see Grimes weaken in the eighth to yield 5 runs, and fall behind 8–4. But in the bottom of the ninth the Dodgers fought back, scoring 3 runs and putting runners on second and third before Hugh McQuillan, brought in to relieve Bentley, could strike out pinch hitter Dutch Ruether to end the game. The victory put the Giants a game and a half in front again. But that margin was short-lived, for the next day, before forty thousand fans in the far more tranquil precincts of the Polo Grounds, Dazzy Vance posted his thirteenth straight victory and his twenty-fifth of the season, 7–2. It was a masterful performance, for Vance was off his game and bested the Giants by mixing pitches rather than by steaming them. Hank DeBerry led the Dodger offense with 3 hits, including a home run. The 2-game showdown had thus ended in a draw, and the Giants retained a half-game lead.

They could not hold it. During the course of the next four days, as rain put holes in the schedules of eastern teams, New York won 2 from Boston but lost 1 to St. Louis, while Brooklyn took 2 from Philadelphia. In one of New York's games against the Braves everything went right for the Giants: With Frankie Frisch going 6-for-7 and Irish Meusel going 5-for-6, the New Yorkers swept to one of the most lopsided victories in major league history, 22–1.[8] Their total of 27 base hits was tops for the majors in 1924. But two days later the lazy offerings of Bill Sherdel of the Cardinals—he had two kinds of pitches, one observer said, "a slow ball and a slower one"—drove them to distraction, and they were unable to capitalize on 13 base hits in a 5–1 loss.[9] The Dodgers were meanwhile finishing their season series with the Phillies, easily defeating them 5–1 in a game that featured 3 hits by Zack Wheat, and then struggling to an 11-inning victory, 8–7, in a game that was won by

Eddie Brown's single. On the evening of September 12, the two teams from Gotham were again in a virtual tie for first place.

The Pirates were having a less successful time. On September 7, Dolf Luque and Carl Mays of the Reds pinned 2 losses on them, and on September 9, Allen Sothoron and Johnny Stuart of the Cardinals duplicated the feat. They got a fine game from veteran Babe Adams—his first start of an injury-filled year—on September 10 and fine hitting from Earl Smith on September 12 to reverse their slide. But the season was offering fewer and fewer days for recovery, and the Pirates, staggered by the doubleheader losses, were now 2½ games behind. They faced, moreover, the difficult task of playing virtually all of the rest of their schedule on the road. But there was at least one basis for hope: Their schedule included 3-game series with both of the New York City teams. The Pirates were not yet out of the race.

The American League: Thoroughbreds in the Homestretch

By contrast with the activities in the National League, the first twelve days of September in the American League featured no head-to-head encounters between the two leading contenders. Instead, two strong teams, each with its eye on the daily work of the other, pushed steadily ahead. They were like a pair of superb runners in the final phase of a long-distance race, picking up the pace as they approached the end. The Nationals, ending their last home stand of the season before wildly enthusiastic crowds of still-stunned Washingtonians,[10] could rely on the regular appearance of Walter Johnson on the mound, and like clockwork the "Big Train," refreshed by a schedule that gave Washington both the second and third off, delivered victories. On September 4, he coasted to a win over the Red Sox, leaving the game in the seventh inning with a 12–3 lead; the Nationals won by a 12–5 score. On September 8, he handily defeated the Athletics, 8–4, going the distance to win his twentieth game, while giving up harmless, bases-empty home runs to Joe Hauser and Bing Miller.

But Bucky Harris also got good pitching from his other hurlers. George Mogridge held the Red Sox to 2 runs on September 6, and Firpo Marberry, after appearing in the ninth inning to save a victory on September 10 against the Athletics, took one of his occasional starting turns on September 11 and bested Eddie Rommel, 7–4. The Nationals continued to bat well. Sam Rice led the way, and by stroking out 3 hits in the second game of the doubleheader on September 10, he extended his batting streak to 17 games. Meanwhile, Goose Goslin, Joe Judge, and Earl McNeely were all batting above .315, and even Bucky Harris, never noted for his skill at the plate, was getting timely blows: The manager initiated Washington scoring on September 6 with a run-scoring triple and closed Washington scoring on September 11 by hitting his only home run of the regular season. When the schedule gave the Nationals a day of rest on September 12, they could reflect that they had won 5 of 7 games since Labor Day and still sat in first place. By a happy coincidence, it was announced on the twelfth that Walter Johnson had been named the "most valuable" player in the American League in 1924.[11]

The Yankees, meanwhile, bayed relentlessly at Washington's heels as Miller Huggins juggled his lineup. Earle Combs was finally healthy again, but when his batting proved rusty, he returned to the bench. Lou Gehrig was assessed and found not yet ready to displace Wally Pipp. Huggins even sought the services of southpaw Vean Gregg, who had not pitched in the majors since 1918.[12] Not all of Huggins's explorations, however, were unsuccessful. Walter Beall, a young pitcher recently purchased from Rochester for $50,000, was thrown into action in September and adjudged splendid—"a Walter Johnson, an Ed Walsh, and a Rube Waddell rolled into one," one fevered writer enthused.[13] On September 3, Beall started against the Red Sox and stifled them for 7 innings; on September 6, he provided 7 innings of relief against the Athletics and struck out 10.

Still, and predictably, the Yankees got their chief impetus from their veteran players. Joe Bush was outstanding, beating the Red Sox on September 2, beating them again with a 2-hitter on September 8, and delivering a game-winning, pinch-hit double with the bases loaded against the Athletics on September 9. And Babe Ruth remained the dynamo of the team. Though playing with an injured arm and a sore ankle, Ruth hit his forty-third home run on September 6, his forty-fourth two days later, and his forty-fifth on September 11. The last of these, with one man on base, tied a game for the Yankees in the eighth, allowing them to win in the ninth. When, like the Nationals, the Yankees rested on September 12, they could look back with satisfaction on a record of 7 victories in the 10 games they had played since Labor Day. As a consequence,

In the closing days of the 1924 season Commissioner Kenesaw Mountain Landis reaffirmed his high authority by imperiously dealing with an incipient scandal.

Rogers Hornsby and John McGraw. The National League's greatest batter and its most successful manager studiously ignore each other. In 1924, Hornsby batted .424 and McGraw won his tenth pennant. Both numbers stand as league records for the twentieth century.

George Kelly, Frankie Frisch, Travis Jackson, and Heinie Groh. The first three members of the Giants' great infield are in the Hall of Fame. And the balding Groh was the best third baseman of his generation.

George "Highpockets" Kelly poses for a high throw. At 6'4", the Giant first baseman was one of the tallest players in baseball. In 1924, he led the majors in runs batted in.

Scrappy Ross Youngs was McGraw's favorite player. The 1924 season was his greatest, but a midsummer illness presaged his death just three years later.

Brooklyn's Dazzy Vance was 31 before he posted the first of his 197 major league victories. He was dominant in 1924, leading the majors in wins, strikeouts, and earned run average.

The leader of the offense that brought Brooklyn back into the race, Zack Wheat was second only to Rogers Hornsby as an offensive force in the National League in 1924.

Coming into his own after more than a decade in the majors, Brooklyn's Jack Fournier led the National League in home runs in 1924.

*Edd Roush, in the words of
John McGraw, patrolled
center field with the "regal
indifference of an alley cat."
He also was twice National
League batting champion.
Notice the tiny glove.*

*Kiki Cuyler posted one of
baseball's great rookie seasons in 1924. His bat was
particularly devastating
when facing the Giants.*

Until a broken wrist side-lined him for three months, the 37-year-old Grover Cleveland Alexander was the most successful pitcher of the 1924 season.

Babe Ruth won his only batting title in 1924. Notice how, like power hitters of our own day, he has released his trailing (left) hand from the bat.

The separated hands gave Ty Cobb a measure of bat control that no player has ever surpassed. Cobb's Tigers had improved in each of the four years under his managerial leadership.

Harry Heilmann was Cobb's greatest pupil and is one of the most successful right-handed batters in the history of the game. The year 1924 being even-numbered, Heilmann did not win the batting title.

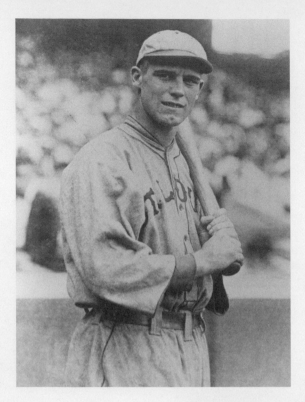

George Sisler. John McGraw once called Sisler a batsman without a weakness. But after a vision-injuring sinus infection in 1923, he never recovered his old form.

Many still regard Eddie Collins as the greatest second baseman of all time. At the age of 37, he led the American League in stolen bases and finished second in the most valuable player voting.

At the age of 27, Bucky Harris led the Washington Nationals to their only World Series victory in his first year as manager.

Earl McNeely, Nemo Leibold, Sam Rice, and Goose Goslin. In Rice and Goslin, Washington's outfield featured two future Hall of Famers. Rice batted safely in 31 straight games during Washington's stretch run; Goslin led the American League in runs batted in.

At the age of 36, the legendary Walter Johnson returned to greatness in 1924. His right arm was at least an inch longer than his left arm.

Firpo Marberry emerged as baseball's first outstanding relief pitcher in 1924. George Sisler said Marberry was "responsible" for Washington's pennant victory.

Fred Lieb, Nick Altrock, Ty Cobb, Babe Ruth, John McGraw, Walter Johnson, George Sisler, and Christie Walsh. Five original inductees into the Hall of Fame grace this photograph, taken before the first game of the World Series.

Paul Zahniser, Byron Speece, Curley Ogden, Joe Martina, Walter Johnson, George Mogridge, Allan Russell, Firpo Marberry, and Tom Zachary. Washington's outstanding pitching corps allowed fewer hits in 1924 than any other American League staff of the decade of the 1920s. All but Zahniser pitched in the Series. Transcendental Graphics.

A photo of two leaders. The Giants' field captain Frankie Frisch shakes hands with the Nationals' manager Bucky Harris. Each batted .333 in the Series. Notice the glove in Frisch's hip pocket.

In the top of the twelfth inning of the first game Artie Nehf scores the go-ahead run on a single by Ross Youngs. Muddy Ruel waits for a throw that doesn't come. George Kelly stands ready to bat next.

Earl McNeely begins a slide into third base in the fourth game while third baseman Freddy Lindstrom awaits the throw and coach Al Schacht cheers McNeely on.

Tom Zachary was the best pitcher in the Series. He needed only 97 pitches to give the Nationals a 2–1 victory in game six in Washington. Notice the posture and position of catcher Muddy Ruel.

OPPOSITE:
Muddy Ruel crosses the plate with the Series-winning run in the bottom of the twelfth inning of the seventh game. Hank Gowdy waits for a throw from Irish Meusel that never came. Notice John McGraw, in civvies, shoving his hat on his head as he leaves the Giant dugout. New York Public Library.

Goose Goslin is thrown out at first base. Bill Terry prepares to whip the ball around the infield.

The Nationals posed for this picture with President Coolidge before the World Series. Under the circumstances you would think more than one of the pennant winners could muster a smile.

and despite the strength of Washington's charge over the same span of days, the Yankees had actually been able to narrow the Nationals' lead to a single game. Thus, with only a game separating first and second place in the junior circuit and a virtual tie in the senior circuit, the combined proximities of the 1924 pennant races—the "closeness index" is what I'll call it—had never been smaller.

Mid-September Excitement

And the story got better. On September 13, when the eastern teams in the American League began their last circuit of the west, the Yankees ripped White Sox pitching for 17 hits on their way to a 16–1 victory. Babe Ruth stroked his forty-sixth home run, quickening hopes that he would at least break the 50 mark for the third time in his career, and Joe Bush, in addition to pitching another complete game, collected 3 hits himself. On the same day, the Nationals sent Walter Johnson against the Tigers, and, assisted by Tiger errors and the relief work of Firpo Marberry, Johnson won by a score of 6–4. Meanwhile, over in the National League and back on the east coast, the Giants pounded out 15 hits against the Cardinals on their way to a 12–2 win. Only the Dodgers lost this day, brought down by careless baserunning and errant fielding against the Reds.

On September 14, both the Yankees and the Nationals lost. The New Yorkers fell to Sloppy Thurston, who pitched a 4-hitter while winning his twentieth game of the season for the victory-starved White Sox. Washington played with uncharacteristic carelessness, leaving 13 men on the bases while falling 5–1 to the Tigers; 4 of Detroit's runs scored on Heinie Manush's grand-slam home run. The Giants continued their winning ways, as Art Nehf not only held the Cardinals to 6 hits but also hit a 2-run homer.[14] The Dodgers sent Dazzy Vance to the mound against Cincinnati, and the toast of Brooklyn recorded his fourteenth straight victory, his twenty-sixth triumph of the season, and another 9 strikeouts. In the third inning he struck out the side in 9 pitches, a feat duplicated on only 4 other occasions in the 1920s. On September 15, while the two National League rivals were idle, the Yankees beat the White Sox 2–0 on a 2-hitter by Sam Jones, and the Nationals lost to the Tigers by the same score, with Rip Collins besting George Mogridge. When these various results were calculated, the American League race featured a tie for the lead, with both the Nationals and the Yankees boasting records of 82 wins and 59 losses, and the National League race found the Giants leading the Dodgers by a single game. Though there had been some juggling of places since September 12, the closeness index was unchanged.

On September 16, the Dodgers had the misfortune to be the victims of one of the most staggering offensive performances that major league baseball has ever seen. Their opponents were the Cardinals, fresh off their series with the Giants, and the final score of the game was 17–5. But the score hides the real story: With 6 hits, 13 total bases, and a record-setting 12 runs batted in, Jim Bottomley almost single-handedly demolished Dodger pitching.[15] One of his home runs—he hit 2—came after Wilbert Robinson (himself the old RBI record holder) chose to walk Rogers Hornsby to get to Bottomley. "Why," the Dodger manager lamented, "did he have to save all those hits for us? Couldn't he have made some of them against McGraw?"[16] The Giants, meanwhile, split a doubleheader with the pesky Reds and increased their lead to a game and a half. In the American League the Nationals took advantage of a Yankee rain-out to take a half-game lead, as Tom Zachary contained the Indians and Sam Rice became the first American Leaguer to collect 200 hits in 1924.

On September 17, however, the American League race tightened again. The Nationals won by 3–2 in what was, for them, a typical game: sharp pitching, some scratch hits, tactical advancement of base runners, and seizing upon an opponent's mistake. Walter Johnson won his twelfth straight decision, and Sam Rice's single allowed him to extend his hitting streak to 24 games, longest of the year in the league. But because the Yankees swept a doubleheader from the stumbling Browns, Washington was forced to cede a share of first place to the New Yorkers. Still, Bucky Harris was growing more outspokenly confident. "The rest of the schedule gives us all the best of it," he noted, explaining that while the Nationals would conclude the season against the feeble Red Sox, the Yankees had engagements with the far tougher Athletics—"rank poison" for the New Yorkers, as he put it.[17] Meanwhile, rain on the east coast meant that no games were played in the National League on September 17.

The bad weather created the need for makeup doubleheaders in the National League on September 18. From their twin bill with the Reds, the Giants managed only a split. In the first game, which they lost 5–3, they could not overcome the results of Edd Roush's bases-loaded triple and Dolf Luque's mastery. In the second game, however, spurred by George Kelly's home run and Ross Youngs' 4 hits, the Giants eked out a 7–5 triumph. Britain's Prince of Wales—the future Edward VIII and then Duke of Windsor—attended part of the second game and saw Kelly's home run. Across the East River in Ebbets Field, meanwhile, the Brooklyn faithful had much to be jubilant about. The first game was a tense one, lasting 12 innings. After Dodger starter Dutch Ruether was knocked from the box and his replacement Burleigh Grimes was forced from the game when hit by a pitch, Wilbert Robinson turned to Dazzy Vance for the Dazzler's first relief appearance of the year. He pitched 4 nearly flawless innings, giving up only an unearned run in the ninth, and when Zack Wheat hit a 2-run homer in the bottom of the twelfth, Vance was credited with his fifteenth consecutive win. "Vance and Victory" indeed! Bill Doak followed this triumph with a fine one of his own, 4–3.

In the American League, on that same September 18, both the Nationals and the Yankees won. Washington's triumph featured a 5-run ninth inning and a pinch-hit single by wonder-batter Wade Lefler in his first plate appearance for the Senators.[18] New York's victory featured a pinch hit home run by Joe Bush and was the ninth triumph in 10 decisions for the red-hot Yankees. And so, after play on September 18, with less than two weeks left in the season, the closeness index was smaller still: The Nationals and the Yankees were tied for the lead in the American League, and the Dodgers stood half a game off the pace in the National League.

The Yankees Crack

Although the conclusion of the 1924 season was turning out to be a fan's dream, everyone knew that each passing day increased the chances that the mounting toll of physical and psychological pressure might lead one of the contenders to buckle. Miller Huggins believed that the pressure was particularly severe on his Yankees: "We have to play twice as hard and put up almost twice as good a game," he declared, "to win a decision now as [Washington does]."[19] It was (and still is) conventional to style these pennant competitions "races." But that term misleads. Each September afternoon in 1924 saw a flurry of diamond activity; each evening saw the results of that activity translated into revised league standings;

each subsequent morning saw a baseball public devouring information about the implications of the previous day's outcomes. With the ticking off of each day, contending teams lurched forward or backward in the standings. It was as if the duels for the pennants were being contested not as dashes to the finish lines but, instead, in a series of freeze frames—with the end of the season drawing remorselessly closer with each succeeding picture. Under such circumstances, tension had ample opportunity to nibble at the resilience of each contending team.

The Yankees were the first to crack, stumbling when they moved into Detroit for a 3-game series. The Tigers had already hinted at their fabled September prowess by taking 2 of 3 from the Nationals a few days earlier. But having thereby pulled themselves to within 4 games of first place, they had promptly lost 3 straight to the surging Athletic team and, given the lateness of the season, effectually eliminated themselves from contention. Their role, therefore, if they were to have one, was to be that of mischief-maker. And this role they now played to the hilt—aided, it must be acknowledged, by some extraordinarily untimely Yankee miscues.

The first game, on September 19, went into the ninth inning tied at 5–5. But then Joe Dugan misplayed a ground ball from Ty Cobb into a 3-base error. With no one out, Miller Huggins ordered that two batters be deliberately walked to set up forces at all the bases, but Fred Haney ruined his desperate strategy by singling, and the Tigers won, 6–5. On September 20, the Yankees' pain was even greater. Two errors by Wally Pipp permitted the Tigers to grasp at another 5–5 tie going into the bottom of the ninth. Once again, in these circumstances, the Tigers loaded the bases with no one out. Facing the prospect of a very damaging defeat, Bob Shawkey, the New York pitcher, found the resources to bear down, first striking out Del Pratt and then getting pinch hitter Bob Jones to pop out. But with Les Burke at bat, Shawkey bore down a shade too hard. He delivered a wild pitch, and in a twinkling Heinie Manush raced in from third to give the Tigers their second straight 6–5 victory. The game also witnessed Ty Cobb's 200th hit of the season.[20] The third game was lower scoring and ended less dramatically. But the result was a 4–3 Tiger victory—the third straight 1-run triumph by Detroit. And, again, it was a New York misplay—in this case a sixth-inning wild pitch by Walter Beall—that allowed the winning run to score in a game in which the New Yorkers actually outhit their hosts. It was a mark of the

Yankees' difficulties that the lame Babe Ruth could muster only 2 singles in 10 at-bats.[21]

Meanwhile, during the three days of Yankee misery in the Tigers' den, the Nationals took 2 of 3 from the St. Louis Browns. In the opening game, played in the rain, it did not matter that George Mogridge was off his form or that Bucky Harris committed 3 errors, for the Nationals scored 9 runs in the first inning and coasted to a 15–9 win. Earl Mc-Neely, Sam Rice, and Goose Goslin all collected 4 hits, and oddly for a game that featured 24 runs, there was nary a home run by either team. The bats were active again on September 20. Walter Johnson (pitching a day early because Tom Zachary had a sore arm) lasted only an inning in the face of the Browns' slugging, Goose Goslin countered with 2 home runs, and the game went to extra innings before St. Louis prevailed, 15–14, on a wild and ill-judged throw from Firpo Marberry, the last of Washington's 5 pitchers.[22] The rubber game, played in wretchedly wet conditions on September 21 and lasting only 7 innings before delays and approaching darkness ended it, went to Washington, 6–4, with Tom Zachary besting Dixie Davis. Again Goslin homered, and an error by the ordinarily sure-handed George Sisler allowed the Nationals to score their winning run. On the evening of the twenty-first, as Washington headed for Chicago, the Nationals rested in the satisfaction of knowing that they held a 2-game lead over the suddenly desperate Yankees. George Sisler was convinced: "I pick the Washington team to win the flag."[23]

The National League Race Tightens

While in the American League only the Yankees were cracking under the strain of a tight race, in the National League both contenders gave evidence of faltering. The Chicago Cubs visited the Polo Grounds and, in stark contrast to their earlier engagements with the Giants, took the last 2 games of a 3-game set with their hosts. Even the single Giant victory (September 19) was costly, for Heinie Groh reinjured his knee sliding into second base and left the field in the arms of Bill Terry. The outcome the next day was decidedly worse for the New Yorkers. Grover Cleveland Alexander went all the way in a 12-inning, 7–3 victory for Chicago—it was his 300th career triumph[24]—and in the eleventh inning, team leader Frankie Frisch joined Groh among the ranks of the disabled when he hurt a finger on his throwing hand sliding into home.

Perhaps unsettled by the injuries to two key teammates at this juncture in the pennant race, the Giants managed only 5 hits and no runs off Tony Kaufmann on September 21. Faced with reports suggesting that neither Groh nor Frisch would play again in 1924, John McGraw refused to lose faith. "The pitchers are showing good form," he said, "and I still think that we have enough hitting power to pull through."[25]

But the Dodgers failed to take advantage of their rivals' problems, instead, losing 2 of 3 to the Pirates. In the contest on September 19, Emil Yde, though not sharp, bested Rube Ehrhardt. Glenn Wright contributed a home run to the Pittsburgh offense. On September 20 matters took a more serious turn for the Dodgers, as the Pirates did what no club had managed to do in ten weeks—beat Dazzy Vance. The score was 5–4, and the star pitcher was not at his best form. But he had overcome that problem on several occasions earlier during the streak. On this day, however, hampered by a crucial error by Johnny Mitchell, Vance found himself in extra innings. And, in the eleventh, Pie Traynor, running from first base with the pitch and then challenging Eddie Brown's notoriously weak arm, scored the winning run on a short single by Rabbit Maranville. The Pirate victory pushed them past the Dodgers into second place, and so another Brooklyn loss would have been catastrophic for the team. But Burleigh Grimes fended off a Dodger collapse, winning the third game for Brooklyn, 2–1, in 10 innings. The winning run was driven in by Brown, who continued a pattern of timely hits, and, with this victory, the Dodgers regained second place.

A day later, on September 22, with the Giants and Pirates idle, Bill Doak bested the Cubs and Vic Aldridge, 2–1, in 12 innings, the winning tally coming on a double by Zack Wheat. Having struggled through 3 consecutive extra-inning games, the Dodgers were once again in a virtual tie for first place, trailing the Giants by only a single percentage point. And the Pirates, written off a week earlier, hovered 1¼ games out. With a 3-game set at the Polo Grounds about to open, Pittsburgh had one final opportunity.

The Giants Clinch the National League Pennant

The Giants' day off on September 22 was not a stroke of good fortune in scheduling. John McGraw knew his team needed an opportunity to regroup, and, much like Branch Rickey trying to avoid playing without

Rogers Hornsby early in the year, he used the occasion of a rainstorm the night of the twenty-first to reschedule the game assigned to the twenty-second for the twenty-fifth. That the charging Pirates were the Giants' next guests only complicated McGraw's concerns. "This time," Barney Dreyfuss told Bill McKechnie, "We ought to lick McGraw and make him like it."[26] The Giants, of course, felt otherwise, and took heart in the thought that the Pirates had a recent record of collapsing in September. Moreover, the Giants had the confidence that goes with being champions. Hank Gowdy, the Giants' veteran catcher, remarked that "no club in the world can beat this team in a pinch."[27] But, with Frisch and Groh out, a pinch of the sort Gowdy might not have envisioned was authentically at hand. And all the while the Dodgers, already hosting the Cubs, felt poised to seize upon the Giants' difficulties.

Athletes like to regard the crucial encounters that separate winners from losers as tests of character. In the three-day test of character that played itself out between New York and Pittsburgh, starting on September 23, it was the Giants who shone. On the twenty-third, using a makeshift lineup that placed George Kelly at second base and Freddy Lindstrom at third (with Bill Terry replacing Kelly at first), the Giants hammered the Pirates, 5–1. Hugh McQuillan pitched well, Jimmy O'Connell delivered a home run, and Hank Gowdy contributed a bases-loaded double. At the same time, only a few miles away, the Cubs beat Brooklyn and Dazzy Vance by a score of 5–4 in the Dodgers' fourth consecutive extra-inning game. For Wilbert Robinson it was a case of going to the well once too often. Early in the season Vance had ordinarily been given four days of rest between appearances to assure his sharpness. But with a pennant on the line, Robinson began to shorten that interval in mid-September. For this game on the twenty-third, he had given the right-hander only two days of rest, and while the Dazzler yielded only 4 hits, 3 were home runs, including Gabby Hartnett's game-winner in the tenth. The loss dropped Brooklyn a game off the pace. On September 24, the Dodgers staved off disaster, as Burleigh Grimes hung on against a late Cub charge to win, 6–5. But the Giants won, too, as Virgil Barnes, despite serving up "his famous home run ball" twice to Earl Smith, outpitched Emil Yde.[28] The size of the Giant achievement in these first 2 games of the Pirate series is underscored by the point that in both of them the Pirates outhit their hosts. The Dodgers' situation was parlous.

On September 25 the Giants completed their sweep of the Pirates, 5–4. Art Nehf was in clear command until the ninth, even hitting his fifth home run of the year, and after buckling temporarily to allow Max Carey a 3-run homer, he struck out the old nemesis Kiki Cuyler to end the game.[29] The strikeout ended the Pirates' hopes, too, since the defeat eliminated them from the race. The unruliness of the happy Polo Grounds crowd prompted the police to afford protection to the Pirates from the seventh inning on. John McGraw savored the sweep of Pittsburgh. The Giants had won as a consequence of good pitching from a staff that observers had thought unreliable and timely hitting from a batting order that observers had adjudged enfeebled. The Giant victory left the Dodgers almost without hope, since they stood 1½ games behind the Giants, with 2 games left for Brooklyn and 3 for New York.

Neither team was scheduled to play on September 26, and so the uncertainty lingered on an extra day. But on September 27, the National League pennant race was decided—without any ambiguity. By defeating the Philadelphia Phillies, 5–1, at the Polo Grounds, the New York Giants won their fourth consecutive flag. Jack Bentley allowed only 4 hits to the visitors, and their single run was unearned. In effect, the Giants doubled the Phillies into submission, as Freddy Lindstrom, Jimmy O'Connell, Bill Terry, and Hack Wilson all hit 2-baggers. At Ebbets Field, meanwhile, the same outcome to the race was assured as the Dodgers lost to the Boston Braves, 3–2. Bill Doak pitched well, but his 10-game winning streak had ended.

Had results been different in the Giant game, a controversial call by Bill Klem, wherein he disallowed 2 apparent Dodger runs on the grounds that a batted ball was foul, might have figured very prominently in the later lore of the season. But in light of the Giant victory, the call had no broader significance. And Dazzy Vance made sure it was completely unimportant when, on the twenty-eighth, he needed only eighty minutes to throw a 5-hitter against the Braves and clinch second place for Brooklyn. It was the twenty-eighth victory of the year for the Dazzler, giving him more wins than any National League pitcher had garnered since Grover Cleveland Alexander's 30 in 1917, and his 9 strikeouts gave him a major league–leading total of 262.[30] Vance had much reason to be proud of this extraordinary season. But it had not been good enough, and he could only regret that it was John McGraw, not Wilbert Robinson, who had the occasion to tell the press, "We have come through the tough part and we expect to be in shape for the world's series."[31]

Washington Clinches the American League Pennant

Although the identity of the Giants' opponent in that series had not yet been confirmed when McGraw spoke, it increasingly appeared that the Washington Nationals would play that role. But if they did, it would not be for want of Yankee effort. When play began in the American League on September 22, the Yankees trailed by 2 games. If they were to win the pennant, the Nationals would have to falter. On that day the New Yorkers fulfilled their own assignment, icing a 10–4 victory over the Indians with 5 runs in the ninth inning. Wally Pipp was the batting star with 2 doubles and a triple. But with Walter Johnson on the mound, the Nationals won, too, coming from behind with 6 runs in the seventh inning. It was Johnson's thirteenth straight victory, and he was aided by 4 hits from Roger Peckinpaugh, 3 from Ossie Bluege, and outstanding fielding from Bucky Harris and Earl McNeely. Sam Rice extended his streak to 29 games.

On September 23 the Yankees again beat the Indians, with good hurling from Bob Shawkey. But the apparently irresistible Nationals also continued to find ways to win, capitalizing on White Sox errors to eke out a 7–6 victory in a cold Comiskey Park. Rice carried his streak to 30 games. September 24 provided a reprise of September 23. The Yankees used a bloop single, an outfield misplay, and a single through a drawn-in infield to score 2 runs, while Sam Jones held the Indians scoreless. Despite the sweep of Cleveland, New York still stayed mired 2 games off the pace, because Washington roughed up Sloppy Thurston to beat Chicago, 6–3, and complete a sweep of the White Sox. Sam Rice pushed his streak to 31 games. It is easy to imagine the frustration felt by the Yankees: They had won 12 of their last 16 contests and not gained a single game on the equally hot Nationals. Their only hope now was that the schedule break, which allowed both teams to rest on September 25, would somehow disrupt Washington's momentum.

For one brief day it appeared that their hope might be fulfilled. The Nationals were winding up their season in Boston, against the now pitiful Red Sox. But, on September 26, everything came together for the home club. Almost against the wishes of the Fenway faithful, who were joining fans around the country in cheering on the Nationals, the Red Sox brought Washington's momentum to an abrupt halt. Alex Ferguson ended the Nationals' 4-game winning streak with a splendid 2–1 game. In so doing, he ended Walter Johnson's personal 13-game winning streak. He was even good enough to end Sam Rice's consecutive-game hitting streak at 31. Both of these streaks had begun to attract national attention before Ferguson checked them. Johnson's was the second longest in the majors in 1924, trailing only Dazzy Vance's; it turned out to be tied for third longest in the entire decade of the 1920s. Rice's streak, the fifth longest in the twentieth century at that point, featured 53 base hits in 136 official times at bat for a batting average of .390. Rice was not a power hitter, and only one of his blows was a home run. But he was the team's best base-stealer, too, and on 5 occasions during the streak he increased the value of a hit by nabbing an extra base.[32] On top of these various disappointments, the Nationals suffered two other blows that day. First, the Yankees pounded out a 7–1 victory over the Athletics, closing to within a game of the lead. Second, Walter Johnson was forced to leave the game in the eighth inning after having been hit on the elbow by a pitched ball three innings earlier. He would not appear again in the regular season. No matter how one looked at it, September 26 was a bad day for Washington.

It was, however, only a bad day, not a harbinger. In the very first inning of their game the following day, Sam Rice doubled and the Nationals scored twice. Then, after falling behind, the Nationals scampered back into the lead. Bucky Harris pumped four pitchers into the game, Goose Goslin collected 3 hits, and Wade Lefler delivered another clutch pinch hit, a double with the bases filled in the fifth inning. The Nationals won, 7–5. And the Yankees simultaneously made matters easier for Washington by giving up the advantage they had gained the previous day. Joe Bush drove in all 3 Yankee runs, but his wild pitch in the seventh inning allowed Jimmy Dykes to score the winning run from second base for the Athletics' 4–3 victory. As a result, Washington needed only 1 more victory or a New York loss—each team had 2 games left—to clinch the pennant.

The ban on Sunday ball in both Boston and Philadelphia gave the two contenders September 28 off, and so the suspense lasted an additional twenty-four hours. But then, on September 29, as the Yankees were idled by rain, Tom Zachary and Firpo Marberry combined their talents to give Washington a 4–2 victory over Boston.[33] Sam Rice again led the way with his speed, singling in the first inning, stealing second, and then racing all the way around to score when the catcher's throw went into center field. But it was a team triumph. Every player in the Nationals' starting lineup got a hit, Washington sparkled on defense, and when the game concluded, the crowd at Fenway Park surged from its seats to salute the new pennant winners as they walked off the field.[34] Back in the rain-soaked nation's capital, baseball fans celebrated the triumph by swarming into the streets and flinging umbrellas at passing cars.

The Nationals' victory registered as an authentic American triumph. On October 1, President Calvin Coolidge welcomed the team to the White House. An estimated hundred thousand people thronged along Pennsylvania Avenue to cheer. As bearers of Washington's first pennant ever,[35] the players were heroes in a town that usually had its mind on other things. It was reported that Walter Johnson blushed on shaking the President's hand. During the tense race of September, baseball had become the leading topic of discussion in the nation's capital. Johnson and Bucky Harris were acclaimed whenever they appeared in public, and after the Nationals left town for the long road trip that concluded their season, radio station WCAP took the unprecedented step of broadcasting the games back to the capital, allowing tens of thousands to follow the team through the hinterlands. Other fans flocked to the various boards erected throughout the city to allow viewers to follow the developments of the games.[36]

Enthusiasm for the Nationals was not confined to the nation's capital. Moved variously by a distaste for New York City's recent dominance in baseball, by generic affection for the underdog, and by a wish to see Walter Johnson have a chance to crown his career with a World Series appearance,[37] fans everywhere became boosters of the Nats. At Sportsman's Park in St. Louis, the September crowds cheered whenever the scoreboard posted a Washington success, and during the Nationals' final series in Fenway Park, the crowd was openly pro-Washington, even going so far as to rise in the top rather than the bottom of the seventh. Most players in the American League were also happy that Washington had beaten New York. Ty Cobb spoke bluntly: "I had the consolation of kicking the Yankees out of the race and I got quite a kick out of that."[38] One great challenge still lay ahead, but there seemed to be little doubt in the nation's capital on October 1 that the Nationals would now humble the mighty Giants. "There isn't a team in the country," Clark Griffith declared, "that can beat Washington in its present mood."[39] He chose an odd attribute to base a prediction of victory on, but as baseball fans well knew, almost anything could affect the outcome of a World Series.

Scandal!

And then, just as the nation's fans were preparing themselves for the excitement of the World Series, newspaper headlines screamed that major league baseball had another game-tampering scandal on its hands. That, of course, was bad enough. Worse was the revelation that the team implicated in seeking to induce an opposing team to throw a game was the National League champion, the New York Giants. The incident that gave rise to the furor occurred on September 27. Prior to the Giants–Phillies game of that afternoon, and with New York only 1 victory away from clinching the pennant, Jimmy O'Connell approached Heinie Sand, the Phillie shortstop, and offered him $500 if he would "not bear down on us today."[40] Sand declined the offer brusquely, the game was played without any strange behavior (Sand in fact scored the only Phillie run), and the Giants, by winning the contest, secured the flag. But Sand recalled that Commissioner Landis had declared that silence about knowledge of bribe efforts deserved no less severe a punishment than offering or accepting a bribe itself, and so after the game he reported the conversation to his manager Art Fletcher. The tale of the overture then made its way upward—from Fletcher to team owner William Baker on September 28, and then from Baker to National League President John Heydler and from Heydler to Commissioner Landis by the afternoon of September 29.

Landis acted quickly. He did not know whether the story was true; if it was accurate, he did not know how many people in the Giant organization, or how many occasions, might be involved. Initially he was confident only of one thing: Although the story had not yet leaked to the press, it would. With the World Series less than a week away, scheduled to involve the very team against which the accusation was made, Landis concluded that if baseball was to be spared another body blow like the disclosures about the 1919 World Series, he would need to move swiftly, decisively, and in a fashion that would reassure the public that major league baseball, and in particular, the imminent World Series was honest. This was precisely the kind of emergency that Landis's appointment had been designed to forestall or—if worse came to worst—to resolve.

Commissioner Landis sped secretly to New York City. On the thirtieth he interviewed Heinie Sand and Jimmy O'Connell. Had O'Connell denied Sand's story, it is not clear what the commissioner would have done. But O'Connell confirmed that he had made the offer, saying that he had been asked to do so by Giant coach Cozy Dolan and adding that he believed Frankie Frisch, George Kelly, and Ross Youngs also knew of the plan. When Dolan was interrogated by Landis about O'Connell's tale, he neither affirmed nor denied it, protesting instead that he could not remember anything about the day. Landis then summoned the three other players whom O'Connell had implicated; all denied the accusation of complicity.

No further evidence was forthcoming, and speed was requisite. Thus, in the newspapers of October 2, when the baseball world first learned that something had been amiss, it also learned of the commissioner's solution. With respect to O'Connell, the matter was easy. He had, after all, confessed to attempting to bribe an opposing player, and so Landis banned him. O'Connell, twenty-three years old at the time, never again played in Organized Baseball. Landis also expelled Dolan, concluding that it was implausible to credit claims of forgetfulness when events of such moment were only seventy-two hours old. For four reasons the allegations against Frisch, Kelly, and Youngs were a different matter. First, they were stars of the game, not bit players. Second, they denied the charge directly rather than offering evasions. Third, O'Connell himself admitted that none of the three had spoken to him directly about the bribe.[41] Fourth, O'Connell's testimony about seeking out Kelly right after offering the bribe was not supported by the accounts of other witnesses. Landis therefore declared their statements "a clear refutation of the charge" and exonerated them completely.[42]

Landis was faulted almost immediately. John McGraw, for example, was enraged at having been kept in the dark about Landis's arrival in New York and his subsequent interrogation of five Giants. As manager of the team under scrutiny, McGraw felt that he deserved prompter notification of Sand's charge. His contempt flared in his reply to a press inquiry about the matter: "I don't know anything about it. I have nothing to say. See Landis. He has all the evidence."[43] Ban Johnson, the American

League President, was enraged that he had had to wait until press reports appeared on October 2 before learning that a corruption investigation had been under way. He went beyond criticizing procedure to lash out at substance. Holding that Landis might be "covering up" widespread malfeasance in the Giant organization, he urged that the World Series be called off.[44] Barney Dreyfuss, the owner of the Pirates, was also unpersuaded by Landis's decision and joined Ban Johnson in urging the cancellation of the World Series.

That was, of course, the last thing that Landis intended to do. Instead, he stated that it was "a pretty good time for gentlemen who are not clothed with responsibility to keep their shirts on."[45] He defended his decision with typical brusqueness: "This was an attempt to bribe a baseball player. The attempt proved abortive. Why call off the world's series?"[46] Thwarted in his effort to prevent the World Series from occurring, Ban Johnson was reduced to seeking consolation in refusing to attend the games, justifying his behavior by reference to "the intolerable condition that had permeated the [Giant] club." But all he earned for his stand was an angry declaration from his old friend Clark Griffith that Ban Johnson was "trying to play baseball politics."[47] Griffith's irritation was understandable since, as owner of the Nationals, he found his own league president proposing to deny his Washington team their first crack at a World Series. The sanest public remark from these heated days came from Dodger owner Charles Ebbets. When asked to petition Landis to have his second-place team represent the National League in the World Series in place of the beclouded Giants, Ebbets declined. "Perhaps," he explained, "the bribe offer was a joke. In any event, the bribe wasn't accepted. The result of the game must stand as played."[48]

In this matter, as in many he handled, Commissioner Landis, though not unconcerned with securing justice, felt that it was secondary to retaining public confidence in the game and his own office. As he well knew, there were reasons to suspect wider Giant complicity in the effort to bribe Sand. For starters, the Giants in general had a tawdry reputation. The club owner, Charles Stoneham, spent the entire 1924 season under indictment for perjury, and John McGraw was famous for his tolerant attitude toward Hal Chase, Shufflin' Phil Douglas, and Heinie Zimmerman, players whose reputations for crookedness were deep-seated and well founded. Then, it was widely known that Cozy Dolan was a close friend of McGraw's, hence unlikely (it was felt) to proceed without his boss's nod. Finally, as Landis heard with his own ears, the testimony from Frisch and Youngs about a bribe offer was not quite as straight-forward as he publicly declared it to be. Youngs said, ungrammatically but not indecipherably, "You hear fellows talking around that boys that are offering money and something like that." And Frisch commented, "On a pennant contender, you always hear a lot of stuff like that, a lot of kidding and some other things."[49] Not exactly unequivocal denials.

It is clear, however, that the evidence to punish McGraw, Frisch, Kelly, and/or Youngs had not been produced. Landis's decision to exonerate them was thus correct, and a later investigation by the District Attor-ney of New York State uncovered nothing to challenge that decision. Nevertheless and inevitably, questions continued to hang over the Giants and the World Series. O'Connell, for example, stirred up some sympathy by weeping in McGraw's presence and later lamenting that "they're making a goat out of me. I've been a damned fool."[50] And Dolan soon got around to saying that in telling Landis he did not remember events, he was really denying the charge—"I always use that expres-sion," he explained.[51] Were these just the virtually predictable efforts of guilty men to deflect or widen blame? Perhaps. But my instinct tells me that it was unlikely that figures as peripheral as Cozy Dolan and Jimmy O'Connell would have initiated a bribe effort without an endorsement from a more central and powerful person. We shall probably, however, never know much more about this strange and (for two men) tragic affair.[52] In any case, the atmosphere of the World Series was suddenly polluted, and while Frankie Frisch could still declare that "I think we will be all right in the series," oddsmakers established the Nationals as nar-row favorites.[53]

Standings at the End of the Season

AMERICAN LEAGUE

Team	Won	Lost	Pctg.	Games Behind
Washington Nationals	92	62	.597	—
New York Yankees	89	63	.586	2.0
Detroit Tigers	86	68	.558	6.0
St. Louis Browns	74	78	.487	17.0
Philadelphia Athletics	71	81	.467	20.0
Cleveland Indians	67	86	.438	24.5
Boston Red Sox	67	87	.435	25.0
Chicago White Sox	66	87	.431	25.5

NATIONAL LEAGUE

Team	Won	Lost	Pctg.	Games Behind
New York Giants	93	60	.608	—
Brooklyn Dodgers	92	62	.597	1.5
Pittsburgh Pirates	90	63	.588	3.0
Cincinnati Reds	83	70	.542	10.0
Chicago Cubs	81	72	.529	12.0
St. Louis Cardinals	65	89	.422	28.5
Philadelphia Phillies	55	96	.364	37.0
Boston Braves	53	100	.346	40.0

The Season in Review

The Pennant Winners

NO OBSERVER was surprised that the New York Giants did well in 1924. Although not every writer had picked them to win their fourth straight pennant, no one had doubted that they would be in the thick of the National League race. In fact, their year-to-year consistency over the course of their four consecutive pennant seasons is impressive: In 1921 they prevailed with 94 victories, in 1922 with 93, in 1923 with 95, and in 1924 with 93. In general, it can be said that they won in 1924 on the basis of their powerful offense. The Giants led the majors in team batting with .300 and in runs scored with 857, an average of 5.6 runs per game. They led the National League in home runs with 95. Six of their regular starting eight batted above .300, with Ross Youngs, in the finest season of his abbreviated career, leading the squad at .356. George Kelly led the team in home runs (21) and the league in runs batted in (136). Frankie Frisch tied for the league lead in runs scored. To reinforce all of this strength, John McGraw, who liked to experiment with platooning, had a fine bench to work with. Bill Terry led the National League in pinch hits, Hack Wilson provided an early-season charge, Hank Gowdy gave the club the most potent backup catcher in baseball, and Jimmy O'Connell, before destroying his career, delivered crucial hits down the stretch. The Giants were hard to shut down and not inclined to defeat themselves in the field.

The reason New York did not run away with the National League flag was that their pitching was inconsistent—better than average, but assuredly not dominant. Four hurlers reached double figures in victories. Virgil Barnes rode his screwball to 16 triumphs. Jack Bentley matched this figure. Art Nehf and Hugh McQuillan added 14 each. But the staff's earned run average (3.62) was only third best in the league, a half-run off the leader's pace. Barnes, in the finest season of his career, was the best of the lot, leading the team in innings pitched and posting a good 3.06 earned run average. As for Jack Bentley, even before the season began, he had invited derision by a public excursion into self-pity, and his subsequent record, combining a very solid 16–5 won–lost record with a mediocre earned run average of 3.78, only fueled the discontents of a multitalented man who was good but wanted to be great.[1] He did, however, defeat the Dodgers 6 times during the year, a vital component in the Giants' final narrow success. Veteran Art Nehf, though still able to throw the occasional masterpiece, was slowly becoming a spot pitcher. He lost only 4 games, but pitched fewer innings than in any year since 1916. Hugh McQuillan had the best earned run average on the team (2.69) and turned in the best year of his career, but he served himself and his teammates poorly by continuing to be a disciplinary problem. This was a team with four solid pitchers but not a single outstanding one. Finally, it should be noted that the Giants succeeded by virtue of their dramatically successful start, for over the entire post–Independence Day span of the season they failed to match the winning percentages of either the Pirates or the Dodgers.[2] Nevertheless, they were seen in their own day as a powerhouse, and posterity has ratified that judgment by placing 7 members of this team in the Hall of Fame.[3]

Virtually everyone was surprised by the success of the Washington Nationals. With a team that had scarcely changed personnel from the squad that the previous year had finished 23½ games out of first place, Washington began slowly, raced to the top in June, slipped back a bit in July, regained the top toward the end of August, and then held off a furious Yankee charge with a sprint of its own. Throughout the season the Nats honored Bucky Harris's spring training promise that the team "would play out the string win, lose, or draw at all times."[4]

The Nationals were a spirited squad—the noisiest, the most aggressive, and perhaps the foulest-mouthed club in the league.[5] Ossie Bluege, for example, an otherwise model citizen, was a celebrated cusser, and Muddy Ruel acquired his famous nickname from "the dirty way he used to talk to opposing players."[6] In their behavior the Nats took their cue from their field boss. Quick to quarrel with umpires and imaginative in his barnyard imagery, Bucky Harris was frequently expelled from games in 1924, on at least one occasion was fined for his abuse of um-

pires, and was finally warned in early September that his next alterca-
tion would end in his suspension. Still, flamboyant invective does not win
pennants, and in the last analysis, the Nationals won the pennant because
they avoided serious injuries to key personnel—only George Mogridge,
Bucky Harris, and Joe Judge were kept out of action for significant
blocks of time—and because they boasted balance and the standard trio
of strengths: good fielding, good hitting, and good pitching.

Most observers believed the Nationals had the best defensive infield
in the American League—"as fine a double play quartet as I have ever
seen," according to George Sisler.[7] Ossie Bluege, the third baseman, had
huge hands and played with a fluid grace; he was, in the view of Luke
Sewell, "the best third baseman"—the framework for this comparison
extends from Pie Traynor to Brooks Robinson—"who ever put a glove
on."[8] Roger Peckinpaugh had slowed down a step from the days when he
had reigned as the league's best shortstop, but he was still very reliable.
Moreover, he joined with Bucky Harris, the second baseman with the
fastest release in baseball, to form—no less an authority than Johnny
Evers is the source of this remark—"the greatest keystone combination
that has ever played in the major leagues."[9] The only reason the Nationals fell off in 1924 from their record-setting double-play pace of the
previous year was that their pitchers were allowing fewer base runners.
First base was patrolled by the sure-handed Joe Judge, who won four
fielding titles in the 1920s and was chosen by F. C. Lane as first baseman on the American League all-star team in 1924.[10] Behind the plate
was Muddy Ruel, who, at midcareer, was finally eclipsing the veteran
Ray Schalk as the consensus choice for the best defensive catcher in the
league. Even on the mound they boasted defensive strength, since either
Walter Johnson or Tom Zachary was the best-fielding pitcher in the
American League.[11]

The Nationals won with their bats as well as their gloves, and their
.294 team batting average was an index of how effective they were at
putting runners on the bases.[12] Goose Goslin emerged into stardom in
1924, batting .344, hitting 12 home runs, and leading the league in runs
batted in, with 129. According to his delighted manager, Goslin was
"one of the greatest natural hitters in the league."[13] And he was not
alone. Though Sam Rice was not a power hitter, during the last phase of
the season he was sensational, hitting safely in 43 of the team's final 44
games and in 57 of the team's final 61 games. He finished the year at .334.

Joe Judge contributed a .324 average;[14] the late-arriving Earl McNeely batted .330. As a whole, the team raised its batting average 20 points over 1923. And it did this with a balanced batting order that, on a typical day, featured (among its position players) four left-handed batters and an equal number of righties.

But the Nationals' offense was most assuredly not like the Giants; and it was absolutely atypical for the 1920s. Not only was their total of 22 home runs for the entire team less than half the figure of 46 that Babe Ruth hit all by himself, it represents the fifth-lowest total for home runs that *any* team—pennant winner or not—has posted in the majors since 1920. Astonishingly, the Nationals hit only 1 home run at home all year.[15] After Goslin's 12, the next highest figure was Judge's 3. In fact, as their mode of offense shows, the Senators of 1924 are best seen as the last redoubt of the days of scrappy inside baseball. They led the league in sacrifices and placed second in stolen bases, they played for the single run rather than the big inning, and they counted on their pitching staff to protect their leads.

And that point leads us to the heart of the argument: Washington's pitching was superb. It featured, above all, Walter Johnson, the league's best hurler. But alongside Johnson in the rotation were Tom Zachary—"Old Tom" to his teammates, because he looked "so sage and crafty and cunning"—whose 2.75 earned run average was second only to Johnson's in the league;[16] and George Mogridge, who for the fourth consecutive year started at least 30 games and pitched at least 200 innings. Since Zachary and Mogridge were lefthanders, Harris had wider flexibility in exercising strategic options on the mound than any other manager in the league.[17] It is true that the Nationals had no regular fourth starter to work with these three. But at crucial moments during the year they got good service in that position from Curly Ogden, the valuable early-season acquisition from the Athletics; Paul Zahniser, a sophomore in the league; and Oyster Joe Martina, a thirty-five-year-old rookie.

The basic reason for the Nationals' success in pitching, however, lies in the culmination of a revolution in mound strategy that Washington had been nourishing for several years. For in a fashion never before seen on a good team, Washington in 1924 relied on relief pitching. Attention to the utility of bringing fresh pitchers to the mound was not new to the club under Bucky Harris. For a number of years, Clark Griffith had avowed that "great depth" in pitching was needed "because of the intense heat" that wilted the nation's capital during the summer,[18] and the Nationals had already been dabbling with relief pitching for long enough to permit the legal spitballer, Allan Russell, to become, during the course of 1924, the first pitcher in major league history to post 200 career appearances in relief. The veteran Russell relieved in 37 games and saved 8. But the star of the relief staff was Firpo Marberry. In his first full-time year with the Senators, the twenty-five-year-old made 36 relief appearances (and 14 starts); he recorded the unprecedented number of 15 saves.[19] In so doing, Marberry launched his career as baseball's first great relief pitcher. Before his career was over, he would become the first pitcher to relieve in 50 games in a season, the first to make 300 relief appearances, and the first to record 100 reconstructed saves.[20]

Throughout his career Firpo Marberry's basic pitch was his fastball. But for 1924, his second season in the majors, he added a curve to his repertoire. On the mound he embodied restless irritation with all batters. He snatched at the ball when it was thrown to him, he was perpetually active as he readied himself to pitch, and he delivered the ball with an animated motion that set his cap a-flying. Muddy Ruel, his catcher, cooperated in the game of intimidation by allowing his warm-up pitches to strike the catcher's mitt with a loud smack. In Ruel's judgment, Marberry lacked the endurance to make a successful starter: "He was invincible for two or three innings, but he couldn't go the distance."[21] In fact, he wasn't really invincible. He blew some save opportunities, as his record of 11 losses shows. But he was very good, and because of his speed he was most effective late in the afternoon—it came to be called "Marberry time"—when the longer shadows made his pitches even harder to pick up. As the season progressed, Bucky Harris's confidence in his star reliever mounted. In the September chase, he called on Marberry 13 times, more frequently than he had turned to the young hurler in any previous month. That's one reason George Sisler later declared his belief that "[Marberry] was responsible for their winning the pennant."[22]

The Nationals posted 25 team saves in 1924, a level that no major league team had reached before.[23] Moreover, if one is to search for the explanation of Walter Johnson's return to dominance in 1924, one need look no farther than his better springtime health and Bucky Harris's relief staff. The Big Train himself remarked that he could no longer pitch as frequently or as long as he had in his prime: "I am not what I used to be as a pitcher."[24] But with Marberry (and occasionally Russell) in the bullpen, Harris needed only 7 good innings from his star in hot weather, knowing that Marberry was ready to finish what Johnson had begun.[25]

Three more measures underscore the effectiveness of the Nationals' mound corps in 1924. First, the opponents' batting average off Washington pitching was only .258, 26 points under the next-lowest average. Second, the pitching staff allowed only 8.6 hits per game, more than a hit below the next-best record and the lowest figure of the decade. Third, the mound staff yielded only 34 home runs all year; in all the seasons since then, only the 1943 Cardinals have won the pennant while yielding fewer round-trippers. Not surprisingly then, the Washington staff led the American League with their earned run average of 3.35, an improvement of almost two-thirds of a run over 1923 and half a run better than any other team in the league. If Washington's offensive strategy harkened back to the opening of the twentieth century, its pitching strategy foreshadowed the mound philosophy of the close of the century.

The Also-Rans

In light of these reflections about the successes of the Giants and Nationals, the reasons for the failures of their rivals become clearer. The Dodgers lacked the depth of the Giants. They were, in fact, in many ways a four-player team. In Dazzy Vance and Burleigh Grimes they had the best pitching duo in baseball, but the rest of the staff, even when fortified by Bill Doak, could not even win half of its games. Robinson worked his two mound stars very hard, and it is likely that the duo's inability to maintain their excellence in the final two weeks of the season was a sign that hurling 300+ innings exacted a toll in arm weariness that even the best of pitchers could not avoid.[26] In Zack Wheat the Dodgers had a batter who hit .375 and who ranked second only to Rogers Hornsby as an offensive force in the National League. In Jack Fournier they had the league-leader in home runs and the runner-up in runs batted in. Three of the four—all but Fournier—are in the Hall of Fame. But beyond this quartet the Dodgers had little to offer. They were last in the majors in stolen bases, last at turning double plays, and notably weak behind the plate. In their season series with the Giants they managed to win only 8 of the 22 games.[27] In light of their poor start, these were fatal shortcomings.

The Pirates lacked the experience of the Giants. Like the Dodgers, they started slowly, as Bill McKechnie tried to work out the articulations between veterans and newcomers. Max Carey and Rabbit Maranville represented the former: Between them they boasted twenty-six years of major league experience coming into the season, and the thirty-four-year-old Carey, famed for his obsession with staying in condition, demonstrated that he had lost none of his speed by taking his ninth base-stealing championship. The Pirates' remarkable rookie corps represented the infusion of youth. Glenn Wright handled shortstop, batting .287 and ranging widely. Ray Kremer won 18 games, with a 3.19 earned run average. Opponents found Emil Yde's jerky underhand delivery still more difficult to pick up, and the late-arriving rookie outshone even Kremer, winning 16 games, posting a winning percentage of .842, and allowing only 2.83 earned runs per 9 innings. Above all, there was Kiki Cuyler, who delivered one of the great rookie performances of all time, batting .354 and finishing second in the league in stolen bases and fourth in slugging. In the 21 crucial games against the Giants, he moved to a still higher level of performance, posting a .432 batting average and leading the Pirates to a 13-to-9 edge in the season's series with the New Yorkers. With an influx of talent of this sort, it is no wonder that the Pirates were but a year away from becoming world champions. But in 1924, in the ultimate September showdown series with the Giants, the Pirates' reliance on the inexperienced cost them dearly, for, being unable to convert an advantage in hits into an advantage in runs, they lost the series and the pennant.

In the junior circuit, although almost winning an unprecedented fourth straight league flag, the Yankees played their poorest ball since 1919. Babe Ruth, Joe Dugan, Bob Meusel, and Herb Pennock aside, Miller Huggins juggled with players who were disappointing. It must have added bitterness to reflect that four Washington standouts—Roger Peckinpaugh, George Mogridge, Muddy Ruel, and Allan Russell—had once been Yankees. Deterioration was most visible in the pitching staff, which delivered only 76 complete games in 1924 in contrast to the 101 of 1923. Mound performance would have been even worse had not Joe Bush revitalized his season in September. And down that exciting stretch, without an obvious relief pitcher to help out in the duel with the Nationals, Huggins was forced to bring such starters as Pennock, Waite Hoyt, and Bob Shawkey out of the bullpen. In part, that's why the Yankees won only 9 of their 22 games with the Nats. Nevertheless, the Yankees made a strong run. For the post–Independence Day portion of the season, New York and Washington turned in identical records of 51 wins and 32 losses (.614). In the period after Labor Day—and without strong support from Ruth—the New Yorkers picked up their pace another notch, winning 16 of 24 games (.667). But it wasn't enough.

The Tigers, meanwhile, with players like Harry Heilmann and Ty Cobb in their lineup, were not wanting in hitters; they led the league in batting average (.298) and in runs scored. As late as August 12 they occupied first place. As a consequence of their competitiveness they drew over a million fans to Navin Field for the first time in club history. But they had an array of problems, too—an unfilled hole at second base, injuries to Lu Blue and Fats Fothergill, and inconsistency from their pitchers. Moreover, troubled by what he felt was a diminution of visual acuity, Cobb had his second-poorest batting season since 1906. Thus, even though the Tigers were strong enough over a short stretch to puncture the hopes of a team as good as the Yankees in September, and strong enough over the longer run to post the fourth consecutive improvement in their won–lost record, they still came up short.

A major reason the 1924 season was so exciting was that no team was dominant. One way to establish this point is to note that the mean winning percentage of the two pennant winners in 1924 was .603, the second-lowest figure since the reemergence of a bipartite major league system in 1901. Another way to bolster the point is to note that the .431 percentage turned in by the White Sox is the second-highest last-place figure in the history of the American League. But if the absence of an overpowering force at the team level helped to make the season a compelling spectacle, another reason for the excitement of the year was that, at the level of individual performance, the campaigns featured some extraordinary athletes and generated some breath-taking achievements.

The Stars

The two strongest hitters of the year were Babe Ruth of the Yankees and Rogers Hornsby of the Cardinals. Each had a mesmerizing season. With a batting average of .378, Ruth (as he had foretold) finally won a batting championship, earning the only major hitting laurel that had thus far eluded him.[28] His 46 home runs were enough to lead the major leagues in that category; only his own 54 in 1920 and 59 in 1921 were higher seasonal figures. Ruth led the league in runs scored with 143 and was second in runs batted in (behind Goose Goslin) with 121.[29] But the most remarkable statistic that he posted—even though he had done better in three recent years—was the 142 bases on balls he received. This figure meant that for the fourth time in five years Ruth had gotten on base more than half the times he came to the plate (.513). His power production remained phenomenal. With a slugging average of .739, he completed the same five-year span with an astonishing slugging figure of .788. "I don't think," John McGraw had recently said of Ruth, "a man ever lived who could put such force behind a ball."[30] Accomplishments of this magnitude leave the commentator groping for adjectives.

And yet, eye-catching as Ruth's statistics were, there were those who maintained that it was Hornsby who had the greater season. Many years later Hornsby declared, "Baseball is my life, the only thing I know and can talk about, my only interest."[31] He demonstrated the intensity of that focus in 1924 when his emergence as Ruth's first clear rival in batting prowess finally drew extensive media attention. In fact, F. C. Lane contended, Hornsby was "the truer, steadier hitter."[32] When the season was over, more grounds for that argument had been laid. Hornsby played in 143 games during 1924 and was held hitless in only 22 of them. In 46 games he had 1 hit, in 47 games he had 2 hits, in 25 games he had 3 hits, and in 3 games he had 4 hits. He struck out only 22 times all year. At the end of April he was batting .429; at the end of May, .404. He slipped to .389 by the end of June. But then he caught fire. At the end of July he was up to .412, and by the end of August he was hitting .434. He slipped a bit in the final month of the season, owing in part to the back injury that sidelined him for a week. Even so, he wound up the season with his fifth consecutive batting championship—he would end his career with seven—and a batting average for the year of .424. This awesome figure stands as the highest seasonal major league batting average of the twentieth century.[33]

Hornsby was, moreover, in the fourth year of a five-year hitting tear the likes of which baseball has never seen, posting a .402 batting average for the entire 1921 through 1925 period.[34] He led the National League in runs, hits, and doubles in 1924, and he stroked out 25 home runs. By posting an on-base percentage of .507, he gave the major leagues the only season of the twentieth century in which two players got on base more than half the times they came to the plate. By leading the league in both hits and bases on balls, he accomplished a feat replicated only three times in the twentieth century.[35] In light of these statistics it is difficult to believe that he struggled with a dislocated thumb in the early part of the summer and a sore back in September. When the season was over, the Cardinal second baseman was asked which pitchers gave him the most difficulty. "There are," he replied with customary bluntness, "no hard pitchers to hit."[36]

Oddly for this year lodged in the middle of the decade of offense, batting success was not the only aspect of baseball that won admiration in 1924. In fact, one of the most remarkable aspects of the year is that it is the only season during the 1920s in which the feats of pitchers merited as much attention as the achievements of batters. This point was underlined when the league awards, created to honor the player who is "of greatest all-round service to his club" (and thus tantamount to the Most Valuable Player awards that were to be initiated in 1931), were conferred on Walter Johnson of the Nationals and Dazzy Vance of the Dodgers.[37] Their windups were as dissimilar as possible: Johnson whipped the ball toward the plate with an easy sidearm motion, while Vance twisted, kicked high, and flashed his shirt cuff as he bore down with his overhand fastball. But each man was dominant in his league, winning a pitching triple crown—that is, leading his circuit in wins, earned run average, and strikeouts.[38] Each was at his best in the closing third of the season, when the pennant chases were hottest. It is impossible to imagine Washington winning the pennant without Johnson; it is impossible to imagine the Dodgers putting a scare into the Giants without Vance.

In winning 23 games, Johnson reached the 20-victory mark for the eleventh time in his career (and the first time since 1919), seizing upon the opportunity Firpo Marberry afforded him to demolish the spreading belief that he was through as a master pitcher.[39] He threw the American League's only no-hitter, the 7-inning job against the Browns on August 25;[40] he threw the major leagues' only 1-hitter, the brilliant effort against the White Sox on May 23. For the sixth time in his career—an American League record he shares with Bob Feller—he was the league's winningest pitcher; for the seventh time in his career—a major league record he shares with Grover Cleveland Alexander—he led the league in shutouts; for the twelfth time in his career—a major league record that is his alone—he led his league in strikeouts. Johnson had unusually long arms, with his right limb extending at least an inch beyond his left. As the Nationals rode this right arm to the pennant, Johnson ripped through July, August, and much of September by reeling off 13 consecutive victories.[41] It was an extraordinary year.[42]

Yet remarkably, in every relevant respect, Vance's season was even better. Having finally learned how to avoid tipping off his deliveries, he posted the greatest season of his career and one of the strongest credited to any twentieth-century pitcher: The man who did not win his first major league game until he was thirty-one years old won five more games (28) than any other major league pitcher, chalked up 104 more strikeouts than his closest rival in either league, and posted an earned run average (2.16) that was half a run better than any other major league pitcher's. No National League pitcher of the twentieth century with as many as 34 decisions has surpassed Vance's winning percentage of .824. In light of the fact that he pitched for a good team rather than a poor one, it is even more remarkable that his winning percentage exceeded by .227 the percentage of his team; only six regular pitchers produced wider margins in the twentieth century.[43] Even in victory streaks Vance bested Johnson, reeling off 15 in a row from July into late September, as the Dodgers mounted their exciting challenge to the Giants. When he was once asked to explain how he acquired the name "Dazzy," Vance replied that it was a childhood way of saying "daisy," adding—superfluously—that to call something a daisy was to commend it.[44] And his "daisiest" season was 1924.

While greatest attention focused on Ruth, Hornsby, Johnson, and Vance, other players posted impressive numbers. Four were veterans of the era of inside baseball who, despite a combined total of seventy-three years of major league experience, gave proof that they could still make their mark in the era of the new offensive advantage. Ty Cobb batted .338, and although he suffered the first major slowdown of his great career in the second half of the season, he played in all but one of the Tigers' games, and was fourth in the league in stolen bases.[45] His success terminated his talk of imminent retirement. His old rival Tris Speaker was still better, batting .344 and posting the third-highest on-base average in the American League. Eddie Collins in turn improved on Speaker. The man, whom many held to be the "smartest baseball man I ever met," hit .349, led the American League in stolen bases with 42, and finished second to Johnson in the league award voting.[46] But Zack Wheat, growing better with age, outshone them all, posting his finest season yet. His .375 average in 1924 precisely matched his average for the previous year, and in 1924 he trailed only Hornsby in total hits in the National League. "I developed," he stated, by way of explanation for the unexpected blossoming of his midthirties, "a contempt for pitchers."[47] Ty Cobb explicitly approved of the remark.

There were other batters who recorded notable seasons. Ty Cobb's greatest pupil, Harry Heilmann, endured a bout of sinusitis and experienced his regular even-numbered-year slip from the peak but still managed to hit .346 and tie for the major league lead in doubles. His coleader was the Indians' Joe Sewell, who anchored his claim to be the American League's outstanding shortstop with brilliant fielding and a .316 batting average. Cincinnati's extraordinarily consistent Edd Roush—"the toughest [batter] of any in the league," in Burleigh Grimes's view—batted .348, led the National League in triples with 21, and burnished his reputation as the league's finest defensive outfielder.[48] Charlie Jamieson of the Indians had a career season with a .359 batting average. Bibb Falk of the White Sox hit .352. Ken Williams of the Browns, despite missing 40 games with a broken ankle, batted .324, drove in 84 runs, and struck out only 17 times in 467 plate appearances. On the other side of the coin, the season showed that Williams's great teammate George Sisler had not recovered his once incomparable batting eye, his .305 average confirming Fred Clarke's devastating judgment that "he looks like a player with only one good eye."[49]

Pitching, too, afforded standouts. Cincinnati's Carl Mays reached the 20-win plateau for the fifth time in his controversial career. Wilbur Cooper of the Pirates reached that plateau for the fourth time in five years, and passed the 200-career-victory mark. Herb Pennock of the Yankees, only thirty years old but in his twelfth year in the majors, won 21 games, a total exceeded in the American League only by Johnson. Burleigh Grimes confused batters to the tune of 22 victories, the fourth time in five years that the biggest winner of the 1920s passed the 20-win mark. Finally, there was Grover Cleveland Alexander. Thirty-seven when the season began, he suffered a broken hand after a spectacular start and so chalked up only 12 victories for the Cubs. His final victory of the season was, however, the 300th of his career, placing him in rarefied company. "He had the control," Freddy Lindstrom explained, expressing the frustrations of several generations of batters. "He'd fix you."[50]

The rookie of the year award did not exist in 1924. If it had, the likely winners would have been Earl Whitehill, Detroit's strong young pitcher, and Kiki Cuyler, the Pittsburgh Pirate outfielder who specialized in bedeviling the Giants.[51] Whitehill was the foundation of Ty Cobb's pitching staff. Although only twenty-four, he led the team in innings pitched (233), complete games (16), and victories (17). A possible rival for Whitehill was Al Simmons of the Athletics. Though still learning about major league pitching, he managed to bat .308 and drive in 102 runs. The work of both of these American Leaguers, however, pales when compared to the achievement of Cuyler. He was the complete ball player, for in addition to his impressive power and speed, he won respect for the range of his outfielding and the strength of his throwing arm. Cuyler's rookie year, in sum, was nothing short of spectacular.

Attendance

The 1924 season was a splendid vindication for those who argued that exciting pennant races pulled in the crowds. Both leagues set new records for total attendance: 4,340,644 in the National League and 5,255,439 in the American League, and while that National League total would be eclipsed in every subsequent season in the 1920s, the American League record of 1924 would stand until 1940. The American League drew almost a million more fans, because in the junior circuit the excitement was present from the very first day, with Red Sox successes dazzling fans for the opening two months and a tight three- (and briefly four-) way pennant race keeping them enthralled from late June on. As a consequence, attendance in Boston rose 95 percent from the level of the previous year, attendance in Washington rose 63 percent, attendance in St. Louis rose 24 percent, and Detroit drew over a million spectators for the first time in the history of the franchise. In the senior circuit the excitement did not come until midway through the season, when the Giants began to stumble. The biggest leap in the National League was enjoyed by the Dodgers, whose attendance of 818,883 represented an increase of 45 percent over the total for 1923. The message in these figures was a baseball truism: Tight pennant races and competitive teams bring out the fans.

Memorable Oddities

It's worth noting before ending that—like all seasons—1924 featured an array of incidents odd enough and achievements bizarre enough to merit inclusion in a chapter about the memorable. On August 2, Bill Sherdel of the Cardinals set a standard for pitching efficiency that can never be surpassed: Called in to relieve, he threw one pitch and, with a triple play, got three outs.[52] On September 6, Urban Shocker of the Browns duplicated the feat turned in by Herman Bell of the Cardinals on July 19 by pitching complete game victories in both ends of a doubleheader. Jesse Barnes of the Braves pitched 268 innings without throwing a single wild pitch. Bill Wambsganss of the Red Sox came to bat 632 times but couldn't hit a single home run. Finally, no listing of strange occurrences would be complete without mention of the Browns–Red Sox game of July 28. The Browns protested their loss, and Ban Johnson upheld the protest, on the remarkable grounds that umpire Brick Owens had required that Tony Rego bat out of order! As most observers of baseball know, one of the pleasures of following the game is sharing thoughts about the records, the feats, and the inanities that arise from the annual schedule of daily contests. The 1924 season certainly provided hot-stove leaguers with much to chew on.

CHAPTER TEN

———— ⚘ ————

The World Series

Getting Ready for the Big Show

T HE 1924 WORLD SERIES was scheduled to begin in
Washington on October 4. After 2 games in the nation's capital,
the teams would move immediately to New York City for as
many as 3 games. If a sixth game was needed, it was to be played back in
Washington on October 9. If a decisive seventh game was needed on October 10, a coin toss would determine the site. That was the taut pre-
scription: 7 games in 7 days. No days off for rest, recuperation, or re-
gathering. In anticipation of intense fan interest in Washington, seventeen
rows of temporary seats were erected in front of the left-field bleachers
in Griffith Stadium, and a few additional seats were squeezed into a corner in right center field.[1] An umpiring team of American Leaguers Tom
Connolly and Bill Dinneen and National Leaguers Bill Klem and Ernie
Quigley was announced.[2] Fred Lieb, president of the Baseball Writers
Association, was designated official scorer.

Lawrence Phillips, the so-called megaphone man who had announced
batteries at Washington home games since 1901, was ready for his first
Series.[3] But national interest in the event required that unprecedented
efforts be made to project information about the games way beyond the
confines of the ballparks. That's why radio stations WEAF in New York
City and WCAP in Washington made plans to broadcast play-by-play
accounts, with veteran New York hand Graham McNamee and Washington broadcaster Stuart Hayes sharing the microphone. Meanwhile,
sportswriters from the hinterlands filtered north and east by rail to cover
the spectacle firsthand, and various newspapers around the country un-
derwrote setting up scoreboards in cities large and small so that fans
might follow events on the diamond virtually as they happened. All of

these moves reflected that national interest in the World Series was un-usually high, first, because it was (finally) not a New York City monop-oly and second, because it had become a morality play, pitting a team with a gallant hurling star against a team that had known too much success in recent years and had now, apparently, ventured into skulduggery in an effort to protect itself. "Johnson at his best," Norman Baxter predicted, "would form a baseball epic that would be written and talked about for generations to come."[4] He was right—but not in the way he expected.

Both clubs had ended their seasons spectacularly, holding off relent-less challenges from strong opponents in riveting pennant races. The fi-nal "closeness index" for the year was 3.5, a figure undercut (before divi-sional play ended the possibility of meaningful comparison) only by the seasons of 1908, 1949, and 1964. Still, though both teams had proved themselves by beating off strong rivals, the Giants seemed the solider squad. They had a higher team batting average, they had scored over a hundred more runs, and they had stroked over four times as many home runs. In almost all respects, they were the model of a major league pen-nant winner of the 1920s—powerful offense and good defense, comple-mented by pitching adequate to its task. Moreover, as the only club to have given Dazzy Vance difficulty during the season, they were not no-tably afraid of Walter Johnson's speed. Finally, the Giants—players and manager alike—had extensive World Series experience. That is why John McGraw ventured the judgment that "the mental strain is more likely to affect the Nats than it is us."[5] Two absences would hurt, however, for Jimmy O'Connell, now banned from baseball, had emerged late in the year as the team's best reserve outfielder, and Heinie Groh, his knee still lame, had anchored the left end of the infield. But the situation might have been worse. At least Frankie Frisch would be available for play, and for the hole at third base, the Giants' vaunted talent-recognition system had already produced, in the youngster Freddy Lindstrom, a fine replacement.

Against this array of strengths the Nationals were far from defense-less. They had the better pitching staff, although George Mogridge was nursing a sore arm as the season ended. In Mogridge and Tom Zachary they featured the best brace of left-handed pitchers in the American League, and this was no small point, since Bucky Harris was aware that the Giants, despite being rich in right-handed batting talent, had per-formed marginally less well in 1924 when forced to deal with southpaws.[6] It would help that the Nationals were familiar with their opponents' playing field (for the Polo Grounds had been home to the Yankees until 1923), whereas the Giants were completely unfamiliar with the peculiarities of Griffith Stadium. Finally, the Nationals certainly had the best pitcher in the Series—although without the cooperation of rain, they could not expect to get three rested starts from Walter Johnson.

Subtler considerations hinted at other problems for Washington. Although they had led the Giants in stolen bases, that fact was indicative less of a superiority in speed—the Giants boasted a complement of speedsters, too—than of Washington's commitment to the now-outmoded strategies of inside baseball. Thus, even though their team average of .294 was scarcely lower than the Giants' .300, they fell far short of the punch of the New Yorkers. In fact, the most remarkable of Washington statistics was their team home run total of 22: The Nats had contrived, on average, to hit only about one home run a week throughout the entire season! Since the Giants had led the National League in homers, it is fair to regard the 1924 World Series as a contest that pitted a fine representative of the old game against a fine representative of the new game. There was a final complication for the Nationals: In contrast with their opponents, they were almost totally inexperienced at coping with the pressures of postseason competition. Only two members of the team had appeared in a World Series, and neither had performed well: Roger Peckinpaugh had batted only .179 for the Yankees in 1921, and his error had allowed the winning run to score in the final game; and Nemo Leibold had managed only .130 for the White Sox in the Series of 1917 and 1919.[7] It goes without saying that the Nationals also had the most inexperienced manager in baseball. It is no wonder that most baseball writers—but not, I must add, the oddsmakers—rated them as underdogs.[8]

The First Game, October 4

The Series opened in Griffith Stadium on Saturday, October 4, before almost thirty-six thousand spectators, including President Calvin Coolidge, whose ceremonial opening throw was wildly errant, and Minnie Johnson, who was seeing her son Walter pitch in the major leagues for the first time. John McGraw, his mind on the talented left-handed batters at the heart of the National order, chose southpaw Art Nehf to duel with Johnson. Though beset by pregame nervousness, Johnson had command of a splendid fast ball that day and tied Ed Walsh's single-game World Series record by striking out 12 Giants during the contest. But Nehf was also strong, confusing the Nationals with an array of curves and minimizing the effectiveness of Sam Rice, Goose Goslin, and Joe Judge. The first run of the game came in the second inning when George Kelly stroked a Johnson fast ball into the temporary seats in left field for a home run.[9] Goose Goslin fell over the low fence trying to grab it. The second run came in the fourth inning when Bill Terry lofted another Johnson delivery into the same temporary stands. Neither ball would have been a home run if the temporary seats had not been erected, and both blows were greeted by a silence from the Washington fans that observers thought eerie. Two innings later Washington scored a run in classic Nat fashion: Earl McNeely doubled down the left-field line, went to third on a groundout, and then scored on another groundout. Going into the ninth inning, the Giants held a 2–1 lead.

Hack Wilson led off the top of the ninth with a single. He was not a fast runner, but John McGraw chose to leave him in the game, and he promptly moved to second on a sacrifice by Travis Jackson. Johnson then bore down to fan Hank Gowdy for the second out. But Wilson was still in scoring position, and so John McGraw had another choice to make: either to bat for the weak-hitting Art Nehf and count on good relief pitching to hold the Nationals in the bottom of the ninth, or to leave his successful southpaw in the game and let him flail away against the fastest pitcher in the Series. Preferring to count on demonstrated mound success, McGraw allowed Nehf to bat. And the veteran surprised everyone by stroking a single to right. That immediately shifted attention to the arm of Sam Rice. A former pitcher, Rice fielded the hit and fired the ball to Muddy Ruel at the plate. The splendid throw beat the lumbering Wilson, and the Giants went away empty from their opportunity. But Nehf still had the lead as he went to work in the bottom of ninth.

He began by striking out Joe Judge. But then Ossie Bluege singled off Travis Jackson's glove, and Roger Peckinpaugh followed with a double. Since Bluege had been running on the pitch, he scored easily, tying the game. The run was greeted by such an effusion of cushions and hats from the jubilant Washington fans that the game had to be temporarily halted to allow the debris to be cleared away. When it resumed, it was the Giants who were in danger, for with the game on the line, Washington still had a runner in scoring position and only 1 out. Art Nehf then showed why McGraw relied so heavily on him, getting both Ruel and Johnson—a good-hitting pitcher—on infield plays. The opening game of the 1924 World Series, the 122nd Series game ever played, thus became the twelfth to go into extra innings.

Through the tenth and eleventh innings, Walter Johnson and Art Nehf continued to show their stuff. The only spot of difficulty for either came in the bottom of the tenth, when the Nationals put 2 runners on base. But Nehf then retired Goose Goslin and Joe Judge without allowing the winning run to score. Johnson, however, was tiring. He opened the twelfth by hitting Hank Gowdy with a pitch, allowing the Giant catcher to take first base. Art Nehf followed with a bloop single,[10] and when Earl McNeely mishandled it, the Giants wound up with runners on second and third with no outs. Deep strategizing followed. John McGraw sent Jack Bentley to the plate to bat for Freddy Lindstrom; Johnson walked him; and McGraw sent Billy Southworth in to run for him. With the bases loaded and no one out, Johnson had the challenging task of dealing with the strength of the Giant order. Against Frankie Frisch he was successful, getting the Giant second baseman to ground to Bucky Harris, whose throw to Ruel forced Gowdy at home. But then fate and Earl McNeely struck again. Ross Youngs, whom Johnson had already fanned 3 times, lofted a fly ball to short center field. McNeely misjudged it, and it fell in front of him as he stood still, allowing Nehf to score. George Kelly followed with a fly to left field that was deep enough to allow Southworth to tag and score the second run of the inning. Bill Terry then got his third hit of the day, a scratch single off Joe Judge's glove. But Frisch could get no farther than third, and when Hack Wilson flied to Goslin, the Giant eruption ended with only 2 runs.

The game was not over. Since Freddy Lindstrom had been removed for a pinch hitter, McGraw shifted Frisch to third, brought Kelly in from center field to cover second, and left Southworth in the game as center fielder. He decided to keep the tiring Nehf on the mound in the bottom of the twelfth. Mule Shirley, batting for a visibly fatigued Walter Johnson,[11] led off the inning by reaching second base when Travis Jackson dropped his pop fly. With 1 out, Bucky Harris singled Shirley home, bringing Washington to within 1 run of New York. Sam Rice followed with a single to center that sent Harris to third. But when Rice tried to reach second on Southworth's brief bobble, he was cut down on a very close play. That left everything up to Goose Goslin. Swinging mightily, he bounced a dribbler to the right of the mound, just out of Nehf's reach. The angular Kelly raced in from second base and snatched the ball with his bare right hand. Then, twisting, he threw off-balance to Terry at first, who in turn caught the ball bare-handed just ahead of the hard-charging Goslin. It was a sensational play: As late as 1942, Bill Terry called Kelly's part of it the greatest fielding play he had ever seen. It was also close: As late as 1934, Goslin was still berating Bill Klem for his call. After the game Bucky Harris poured "a profane attack of extraordinary viciousness"—Klem's words—on the umpire, and when Klem showed some inclination to answer Goslin's epithets with invective of his own, Commissioner Landis felt compelled to call the umpire aside for a quiet chiding.[12] But the play was important chiefly because it secured the game for Nehf and the Giants, by the narrow margin of 4–3. Though a satisfied John McGraw pronounced the contest the greatest World Series game ever played, he also noted with characteristic candor that "we just outplayed them."[13] Meanwhile, an angry Bucky Harris, though willing to face down second-guessers with the pronouncement that "Johnson pitched a wonderful game," was left to contemplate the task of winning 4 of 6 games from the Giants without any immediate help from the Big Train.[14]

The Second Game, October 5

Having prevailed in the Saturday game behind one of his brace of southpaws, John McGraw chose his other left-hander, Jack Bentley, for the game on Sunday, hoping to jump to a 2-game lead before allowing the Nationals to feed off right-handed pitching. But his plan went awry in the very first inning when, with 2 outs, Sam Rice singled off Bentley and Goose Goslin homered into the new seats in right center field. Washington scored a third run in the fifth inning when Bucky Harris, who had homered only once all year, popped a pitch into the temporary left-field seats.[15] Meanwhile, Tom Zachary kept the Giants scoreless through 6 innings, aided by good fielding and 2 double plays. In the seventh inning, however, the Giants began to twitch. George Kelly led off with a walk, and Irish Meusel followed with a single, sending Kelly to third. Hack Wilson then blighted a possible rally by grounding into the Giants' third double play, but Kelly raced home, and the score was 3–1. And that's how it remained until the ninth inning, when the Giants stirred again. Frankie Frisch singled and then, with 1 out, George Kelly stroked a long single to right, permitting the speedy Frisch to score all the way from first on a close and disputed play at home. Irish Meusel moved Kelly to second on a ground ball that Harris was barely able to stop, and Kelly then scored on Hack Wilson's single to right, just beating Sam Rice's throw in the second exciting dash to the plate of the inning. That run tied the game, and Harris, fearful of allowing the Giants to grab the lead from tired Zachary (for Wilson had taken second on the throw to the plate), summoned Firpo Marberry from the bullpen. Fortunately for the Nationals, Marberry was invincible: He threw 3 pitches—all strikes—and Travis Jackson flipped his bat away to take his position in the field.

In the bottom of the ninth, John McGraw made the first of several World Series decisions he was later widely criticized for. Jack Bentley began the inning by losing Joe Judge to a base on balls after getting him to a 1-and-2 count, and when Ossie Bluege executed a splendid sacrifice, Judge went to second. Roger Peckinpaugh was the next batter. Since he had stroked out 2 hits the previous day and was scheduled to be followed by the still-hitless and notoriously slow Muddy Ruel, most people expected McGraw to have Peckinpaugh intentionally passed, both to set up a force play (and potential double play) and to get at a poorer hitter. When Frankie Frisch realized that McGraw wanted to have Bentley pitch to the National shortstop, he was so disbelieving that he called time to remonstrate with his manager. It was to no avail. McGraw abided by his first impulse, and, as Giant fans feared, it turned out to be misguided. Peckinpaugh laced a 2-and-1 pitch sharply past Freddy Lindstrom, and to tumultuous cheering the game was over. By a 4–3 margin—the same score as that of the previous day—the Nationals had won. The hit was particularly satisfying for Peckinpaugh, because it began to even the score for the error he had committed in the 1921 World Series.

The game brought official scorer Fred Lieb briefly into the limelight, for he was obliged to defend two of his board's decisions against criticism. The first challenge was of the character of Peckinpaugh's hit: It was, Lieb declared, properly scored as a double and not a single, since a batter who drives in a game-winning run should get as many bases as the base runner advances. The second challenge involved the decision to award the victory to Tom Zachary and not to Firpo Marberry. Lieb was sensitive on this point, because his board of scorers had, in fact, first opted for the reliever and then changed to the starter. Today, the matter would be uncontroversial: Marberry was the pitcher of record when the winning run scored, and so Marberry would receive the credit. But in 1924 the scorers finally decided that "the common sense thing to do" was to honor Zachary for his 8⅔ innings of strong work.[16] All of these quibbles were, of course, marginalia. The key point, as the teams took the overnight train from the smallest major league city to the largest, was that the Nationals had tied the Series at a game apiece and could begin to test the right-handers on the Giant staff.

The Third Game, October 6

The next game of the Series, although not as exciting as the first two, did not lack elements of drama.[17] But what first caught everyone's notice on Monday, October 6, was the unusual composition of the home crowd: There were almost as many National fans among the forty-seven thousand people packed into the Polo Grounds as there were Giant fans. John McGraw chose Hugh McQuillan to pitch the first game in New York. In response, Bucky Harris made a lineup adjustment, replacing the right-handed Earl McNeely with the left-handed Nemo Leibold in center field. Leibold, a clean member of the Black Sox, thus became the first player from that team to make it back to a World Series. For mound duty, Bucky Harris chose Firpo Marberry, even though he had pitched to the final batter the previous day and was therefore not entirely rested. The decision was a modestly surprising call, for although Marberry had made 15 starts during the season, those appearances had generally been designed to allow the regular starting staff a needed measure of rest. And because George Mogridge, despite reports about a lame arm, was in fact available, it was also a gutsy call by Harris.

The outcome proved it a mistaken one as well. Marberry was not sharp, and before he left after the third inning, the Giants had taken a 3–0 lead. The Nationals' situation might have been still worse had not Hack Wilson grounded into his third double play in as many games. Harris himself compounded Marberry's problems by dropping a double play throw in the second inning. And as a final complication for the Nats, Roger Peckinpaugh was forced to leave the game early when a tendon injury incurred during his ninth-inning heroics of the previous day proved immobilizing. Because his regular substitute, Tommy Taylor, had a bandage on his own injured hand (a casualty of pennant-winning revelry in Boston), Harris was forced to deal with Peckinpaugh's departure by shifting Ossie Bluege to shortstop and bringing Ralph Miller in to cover third, even though Miller had not played that position in a major league game since 1921.

Still, the Nationals made a game of it. Joe Judge stroked out 3 hits, Goose Goslin actually bunted to get on base, and Bennie Tate made the first of three pinch-hitting appearances in the Series—all of which eventuated in bases on balls. Bucky Harris sent 4 pitchers to the mound in an effort to hold the Giants within striking distance. But New York was not to be checked. George Kelly continued his strong hitting, and Rosy Ryan, who was the pitcher of record for the New York victory, used the upper deck in right field as the target for the first home run of his career. Twice Frankie Frisch, now playing with an injury to his left hand as well as his right, made exciting, over-the-shoulder catches in short center of balls off the bat of Goose Goslin. John McGraw was determined not to let the game slip away, and in the top of the ninth, when the Nationals sent 8 batters to the plate, he used 3 pitchers to thwart them. The star hurler of the inning and the game was the veteran Mule Watson, whom McGraw summoned to the mound to protect a 2-run lead after the Nationals had loaded the bases with only 1 out. The first batter Watson faced was Ralph Miller; Watson got him to foul out to Freddy Lindstrom at third base. The next batter was the luckless Muddy Ruel; Watson retired him on a grounder to short. The Giants won 6–4, and since Watson never again pitched in a major league game, it should be noted that he went out in style. Meanwhile, the Nationals' loss meant that in order to win the Series, they needed to win 3 of the remaining 4 games.

The Fourth Game, October 7

The fourth game, played on Tuesday, October 7, pitted Washington's steady southpaw, George Mogridge, against New York's other strong right-hander, Virgil Barnes. To the great delight of a crowd of almost fifty thousand, the game turned into the Goose Goslin show, as the National left fielder played major roles in the middle of each of Washington's three scoring rallies, lending point to Ossie Bluege's remark about him: "Goose was a great hitter. You couldn't throw a fastball by him."[18] Prior to the game, Babe Ruth had moved onto the field, ostensibly to give Goslin advice about how to hit in the Polo Grounds.[19] Though staged as a stunt, the Babe's counsel may have been sound, for when the afternoon was over, Goslin had collected not only a home run—a 3-run shot deep into the right-field stands—but also 3 singles. In the process he had driven in 4 runs and scored twice. "I sure do owe a lot to the Babe," he smiled after the game.[20] But—and one imagines the smile broadening with this remark—"I'll be giving that lad lessons next year."[21] Goslin even shone in the field, making a spectacular running catch of a long blow off Hack Wilson's bat in the fourth inning. He received assistance from Earl McNeely, reinserted in the lineup after Nemo Leibold's disappointing performance the previous day, and from Ossie Bluege, both of whom collected 3 hits. Bucky Harris played second with a panache that invited comparisons to Frankie Frisch's performance of the previous day.[22] Mogridge, meanwhile, baffled all the Giants except Freddy Lindstrom. The New Yorkers got an unearned run in the first inning and added a second in the sixth when George Kelly doubled and scored. Still, Mogridge sailed into the eighth inning with a 7–2 lead.

But then Mogridge's "snake-like left arm" wearied.[23] He walked Ross Youngs, and after getting George Kelly to fly out, he walked Irish Meusel. When his first two offerings to Hack Wilson were also outside the strike zone, Bucky Harris summoned Mogridge and Joe Judge to a squatting conference near the mound, where he got his pitcher to acknowledge that he was too tired to protect even a 5-run lead. Harris then summoned Firpo Marberry for his third appearance in as many days. Marberry promptly yielded a double to Wilson, which scored Youngs. But a fine relay from Rice to Harris to Ruel on that hit caught Meusel at the plate for the second out of the inning,[24] and when Travis Jackson grounded out to first, Marberry enjoyed the satisfaction of knowing he had done his job.

The ninth inning was trickier. After Washington went down in order in the top of the inning, Hank Gowdy led off the bottom half with a single to right. Trying to catch Gowdy taking too wide a turn, Rice threw the ball behind him to first. But the ball hit the base and bounced into the Giant dugout, allowing Gowdy to move all the way to third base. Jack Bentley came to the plate as a pinch hitter and struck out. But then Freddy Lindstrom got an infield single that scored Gowdy, and Frankie Frisch walked. The second out came when Ross Youngs grounded the ball to first, allowing Joe Judge to throw to shortstop Ossie Bluege to force Frisch. So now there were 2 outs, but runners were at the corners, and George Kelly, thus far the Giants' greatest weapon in the Series, was coming to the plate. Marberry, however, born with the instincts of a great relief pitcher, was often at his best in situations like this one, especially when a late afternoon shadows obscured a clear view of his fast ball. Kelly had no chance against Marberry's speed: Just like Travis Jackson in a similar situation at the end of game two, he struck out on 3 pitches. With that, the Nationals tucked away a 7–4 victory and again tied the Series. Thanks to Marberry—"the greatest relief pitcher in the big leagues," according to Bucky Harris—the Series was down to a 2-of-3 match.[25] And Walter Johnson was ready to return to the mound and avenge his first-game loss. "They can't lick us, pal," Clark Griffith boasted to all who would listen.[26]

The Fifth Game, October 8

Johnson's presence on the mound explained the noisy ambivalence of the spectators at the Polo Grounds for the fifth game. For even as they cheered for the home team with greater enthusiasm than in the two previous contests, so too did they applaud Johnson, rocking the ballpark with their shouts when he ambled to the mound. It only increased their interest that Johnson had talked of ending his career after completing the 1924 season, thus raising the possibility that the October 8 game would be his final major league appearance. Under these circumstances, the apparently contradictory partialities of the fans, while surprising in their scope, are understandable. On the eve of this momentous appearance, Johnson professed optimism: "Give me a few runs tomorrow, that's all I want."[27] To hurl against the Big Train, John McGraw chose Jack Bentley, whose performance in the second game had been frustrating, but whose left-handedness seemed the best weapon the Giants possessed for stopping the fired-up Goose Goslin. Since Roger Peckinpaugh was still ailing, the Nationals continued to cover shortstop with a third baseman (Ossie Bluege) and third base with a .133 hitter (Ralph Miller).

The game itself was a massive disappointment for Johnson's fans, its script crafted by a spinner of nightmares—not a forger of fairy tales. Although Goslin beat out an infield hit in his first at-bat to extend his hitting streak to 6 in as many plate appearances and then hit a home run in his final appearance to tie Babe Ruth's mark of 3 World Series home runs, it was the Giants who had the batting eye. Or rather, it was Johnson who gave them choice offerings. His measly strikeout total of 3 testified to the absence of velocity from his pitches. And without speed, Johnson had only control and a mediocre curve with which to try to chasten the best-hitting team in baseball. They were not weapons enough. The Giants collected 13 base hits, including a double by Frankie Frisch, a tremendous triple by Bill Terry, and a home run by Jack Bentley. Nevertheless, through seven innings the game remained tight, as Johnson benefited from Washington's strong defense to keep the Nationals only a run off the Giants' pace.[28]

In the eighth inning, however, Walter Johnson's inability to reach back for smoke in the pinch finally caught up with him. George Kelly led off by singling to left, and Bill Terry, receiving Johnson's fullest respect, walked. Hack Wilson bunted to advance the runners, but when the ordinarily sure-handed Johnson mishandled the ball, the bases were full. The Giants' task then was to get 3 runners in, and they accomplished it with dispatch. Travis Jackson's sacrifice fly scored Kelly. Hugh McQuillan's looping single scored Terry. And Freddy Lindstrom's sharp single scored Hank Gowdy, who had taken Wilson's place on the base paths when he had forced Wilson at second. Lindstrom, who had not reached his second birthday when Johnson pitched his first major league game, touched the Big Train for 4 singles during the Giant bombardment.[29] These 3 runs made the score 6–2, and that is how the contest ended.

"I couldn't hold them," Johnson remarked quietly after the game. He was patently right, and he was particularly sad because the failure would mean that "I'll finish up my career in the big leagues with two world series defeats."[30] That view seems to have been Clark Griffith's, too, when, putting his arm around Johnson's shoulder, he told his star after the game: "Don't think about it anymore, Walter. You're a great pitcher. We all know it."[31] Bucky Harris, however, did not have time for considering the dimension of epic tragedy—age inexorably yielding to youth—that writers tended to see in Johnson's second defeat. His job was to ready his squad for the sixth game, and his public mood found expression in his cocky remark: "We'll get them in the seventh game."[32] As far as Harris was concerned, the sixth was in the bag.

The Sixth Game, October 9

The remorseless momentum of the Series—7 games in as many days—left neither players nor managers much time for psychological regrouping or physical recuperation. As the teams moved back to the nation's capital to spend the night there, John McGraw and Bucky Harris made plans for the endgame portion of the match. By now both knew that, by determination of a flipped coin, the seventh game, if it was necessary, would be played in Washington. The Giant manager was proudly hungry for a fourth World Series title, a figure that would move him past Connie Mack into undisputed first place among managers. And because he had agreed to lead a baseball tour of Canada and Europe starting on October 11, he was eager to claim that title quickly so that he would have a day of rest before his travels. Since he had Art Nehf, winner of the exciting opener, rested and ready for duty on the ninth, he had grounds for measured confidence. It was, however, always wise to plan for a disappointment. If a seventh game should be necessary, McGraw intended to lead with Virgil Barnes, knowing, like everyone else, that for the final game of a World Series one's entire pitching staff is effectively on call.

Bucky Harris's burden was greater. He felt, of course, the sting of wise-after-the-fact second-guessers who scolded him for sticking with an obviously struggling Walter Johnson in the eighth inning of the fifth game. But managers cannot dwell on misjudgments they have made. Looking ahead, he planned to bring Roger Peckinpaugh back into action for the sixth game, even though the internal hemorrhaging on his leg was visible and ugly. "I'll get into that game," the mysteriously prescient Peckinpaugh said, "if I break the leg."[33] Harris also planned to send Tom Zachary, winner of game two, back to the mound. Though he had enjoyed only three days of rest, Zachary was a southpaw, and his presence would mean the benching of Bill Terry, who had thus far terrorized Washington right-handers with 6 hits and 3 walks in 15 plate appearances.

The fans who witnessed the contest in Griffith Stadium on Thursday the ninth could scarcely have hoped for a finer baseball game. Just before the opening pitch, everyone rose in silence to honor Jake Daubert, the Cincinnati veteran who had died from complications following an appendicitis operation that morning. Tom Zachary then got off to a bumpy start. He yielded a double to Frankie Frisch, and after a rundown play retired Frisch, while leaving Ross Youngs at second base, George Kelly stroked out a single to drive in the first run of the game. The Nationals were spared greater damage when Sam Rice made a leaping catch to rob Irish Meusel of an extra-base hit and end the inning. Art Nehf also began awkwardly. He yielded a walk and a single, but by picking Bucky

Harris off first, he quashed Washington's opportunity. The two pitchers then settled down. Between Frisch's second double in the third inning and the opening of the ninth inning, Zachary tantalized the Giants with slow curves and allowed only Hack Wilson to reach first base. In his shutdown of the Giants' offense he was the beneficiary of two additional dazzling catches by the wide-roving Sam Rice. But Art Nehf, except for the fifth inning, was equally sharp. In that fifth, however, Roger Peckinpaugh singled, advanced to second on Muddy Ruel's sacrifice, and went on to third when Zachary grounded out to first unassisted. At that juncture, with 2 men out, Nehf briefly lost his control and walked Earl Mc-Neely on 4 pitches. That mistake was compounded when McNeely was able to steal second. Bucky Harris, offered this splendid chance to redeem himself for his first-inning lapse, came through with a single, and the Nationals took a 2–1 lead.

And that was the score going into the ninth inning. Ross Youngs led off against Tom Zachary by fouling out. But George Kelly then got the potential tying run on base by singling. John McGraw sent Billy Southworth in to run for Kelly. When Irish Meusel hit a ground smash up the middle, a leaping Roger Peckinpaugh was just able to knock it down. Knowing he needed to get the ball quickly to Harris at second if the speedy Southworth was to be forced, he flipped it blindly with his gloved hand. The lurching effort, though successful, was too much for his insufficiently healed leg muscles, and he crumbled on the infield. To render the field even more battlelike, Harris's hurried relay to first skipped into Joe Judge's leg, leaving the first baseman on the ground, also twisting in pain. The game was halted so that first aid could be administered to the wounded, and while the pause allowed Judge to rise from what was only a painful bruise, Peckinpaugh could not walk unaided and was assisted from the field. His World Series was obviously over, and the crowd, recalling that his ninth-inning doubles had tied the first game and won the second and that he had stroked out 2 hits in the current contest, was too horror-struck to applaud him as he left. "This isn't the time to clap," one fan explained to an inquiring writer. "It's the time to pray."[34]

To deal with the loss of Peckinpaugh, Harris moved Ossie Bluege to shortstop but, recalling Ralph Miller's poor throwing from third, sent in Tommy Taylor, splint and all, to patrol the hot corner. It didn't matter in the short run: Zachary ended the game by fanning Hack Wilson on 3 pitches. The Washington hurler had pitched a superb game. Though allowing 7 hits, he had walked no one and thrown only 97 pitches to get 27 outs. His sixth inning was a study in minimalism, as he retired 3 batters on 3 pitches. As a result of his strong effort, the Nationals had once again knotted the Series. But that led to the longer run: The match was down to a single contest, and Washington would have to play it without its most consistent hitter and with its third baseman sporting a bandage on his battered throwing hand.

The Final Game, October 10

In the twenty hours before the final game, both managers gave much thought to the shaping of its outcome, with Clark Griffith joining in on the Washington planning. Paramount for the Nats' leadership was the need to confine the damaging bat of Bill Terry. That was the point of the scheme that Harris revealed to his players on the evening of the ninth. Washington would start right-hander Curly Ogden on the mound, inviting John McGraw to place Terry in the Giant lineup. If McGraw accepted the invitation, Ogden would be promptly replaced by left-hander George Mogridge, presenting McGraw with the choice of leaving Terry in the game to face southpaw pitching that he had trouble with or removing him even though Washington had an array of right-handers who might subsequently be called on. The Giants, however, learned of this plan that same evening, and the Nationals soon thereafter learned that the Giants were aware of the scheming.

This situation set the stage for some heavy cerebration. Giant players urged McGraw not to bite—that is, to start Terry and leave him in the game, whatever Washington did, since the National staff (with Zachary presumably not available) was preponderantly right-handed. Washington players urged Harris to abandon the plan, since New York was aware of it and Ogden was not as good as Mogridge.[35] As game time on the tenth approached, John McGraw sowed some independent doubts of his own by warming up three different hurlers—Virgil Barnes, Jack Bentley, and Art Nehf—and leaving Harris to guess who might really start. As these various machinations suggest, when the world championship is on the line, any lawful step that might throw an opponent off balance is felt to be warranted. Meanwhile, the oddsmakers, assuming that the left-handed Mogridge would be the chief pitcher and sensing that the home field gave Washington a modest advantage, installed the Nationals as 11–10 favorites.

A surprisingly small crowd—fewer than thirty-two thousand—attended the final game of the Series. This was not a reflection of diminished interest. Rather, it was the consequence of scalpers being unable to find ways to market the large number of tickets they had secured.[36] But those who attended saw the greatest World Series game ever played. Bucky Harris stuck with his plan, sending Curly Ogden to the mound. "We'll see what they can do with Curley's curves," the manager deadpanned to the press. "Don't worry. He'll come through."[37] John McGraw responded as expected—but what choice did he have?—by inserting Bill Terry at first base and placing George Kelly in center field. Harris planned to remove Ogden after he had pitched to one batter, and Ogden actually started walking off the mound after striking out Freddy Lindstrom to open the game. But the strikeout was so impressive that Harris decided to see whether his young pitcher was genuinely strong. The walking of Frankie Frisch quickly persuaded the Washington manager that he should revert to his original plan, and so he brought George Mogridge out from under the stands, where he had been secretly warming up, to replace Ogden. Mogridge quickly ended the modest Giant threat by striking Ross Youngs out and getting George Kelly on a ground ball to third. That last play relieved Harris, since it demonstrated that Tommy Taylor could fire a ball to first even with his damaged knuckle. In the bottom of the first, Virgil Barnes came out to pitch and put the Nationals down in order.

The game remained scoreless through the second and third innings. Washington, in fact, was completely baffled by Virgil Barnes. The Nationals could not even hit a ball into the outfield, and by the end of the third inning they still had not placed a runner on base. The Giants, on the other hand, showed sparks of offensive life. In the second inning they mustered a threat when, with 2 outs (one of them by Terry, whom McGraw left in the game), an error by Tommy Taylor allowed Travis Jackson to reach first, and a single by Hank Gowdy placed a runner in scoring position. Had Ossie Bluege not already made a sensational stop of a sharp grounder hit up the middle by Hack Wilson and then caught Wilson at first, the Giants would have scored. But Mogridge ended the danger in the second by striking out Virgil Barnes. And he retained command in the third, allowing only a bunt single to Frankie Frisch.

In the top of the fourth inning John McGraw allowed Bill Terry to bat again, and the Giant first baseman struck out: Bucky Harris's strategy was reducing Terry to a nullity. When the next two Giant batters grounded out, Mogridge finally had a perfect inning to his credit. In the bottom of the fourth, Earl McNeely struck out to become the tenth consecutive batter to be set down by Virgil Barnes. But then Bucky Harris struck one of Barnes's offerings and planted it in the temporary seats in left field for a home run. At a stroke the Nationals got a 1–0 lead, and the crowd exploded in joy. Sam Rice followed with a smash that seemed destined to break his slump, but Hack Wilson grabbed it just before it hit the ground. Goose Goslin, also slumping, grounded out to end the inning. The fifth inning saw more of the exciting defensive play that the Series featured—a racing catch by Harris of a pop fly from Hank Gowdy's bat and a sharply executed 3-to-1 play by Bill Terry and Virgil Barnes—but there was no additional scoring.

Then came the Giant sixth inning—for the Nationals, a self-inflicted disaster. Ross Youngs led off by working George Mogridge for a base on balls, and George Kelly singled him to third. With Bill Terry due up next, John McGraw was confronted with precisely the painful choice that Bucky Harris had intended to press upon him. But if painful, the choice was not really difficult, for Terry's feeble batwork in his two previous appearances gave McGraw no option but to send in the right-handed Irish Meusel at this moment of opportunity, even with the expectation that Harris would respond by replacing Mogridge with the right-handed Firpo Marberry. And so Terry left the game and the Series, Marberry moved to the mound, and Meusel hit a fly to right that was deep enough to score Youngs. But Marberry was not yet sharp, and Hack Wilson followed Meusel's fly with a single to center, sending Kelly to third. A double play could still have gotten the Nationals out of the inning in good shape, but when Travis Jackson hit a grounder to first, Joe Judge bobbled it, allowing Kelly to score and Jackson to take first. And when Hank Gowdy sent a grounder to shortstop, Ossie Bluege let it slide under his glove, permitting Wilson to score from second. It was "my worst error ever," Bluege said later.[38] Two errors and 2 runs on 2 potential double play balls—it was very uncharacteristic National form.

The Giants might have scored again, for with Jackson now on third, Barnes flied to right. But recalling how he had once been burned by Sam Rice's powerful arm, third base coach Hughie Jennings held Jackson, only to see Freddy Lindstrom end the inning by striking out. Still, as announcers are wont to say, the damage had been done. The fault was hardly Marberry's, but he and the Nationals now trailed 3–1.

From the bottom of the sixth inning through the top of the eighth, Virgil Barnes and Firpo Marberry commanded the opposing batters. Neither team mounted a serious threat. The bottom of the eighth opened in a fashion that suggested that Barnes still had the Nationals' number, as Ossie Bluege fouled out to Hank Gowdy. But Bucky Harris then dispatched Nemo Leibold to bat for the injury-hampered Tommy Taylor, and the veteran slashed a double to left that glanced off third base. Muddy Ruel was the next scheduled batter, and Harris was faced with a dilemma. Superb as Ruel was as a defensive player, he had been a bust as a hitter, with no hits to his credit in 19 at-bats. Comment about Ruel's plight had been a rising theme in the press. Harris chose to stick with his catcher, and Ruel rewarded his manager by getting his first hit of the Series on a smash that George Kelly knocked down but could not control.[39] Harris then sent Bennie Tate in to bat for Marberry, and for the third time in as many pinch-hitting appearances in the Series, the patient Tate worked the pitcher for a walk. The bases were now loaded with 1 out. Earl McNeely lofted a fly to short left, and Leibold, on third, chose not to challenge Irish Meusel's arm, even though it was not remotely as strong as his brother Bob's. That left Bucky Harris if Barnes were to extricate himself from the inning. Hank Gowdy took a moment to confer on strategy with John McGraw before settling in behind the plate to let Barnes work on the Washington manager, whose home run had accounted for the only Senator run thus far. Harris stroked a grounder to the left of Freddy Lindstrom at third, apparently an easy play. But just as Lindstrom reached to snag it, it took a "wicked hop" back over his head and sailed into left field.[40] Both Leibold and Ruel scored on what could only be adjudged a single, and the game was tied. Having seen enough, a disgusted McGraw brought Art Nehf in from the bullpen, and the stylish left-hander made short order of Sam Rice to end the inning. But going into the ninth the game was knotted, 3–3.

Since Firpo Marberry had left the game for a pinch hitter in the bottom of the eighth, Washington needed a new pitcher. The crowd had seen that Walter Johnson was warming up, and even as the Nationals batted in the bottom of the eighth, many took up chants of "We want Johnson!" and "Walter, Walter, Walter!" And Johnson was in fact Harris's choice. "You're the best we've got, Walter," Harris is reported to have explained to his pitcher.[41] That statement was probably true: Tom Zachary was exhausted, George Mogridge and Firpo Marberry had already pitched, and the other members of the staff were patently not in Johnson's league. But Harris had a further calculation in bringing on a man who had not pitched an inning of relief in 1924.[42] In October, evening came early, and in the dimming light Johnson's fast ball, always assuming he still had it, would be even harder to hit than it usually was. Still, the risks were obvious. Johnson was pitching with only one day of rest; feats he could pull off in his youth he might no longer be capable of. Then, too, his confidence might be frayed; after all, the Giants had beaten him twice already. And finally there was the personal consideration: Like everyone else on the Nationals, Harris had enormous concern for Johnson's well-being and could only wonder what a third failure would do to the man whom so many revered. Christy Mathewson, in ill health but in attendance, was better positioned than anyone else to understand the mélange of feelings that Johnson was coping with as he strode to the mound. "Poor old Walter," he muttered, "it's a shame to send him in."[43] The crowd, however, felt otherwise: Griffith Stadium was his home, and a roar of extraordinary intensity swept through its precincts as Johnson began his slow walk to the mound.

A tense ninth inning followed. Freddy Lindstrom opened the top of it harmlessly enough by popping out to Ralph Miller, the replacement Bucky Harris had sent in to cover third. But Frankie Frisch then cracked a ball to center field, and before Earl McNeely could run it down and return it to the infield, Frisch was on third with the potential lead run. Johnson then pitched with excessive care to Ross Youngs and lost him to a base on balls. The suspicion rapidly spread that, with Frisch darting skittishly at third, the Big Train would once again be unable to handle Giant batting. But then Johnson called on his famous reserve powers—the ability to "reach back for a little bit extra"—and with a quick speed that reminded spectators of the Big Train in his youth, he struck the dangerous George Kelly out on three bolts of lightning.[44] It did not matter that Youngs had stolen second, for Johnson ended the inning by inducing Irish Meusel to ground out to third. He had emerged unscathed from the threat.

It was then the Nationals' turn to apply the pressure. With one out, Joe Judge singled to center. Ossie Bluege followed with a grounder to Kelly, and when Travis Jackson mishandled Kelly's poor throw to second, Judge wound up on third and Bluege on first. With the potential Series-winning run only 90 feet from home plate, John McGraw turned to the book—in fact, *his* book—for two crucial defensive decisions. First, he replaced the left-hander Art Nehf with the right-hander Hugh McQuillan in order to reduce right-handed Ralph Miller's chances of success at the plate.[45] Then, he chose not to pull his infielders in but to position them at double play depth.[46] Baseball, McGraw liked to say, is a matter of percentages, and he called this one right. With the game on the line and the crowd on its feet, Miller hit into a Jackson-to-Frisch-to-Kelly double play, ending the inning. Like Johnson in the top of the ninth, McQuillan had escaped unscathed. And like the first game of the World Series, this last one went into extra innings tied at 3–3.

The tenth inning found the pitchers in command. Walter Johnson walked Hack Wilson, but then struck out Travis Jackson and got Hank Gowdy to ground into a double play. Hugh McQuillan retired Muddy Ruel, Johnson, and Earl McNeely in order. The eleventh inning, however, saw the renewal of offensive challenges. In the top of the inning Heinie Groh strode gimpily to the plate to bat for McQuillan and, in his only World Series appearance, singled to right. His duty done, he was replaced on first base by Billy Southworth. Freddy Lindstrom sacrificed Southworth to second, leaving a runner in scoring position with three future Hall of Famers, Frankie Frisch, Ross Youngs, and George Kelly, scheduled to bat. The first of these three had collected 10 hits thus far in the Series and had tagged Johnson for a triple in the ninth inning. Once again Johnson reached back for a little bit extra, and after 2 strikes he got Frisch to swing at an outside pitch and become Johnson's third strikeout victim, the first time in 50 World Series at-bats that the Giant star had fanned. Playing the percentages, Johnson gave the left-handed Youngs his fourth walk of the game, a World Series record. Then he turned his speed loose on Kelly, notched up his second strikeout of the big Giant first baseman, and walked proudly from the mound. The performance had been vintage Johnson, and deafening roars of support rolled through the stadium.

Once again the pressure was on the Giants, and John McGraw brought the gyrating Jack Bentley in from the bullpen—he used all four members of his starting staff in this final game—to hold the Nationals. Bentley retired the first 2 hitters readily, but then Goose Goslin hit a looping double to right. After consultation, the Giants decided to walk Joe Judge, who had pounded their pitching for a .385 average in the Series, and pitch to Ossie Bluege. As an added precaution, McGraw temporarily switched Irish Meusel and Ross Youngs, putting the stronger-armed Youngs in left field, where the right-handed Bluege was likelier to hit a ball that reached the outfield. But Bluege's batted ball got only as far as Travis Jackson, who threw to Frisch to force out Judge. Bentley had held.

The game was nearly three hours old as the twelfth inning began, and the shadows, which had aided Walter Johnson since his entry into the game, were now growing deep enough to warrant speculation that the twelfth might be the final inning. Moreover, as the sun moved behind the grandstand, defensive players, and especially those on the left side of the field, could be distracted by the intensity of its slanting rays through the haze that a cigarette-smoking crowd had been generating all afternoon. Johnson yielded a single to Irish Meusel in the top of the twelfth, but followed by striking out Hack Wilson, getting Travis Jackson to hit into a force play, and retiring Hank Gowdy.[47] Plate umpire Bill Dinneen later acknowledged that visibility was becoming so poor that he "was doing some lively guessing on where the ball crossed or didn't cross the plate."[48] As for Jackson, his out gave him an 0-for-6 day, a record of futility in a World Series game that has been matched but never surpassed.

Johnson's success again put Jack Bentley on the spot, although the Giant hurler may have taken comfort from the thought that he would be facing the bottom third of the Washington order. He started off well, inducing Ralph Miller to ground out to Frankie Frisch. But then the Giant nightmare began. Muddy Ruel stepped in, the most ineffectual World Series hitter among regulars on both teams. In apparent consistency with his earlier hitting, he popped the ball foul near the plate. But Hank Gowdy, neglecting a primary instruction for all catchers, flipped his mask in his own circling path, then stepped in it, tried desperately to kick it off, lunged at the ball, and saw it slide off his groping glove onto the ground about 10 feet from home plate. Given this unexpected second chance—"I felt like a sinner forgiven"—Ruel lashed a double to left, just on the fair side of third base.[49] Instead of 2 outs and no one on base, the Nationals had one out and a runner in scoring position. Walter Johnson was the next scheduled batter, and by letting him hit, Bucky Harris showed that he would be counting on his star even if a thirteenth inning were played. Johnson stroked a ground ball to Travis Jackson's right. And again disaster struck the Giants. The overeager shortstop bobbled the ball, and Johnson reached first on this second error of the inning. Ruel bluffed a dash to third, but held at second. All the elements were now in place for one of the most celebrated moments in baseball history.

The batter was the right-handed Earl McNeely. In contemplating offensive moves, Bucky Harris knew that Muddy Ruel was one of the slowest runners on his generally fast team. But because both Bennie Tate and Mule Shirley had already been inserted and withdrawn, he had no one else to put behind the plate if the game went to 13 innings, and so he had to stick with Ruel. On the other bench, John McGraw, in aligning his defense to deal with McNeely, made two crucial decisions. First, fearing that McNeely might attempt a bunt, he instructed third baseman Freddy Lindstrom to play even with the bag, rather than deep, and about 12 feet off the line. Second, disregarding his own action in the eleventh inning when Ossie Bluege had been at bat with a runner in scoring position, and disregarding too the "book" that stamped McNeely a pull-hitter, he kept Irish Meusel in left field rather than bringing the more powerful arm of Ross Youngs over to the area where play was likeliest to develop.

Bentley went to work on McNeely, hoping that he could get the batter to hit into a double play. And it almost worked. McNeely struck the ball sharply toward third. Lindstrom prepared himself, hands at his chest, to launch a round-the-horn double play. Ruel registered the flashing hope that Lindstrom might somehow be tricked into tagging him rather than going for the twin-killing. But before anyone could act on these trained responses . . .

. . . THE BALL TOOK A CRAZY HOP OVER LINDSTROM'S HEAD!

The third baseman leaped hopelessly, Ruel shifted to maximum speed, Irish Meusel raced to his right to pick up a ball that was unexpectedly in the outfield, and Al Schacht, coaching at third base, pointed Ruel toward the plate. As the Nationals surged to the step of their dugout to exhort the improbable sprinter on his dash toward home, Meusel reached the ball, picked it up, and concluding that his throw could not beat Ruel, put it in his pocket! When Muddy Ruel touched home plate, the Washington Nationals became champions of the world.[50]

Analyzing the Improbable

We have seen, said Commissioner Landis that evening, "the greatest game ever played."[51] Such assertions are always advanced as much to challenge as to describe. But the claim was credible then, and at a distance of more than three-quarters of a century, it remains plausible. The contest featured some superb feats, an array of exciting turns, recurring occasions of high tension, several strokes of improbable fortune, and the richest human interest story ever to weave itself through a championship baseball game.

The final play invited a cacophony of comment. People speculated about the chances that *two* baseballs would take bad hops on Lindstrom. They sought out the culprit pebble—Lindstrom was inclined to blame a pebble—though none was ever produced and, according to some spectators, the two balls had not been hit along the same trajectory. We know, at least reputedly, the fate of the memorable twelfth-inning ball: It went to Walter Johnson, and over half a century later his daughter could produce it.[52] People noted that had John McGraw stationed Lindstrom deeper or had he chosen to position Ross Youngs in left field, the play on McNeely's blow would probably not have produced a run. People also wondered whether the sun had blinded Lindstrom at the crucial moment; some thought that the bounce had not in truth been terribly erratic.[53] Few actually blamed the rookie[54]—still (as the twenty-first century opens) the youngest player ever to appear in a World Series game—but he himself was so distraught at his failure to field McNeely's hit that he drank himself into unconsciousness as the Giants' train rolled back to New York City that night.

Still, if the game was so good that it had no goat, it clearly had a hero. Almost as soon as the winning run scored, Hank Gowdy and Frankie Frisch sought out Walter Johnson to congratulate him. Johnson himself was seeking out Bucky Harris: "I want to thank you for letting me go today."[55] Clark Griffith, though declining to make a speech, allowed himself to remark that "it happened just as I wanted [it] to, with Walter winning it for us."[56] Even Jack Bentley, victim of McNeely's hit, could be mellow. "Cheer up, boys," he told his downcast teammates that evening, "it just looks as though the Good Lord couldn't stand seeing Walter Johnson get beat again."[57] As a tale of secular redemption, the seventh game cannot be beat.

Comment on the game usually turned to comment on the World Series itself—"the most remarkable Series ever played," in James Harrison's representative judgment.[58] In 1924 that was a fairly easy call: Only two World Series had gone to their final game, and only in 1912 had the final game been won in the bottom of the final inning. What is interesting is that, again at a distance of over seventy-five years, the claim for the 1924 Series remains plausible. After all, Washington scored fewer runs than New York, stroked out fewer hits, and committed more errors—and nevertheless won. It is true that Washington was not without its statistical triumphs: The Nationals engineered more than twice as many double plays as the Giants, they stole more bases, and—a startling fact—they hit more home runs. Taking into consideration the styles that had brought the two teams to the Series and—home run figures aside—the statistical comparison of performances in the Series, it would appear that Noel Hynd's contention that the 1923 World Series witnessed the end of inside baseball as a winning strategy is wrong. In 1924 it was actually the scientific team that won.[59] That may explain in part why a soured John McGraw was not gracious in defeat, remarking, "They got the breaks. . . . I don't see how Washington can be called a better ball club than the Giants."[60] To some sportswriter friends he spelled out the implication of that comment: "The better team did not win."[61] Well, maybe. But there seems no reason to doubt that the quicker, sharper, better-managed team triumphed.

Each team had players who turned in outstanding performances. Bucky Harris's 2 round-trippers doubled his regular season total. Roger Peckinpaugh (.417), Joe Judge (.385), and Goose Goslin (.344—coincidentally, also his season average) were Washington's hitting stars. Moreover, Goslin's 3 home runs, although one-fourth of his season total, allowed him to share with Babe Ruth the World Series record for home runs. And even though Muddy Ruel (.095) and Sam Rice (.207) were batting disappointments for Washington, both were stellar on defense, and Rice had played (as it later was discovered) with a disabling shoulder ailment. For the Giants, the remarkably reliable Frankie Frisch (.333) turned in his fourth consecutive Series with an average of .300 or above, and Bill Terry punished Washington pitching with a .429 average. (George Kelly, on the other hand, after savaging the Nats' pitching in the early games, struck out twice with runners in scoring position in the extra innings of the final game and wound up at only .290.) Washington's ability to throw left-handed pitchers at New York had paid off, as George Mogridge and Tom Zachary were credited with 3 of the Nationals' 4 victories. The star of the Series was clearly Tom Zachary, who twice used his curve and knuckleball to bring the Nationals back from 1-game deficits, while registering an earned run average of 2.04 in 17⅔ innings of pitching. When asked how he explained his success in the pressurized atmosphere of a World Series, Zachary disarmingly replied, "Oh, just like I do it every day. There are only nine innings to a world series game, the same as to any other."[62]

In the duel between the two managers as tacticians, Bucky Harris won hands down. Both he and John McGraw made mistakes, but Harris made fewer and less consequential ones. And when one realizes that he maneuvered McGraw into removing his .429 hitter in the final game, it can only be concluded that the youngster taught the veteran a lesson. Harris was the first manager to win a World Series in his rookie year of managing, and although others have now accomplished that feat, he is still the only manager under the age of thirty to have won a World Series. Many years later he was quoted as saying that there were only two things a manager needed to know: "when to change pitchers and how to get along with players."[63] The 1924 Series is conclusive evidence that when he said that he knew he was talking shit.

When the final game was over, fans raced onto the field. They threw hats, cushions, programs, coats, canes, and shredded newspapers into the air, all the while ignoring the presence of President Coolidge, who had sat through the entire game.[64] The crowd swarmed deliriously about the diamond, ripping off parts of Earl McNeely's shirt—displeasure at his midseason replacing of Wid Matthews was now forgotten—and groping to touch the hands of Walter Johnson and Bucky Harris. Finally, with the assistance of the capital police, the Washington players were enabled to withdraw from the bedlam. The Giants meanwhile made their way to their dressing room largely unobstructed and within two hours were on their way back to New York. Though angry and disappointed, John McGraw had the distraction of a European tour lying just ahead. He did not, however, neglect his players, throwing a consolation party for them and their wives that very night at the Biltmore Hotel, where, among other festivities, he sang songs with George M. Cohan. As for the Nationals, after they reached their dressing room, they broke into uproarious celebrations, as Bucky Harris raced about the room naked, but with his hair carefully combed, to thank his men, while Clark Griffith, whose chief hatreds were the New York Yankees and John McGraw, puffed his ubiquitous cigar and basked in the thought that he had bested them both. Still later, as the players moved out into the nation's capital for celebrations with friends, they often found themselves stopped and saluted and sometimes called upon to deliver brief speeches ex tempore. Walter Johnson dined out with his wife and was presented at his restaurant table with two hundred telegrams of congratulation.

The capital city witnessed a general relaxation of deportment: Happy crowds (sometimes of cross-dressers) roamed through the city sporting white ribbons with the slogan "I told you so," mounted patrolmen were indulgent toward all disorderliness short of major vandalism, traffic rules were widely abandoned, drivers competed in efforts to induce their machines to explode with celebratory backfires, horns sounded, confetti flew, open gunfire was tolerated, and "Bucky for President" signs—it was, after all, an election year—proliferated. "Even if I live to be 100 years old," Bucky Harris wrote, "I don't think I'll ever see another day like this."[65] A writer for the *Washington Post*, seeking the comparison that would capture the giddiness of the crowd, declared that the celebration was "an armistice day and mardi gras blended into one."[66] With a total gate of $1,093,104, the 1924 World Series established a new record for receipts for the October classic. This revenue gave Bucky Harris the pleasure, a few days later, of distributing World Series checks of $5,959.64 to each player—a sum virtually equal to the mean major league salary in 1924.[67] The trainer also received a full share. In an unusual gesture, the Nationals agreed that payments, albeit much smaller, should go to Wid Matthews, Wade Lefler, the team batboy, and the team grounds squad. Lefler, who had delivered 3 pinch hits in 4 plate appearances in September, quickly complained about the miserliness of his reward. But his was one of the few discordant notes in the hour of triumph, a reminder perhaps that no human achievement goes without its critics.

Epilogue

On the evening of October 10, Commissioner Landis joined Fred Lieb on the balcony of the Raleigh Hotel to gaze out on the throngs clogging Pennsylvania Avenue. Already sportswriters were elaborating the thesis that the success of the extraordinary World Series had saved baseball—that the national fervor it had aroused had obliterated the rumors of scandal, which only a week earlier had threatened to engulf the fall classic.[68] Landis hoped that this analysis was valid. But according to Lieb, who wrote of the incident later, Landis was, in fact, melancholy that night. "Freddy," he asked, "what are we looking at now—could this be the highest point of what we affectionately call our national sport?" The commissioner followed this remark with some ruminations about ancient Greece and Rome. And then he rephrased the question: "I repeat, Freddy, are we looking at the zenith of baseball?"[69] I am not sure exactly what the ruminating Landis had in mind in putting this question so persistently. But I suspect that his question was predicated on the belief that major league baseball had just passed through a season so fine and capped it with a World Series so exciting that the combination was unsurpassable. I think, in that judgment, the commissioner was and remains right.

NOTES

Chapter 1. Waiting for the Cry, "Play Ball!"

1. In 1924 the Hot Springs gathering drew perhaps as many as one hundred players, including such notables as Stan Coveleskie, Burleigh Grimes, Harry Heilmann, Walter Johnson, Babe Ruth, Ray Schalk, Luke Sewell, and Urban Shocker. The Indians and the Nationals were particularly well represented. Unfortunately for those who gave up time to enjoy the hospitality of Hot Springs, the weather in early 1924 was cold and rainy.

2. "Humors and Tragedies of Baseball Training-Time in Dixie," *Literary Digest* 59 (April 9, 1921): 64.

3. Quoted in Charles C. Alexander, *John McGraw* (New York: Viking Press, 1988), 249.

4. Groh later laughingly noted that he had been present at so many famous moments in baseball history—Snodgrass's muff, the Toney–Vaughn double no-hitter, the Black Sox World Series, and (soon) the Lindstrom "pebble"—that he was called "the ubiquitous Mr. Groh." Lawrence S. Ritter, *The Glory of Their Times: The Story of the Early Days of Baseball Told by the Men Who Played It*, enlarged ed. (New York: William Morrow, 1984), 299.

5. Joe Williams, *The Joe Williams Baseball Reader*, ed. Peter Williams (Chapel Hill, N.C.: Algonquin Books, 1989), 99. People began calling Wilson "Hack" after they noted a resemblance to a wrestler named Hackenschmidt.

6. Though "saves" were not a recognized statistic in the 1920s, post facto reconstruction of the era shows that Jonnard led the National League in both 1922 and 1923 with 5 in each year.

7. These terms refer to the play-for-1-run strategy of the first two decades of the twentieth century.

8. Alexander, *McGraw*, 4.

9. Frank Graham, *McGraw of the Giants: An Informal Biography* (New York: G. P. Putnam's Sons, 1944), 179–80. The statement was not factually accurate.

10. William Knowlton Zinsser, *Spring Training* (New York: Harper & Row, 1989), 141; Ritter, *Glory*, 301. Roush was so great an athlete that, when he broke his right arm in 1912, he learned to throw left-handed. Roush has been oddly denigrated lately. Bill James, for example, states that he was not as good as Bobby Doerr or Phil Rizzuto, in *The Politics of Glory: How Baseball's Hall of Fame REALLY Works* (New York: Macmillan, 1994), 142, 433. That judgment is

absurd. Roush was one of the greatest hitters and defensive outfielders of his day. In fact, if the rules controlling official records had been the same in 1918 as they were before 1910 and after 1920, that is, for the great majority of baseball history—Roush would have won the batting title in 1918, too, and been one of a handful of players to have three consecutive titles. See Joseph M. Wayman, "Roush's Ruled-Out Batting Title," *Baseball Research Journal* 22 (1993): 9–10.

11. Among Latin pitchers only Dennis Martinez (with 245), Juan Marichal (243), and Luis Tiant (229) won more games than Luque's 193 during their major league careers. Luque won another 93 games playing winter ball in Cuba. Only Marichal, at 2.89, has a lifetime earned run average that is lower than Luque's 3.24. A useful article is Peter C. Bjarkman's "First Hispanic Star? Dolf Luque, of Course," *Baseball Research Journal* 19 (1990): 28–32.

12. Ritter, *Glory*, 208.

13. On Rixie, see Ted Farmer, "Eppa Rixie, Virginia Squire," *Grandstand Baseball Annual 1996*: 57–60.

14. Frederick Lieb, *Baseball as I Have Known It* (New York: Coward, McCann, and Geoghegan, 1977), 133.

15. *Baseball Magazine* 32 (February 1924): 386. Kenneth D. Richard argues that Mays was the third-best pitcher of his era, behind only Walter Johnson and Grover Cleveland Alexander. See his "Remembering Carl Mays," *Baseball Research Journal* 30 (2001): 122–26.

16. *Sporting News* (St. Louis), April 17, 1924.

17. On these four, see Lyle Spatz, "The Best NL Rookie Crop? The 1924 Pirates by Far," *Baseball Research Journal* 16 (1987): 57.

18. Hollocher committed suicide in 1940; undiagnosable physical symptoms had never left him, and it is probably fair to conclude that he was psychologically troubled. See Arthur Ahrens, "The Tragic Saga of Charlie Hollocher," *Baseball Research Journal* 15 (1986): 6–8.

19. Charles Alexander, *Rogers Hornsby: A Biography* (New York: Henry Holt, 1995), 86.

20. Quoted in Honig, *Man in the Dugout*, 48.

21. Rogers Hornsby, *My Kind of Baseball*, ed. J. Roy Stockton (New York: David McKay, 1953), 60.

22. Robert W. Creamer, *Stengel: His Life and Times* (New York: Simon & Schuster, 1984), 157.

23. Harold Kaese, *The Boston Braves* (New York: G. P. Putnam's Sons, 1948), 196.

24. "The Sad Life of a Losing Manager," *Baseball Magazine* 32 (March 1924): 438.

25. Grimes would proceed to win more games in the decade of the 1920s than any other pitcher in the major leagues. See Tom Knight, "Burleigh Grimes: Not Just a Spitballer," *National Pastime* 16 (1996): 72–73.

26. *Sporting News*, April 17, 1924.

27. Honig, *Man in the Dugout*, 37.

28. John Durant, *The Dodgers: An Illustrated History of Those Unpredictable Bums* (New York: Hastings, 1948), 22.

29. *Total Baseball* uses a measure called Total Player Rating (TPR) to assess the quality of players' performances. Ruth's TPR of 10.8 for 1923 is the highest for any player in any twentieth-century season. TPR is designed to improve on the two kinds of statistics which for many decades have been the conventional metrics: those assembled simply by aggregating (e.g., the number of home runs a batter hits in a season or the number of wins a pitcher is credited with) and those assembled by calculating ratios (e.g., batting averages and earned run averages). TPR is a more sophisticated measurement, incorporating (for batters) the calculable average importance of discrete offensive events (e.g., singles, triples, and ground outs) and adjusting the raw figures to take into account differences by era and ballpark. A good introduction to the subject is the section titled "Sabermetrics" in John Thorn, Pete Palmer, and Michael Gershman, eds., *Total Baseball*, 7th ed. (Kingston, N.Y.: Total Sports, 2001), 532–42.

30. Barry Bonds was walked 177 times in 2001.

31. In May he modified that judgment slightly: "I'd rather hit seventy homers than lead the batters." *New York Times*, May 1, 1924.

32. *Sporting News*, April 10, 1924.

33. Ibid., March 27, 1924.

34. "Sixteen Years as a Big League Star," *Baseball Magazine* 32 (March 1924): 437.

35. On Heilmann, see Jamie Selko, "Harry Who? The Story of Harry Heilmann's Four Batting Titles," *National Pastime* 15 (1995): 45–50.

36. Lee Allen, *The American League Story*, rev. ed. (New York: Hill & Wang, 1965), 113.

37. *Sporting News*, November 22, 1923.

38. Aided by the era he played in, Uhle has the highest lifetime batting average, .289, of any player who was essentially a pitcher for the duration of his major league career.

39. Sewell's most remarkable year lay ahead: In 1925 he would have 672 plate appearances (608 official at-bats) and strike out only 4 times.

40. Sisler had batted .4198 in 1922. Ty Cobb, credited with .420 in 1911, had batted .4196. Some sources lower Lajoie's 1901 average to .422, but the point still holds.

41. John McGraw, *My Thirty Years in Baseball* (New York: Arno Press, 1974; originally published, New York: Boni and Liveright, 1923), 215.

42. *Sporting News*, February 28, 1924.

43. For an appreciation of Sisler, see Paul Warburton, "George Sisler," *National Pastime* 19 (1999): 93–97.

44. Joe Hauser is one of baseball's great enigmas. He stands with Mark McGwire and Sammy Sosa as one of only three players ever to hit over 60 home runs in more than one season. Hauser's two seasons were both minor league years— 63 for Baltimore in 1930 and 69 for Minneapolis in 1933. A broken leg in 1925 would effectively end his play at the major league level. See Stew Thornley, "'Unser Choe' Hauser: Double 60," *Baseball Research Journal* 20 (1991): 20–21.

45. *Sporting News*, January 24, 1924.

46. Tyrus Raymond Cobb and Al Stump, *My Life in Baseball: The True Record*

(Lincoln: University of Nebraska Press, 1993; originally published, New York: Doubleday, 1961), 159. Schalk was the first catcher to back up at first base on grounders hit to the infield.

47. On Falk, see Charles Kaufman, "Bibb Falk: Can You Fill Shoeless Joe's Shoes?" *National Pastime* 19 (1999): 103–6.

48. The remarks were made by Cincinnati baseball writer W. A. Phelon, in "Who Will Win the Big League Pennants?" *Baseball Magazine* 32 (May 1924): 533.

49. Arthur Daley, *Times at Bat: A Half-Century of Baseball* (New York: Random House, 1950), 61.

50. Basically the team used Tampa as its spring training base. But training for many veterans began at Hot Springs, and it was there that Bucky Harris first began working with his men.

51. *Sporting News*, April 17, 1924.

52. Marberry acquired the nickname, which he disliked, from a presumed resemblance to the heavyweight boxer, Luis Firpo.

53. Unlike the other three playing managers in the American League—Ty Cobb, George Sisler, and Tris Speaker—Harris was not a star. That fact underlines Griffith's remarkable confidence in him, for by doubling his salary, Griffith forwent most of the financial advantage that had induced some owners to turn to playing managers. Oddly enough, since Roger Peckinpaugh had briefly managed the Yankees in 1914 at the age of twenty-three, Harris was now managing an older man who had borne identical responsibilities at an even earlier age.

54. Shirley Povich, *The Washington Senators* (New York: G. P. Putnam's Sons, 1954), 107.

55. *Sporting News*, February 28, 1924.

56. In fact, an illness may have accounted for Goslin's lethargic, uninspiring work. But whether indolence or infection explained his lethargy, Harris's refusal to countenance sluggish play caught the attention of observers.

57. *Washington Post*, March 7, 1924. During an off-season interview, Johnson had said—another of these quotations almost too good to be true—"If I had the chance to go to a pennant-winning team and play in a world series, I'd rather stay right here with my old team." "How Baseball's Biggest Pitcher Reached the Top," *Literary Digest* 79 (November 10, 1923): 67.

58. *Washington Post*, March 10, 1924.

Chapter 2. From Opening Day to Memorial Day

1. *New York Times*, April 26, 1924.

2. *Sporting News* of May 8, 1924. The Reds were scoring one run for every 2.8 base hits. The league ratio at the end of the year would be 1:2.2; the Reds' ratio, 1:2.4.

3. On Shocker's quarrel with management, see Steve L. Steinberg, "Free Agency in 1923? A Shocker for Baseball," *National Pastime* 20 (2000): 121–23.

4. *Sporting News*, May 8, 1924.

5. Lee Allen, *The Cincinnati Reds* (New York: G. P. Putnam's Sons, 1948), 171.
6. *Sporting News*, May 22, 1924.
7. This accounts for Branch Rickey's odd judgment: "Walter Johnson was not a pitcher in the generally accepted sense of the word. He was a thrower." Branch Rickey and Robert Riger, *The American Diamond: A Documentary of the Game* (New York: Simon & Schuster, 1965), 131.
8. Sam Crawford used "swoosh." Ritter, *Glory*, 57. Roger Peckinpaugh used "swish." Honig, *Man in the Dugout*, 215.
9. *Sporting News*, May 22, 1924.
10. Ibid., June 6, 1924.
11. This is the second-shortest complete game in American League history.
12. This Dutch Leonard (Hubert Benjamin Leonard), whose major league playing career extended from 1913 to 1925, should not be confused with a later Dutch Leonard (Emil John Leonard), whose major league career began in 1933 and ended in 1953.
13. Hollocher was reported to have signed for $12,000, a good salary for the era. Even more remarkable, the Cubs yielded to his argument that he deserved more money for his labors of 1923.

Chapter 3. The Business of Baseball

1. Edward Mott Woolley, "The Business Side of Baseball," *McClure's Magazine* 39 (July 1912): 248.
2. On the duties of a trainer in 1924, see "Confessions of a Big League Club Trainer," *Baseball Magazine* 32 (February 1924): 415–16; on the duties of a property manager in 1924, see "Behind the Scenes in a Big League Clubhouse," *Baseball Magazine* 34 (April 1925): 504.
3. In 1924, Sunday ball was prohibited in Boston, Philadelphia, and Pittsburgh, which affected the home scheduling of five clubs. These teams sometimes made day trips to other cities so that they could play on a Sunday.
4. The cost of the contract of a highly touted minor leaguer could be great. In the two years prior to the 1924 season, the Tigers paid $50,000 for Red Wingo, the Giants paid $65,000 for Jack Bentley, the Athletics paid $70,000 for Paul Strand, and the White Sox paid $100,000 for Willie Kamm.
5. David Quentin Voigt, *American Baseball*, vol. 2: *From the Commissioners to Continental Expansion* (University Park: Pennsylvania State University Press, 1983), 224; *Sporting News*, January 24, 1925; U.S., House of Representatives, *Organized Baseball: Report of the Subcommittee on the Study of Monopoly Power of the Committee on the Judiciary*, 82d Cong., 2d sess., House Report 2002 (Washington, D.C.: Government Printing Office, 1952), 109; *Sporting News*, December 13, 1923.
6. For example, Bozeman Bulger's sources led him to a figure of $598,000 for his unidentified club in 1922. "The Baseball Business from the Inside," *Collier's* 69 (March 25, 1922): 29.

7. Uniforms did not bear numbers in 1924, but the scoreboard identified batters with arbitrary numbers that corresponded with numbers printed in the scorecards. This system allowed the numbers to be changed at intervals, thus undermining the utility of fans' retaining scorecards for future use and compelling them to purchase new ones each time they attended a game.

8. Harold Seymour, *Baseball: The Golden Age* (New York: Oxford University Press, 1971), 344. Of the approximately 85 percent of revenues that came from gate receipts, about 65 percent came from the home gate and about 20 percent from the road gate. U.S. House Report, *Organized Baseball*, 6.

9. It was policy in the 1920s to offer the same schedule of ticket prices in all major league cities. Throughout the 1920s, bleacher seats cost 50 cents, grandstand seats cost $1.00, and box seats cost $1.50. Each club was free, however, to designate as many (or as few) of its seats as it wished to any of the standard categories and hence had some control over the gate.

    For profits, see U.S. House Report, *Organized Baseball*, 93. Robert Burk reinforces that figure when he says that average annual profits during the 1920s came to $115,000 per club. If that figure holds for 1924, the average club profit was about 20 percent. Robert Burk, *Much More Than a Game: Players, Owners, and American Baseball since 1921* (Chapel Hill: University of North Carolina Press, 2001), 4.

10. U.S. House Report, *Organized Baseball*, 191.

11. Salary information was, in general, not public. Owners were not eager to give their players leverage for bidding against one another, and players tended to be closed-mouthed about the information. Voigt, *American Baseball*, vol. 2, 223 provides the "average salary" figure. Figures for individuals come from *Time 3* (January 21, 1924): 24; Seymour, *Golden Age*, 346–47; Alexander, *Hornsby*, 92; Burk, *Much More Than a Game*, 20.

12. *Sporting News*, February 28, 1924.

13. Burk, *Much More Than a Game*, 22.

14. Francis Wallace, "College Men in the Big Leagues," *Scribner's* (October 1927), 493.

15. Seymour, *Golden Age*, 353.

16. Quoted in Ritter, *Glory*, 273.

17. *Sporting News*, February 21, 1924, 7.

18. Voigt, *American Baseball*, vol. 2, 95.

19. Quoted in U.S. House Report, *Organized Baseball*, 153.

20. In practice, players still had a measure of power. By making nuisances of themselves, they could create conditions in which an owner might conclude that they would be more valuable sold for cash. This tactic to force a trade or sale was deplored in the press, but it was probably engaged in more frequently than was generally recognized.

21. McGraw, *My Thirty Years*, 252. It is odd that the empirical evidence of the inefficacy of the reserve rule as a device for equalizing the distribution of talent was so rarely cited. At the opening of the 1924 season, the Giants had 9 twentieth-

century pennants to their credit, the Red Sox and the Athletics had 6, and the Cubs had 5, while the Browns, Cardinals, and Senators had none.

22. Seymour, *Golden Age*, 322.

23. The owners were choosing wisely. Having decided they needed a despot, they wanted one whose instincts were consistent with theirs. In 1915, when hearing testimony in the Federal League case, Landis had said that "both sides must understand that any blows at the thing called baseball would be regarded by this court as a blow to a national institution" and—even more comforting to the ears of owners—"I am shocked because you call playing baseball 'labor.'" Lee Lowenfish and Tony Lupien, *The Imperfect Diamond: The Story of Baseball's Reserve System and the Men Who Fought to Change It* (New York: Stein and Day, 1980), 90.

24. Ibid., 104.

Chapter 4. From Memorial Day to Independence Day

1. *New York Times*, June 8, 1924, section 1, part 2, 1.

2. In a 10-inning game on September 2, 1996, Mike Greenwell drove in all the Red Sox runs in a 9–8 victory. Bob Johnson of the Athletics had equaled Kelly's feat on June 12, 1938, in an 8–3 win over the Browns.

3. *Sporting News*, June 19, 1924, took editorial exception to this decision. Scoring rules, it asserted, were subordinate to playing rules, which clearly stated (section 7, rule 48) that a player must "touch all the bases in regular order."

4. *New York Times*, July 1, 1924.

5. The words are Bob O'Farrell's, quoted in Ritter, *Glory*, 252.

6. *Sporting News*, June 19, 1924.

7. The following winter, when told of the statement that no pitcher could fool Hornsby, the Rajah reminded the writer of this day. "For me to say Vance wasn't fooling me, that day, would be ridiculous, wouldn't it?" James M. Gould, "Will Rogers Hornsby Ever Hit .500?" *Baseball Magazine* 34 (March 1925): 476.

8. He had also been the winning pitcher in 2 of the 3 Dodger victories against the Giants. By way of contrast, Fournier had padded his statistics by feasting on Giant pitching, 7 of his 16 home runs having come off McGraw's mound staff.

9. Pitchers were given greater latitude in the 1920s than in later years in bluffing a runner on first; balks were rarer, and base runners' leads shorter.

10. U.S. House Report, *Organized Baseball*, 63.

11. *Sporting News*, June 26, 1924.

12. Very early in this same game, Ruth collided with another player and was unconscious for about five minutes. It tells us much about his value to the team and the assumptions of the time that he was allowed to stay in the game and hit his towering home run.

13. Ruth did not stint even when the pressure was off. Always eager to please the crowd, he hit the longest home run ever seen in Louisville in an exhibition game held there on June 2.

14. Quoted in Ritter, *Glory*, 246.

15. *Sporting News*, June 19, 1924. The same journal provided an additional (and telling) anecdote in its July 10 edition. Umpire Billy Evans reported that the Tiger catcher Johnny Bassler had admonished pitcher Bert Cole, just before the pitch that hit Bob Meusel: "Well, if you must hit Bob, don't hit him in the head."

16. George Sullivan and John Powers, *Yankees: An Illustrated History* (Englewood Cliffs, N.J.: Prentice-Hall, 1982), 31.

17. *New York Times*, June 21, 1924.

18. When he learned of his suspension, Sisler was furious: "Umpire Holmes misrepresented matters to Ban Johnson. I said nothing warranting Holmes in putting me out of the game." *Sporting News*, June 26, 1924. Holmes was also upset, for after the game he had been attacked by an angry St. Louis crowd. He speculated that a conspiracy on "the part of gamblers" lay behind his troubles. *New York Times*, June 26, 1924.

19. *Sporting News*, July 3, 1924.

20. Prothro's performance was diminished by a foot injury that he tried to play through. His basic difficulty, however, was that Harris thought him lazy. He sent him to Memphis before June was over.

21. *New York Times*, June 25, 1924.

22. *Washington Post*, June 25, 1924.

23. Ibid., June 26, 1924, section 2, 1.

24. *Sporting News*, July 3, 1924.

25. That's an accomplishment worth reflecting on. Fourteen contests is a significant run of games. The average American League team scored just under 5 runs a game in 1924. In short, for almost one-tenth of the season, the Senators' pitching staff held the opposition to about one-quarter of its ordinary scoring pace.

26. No team had actually played half of their scheduled games yet. The Tigers, with 74 games in the books, had played the most.

Chapter 5. The Players

1. Burk, *Much More Than a Game*, 310.

2. The truly oldest player in 1924 was Nick Altrock, the coach of the Senators, who appeared in a game at the end of the season at the age of forty-eight, essentially as an amusement. Babe Adams of the Pirates deserves mention, too. He was a bit older than Quinn, forty-two in May, and pitched well in 39⅔ innings.

3. "Country Boys in the Big Leagues," *Literary Digest* 85 (April 18, 1925): 60–62.

4. Among the players figuring in this book who attended college are Max Carey, Eddie Collins, Kiki Cuyler, Bibb Falk, Frankie Frisch, Harry Heilmann, Waite Hoyt, Travis Jackson, George Kelly, Freddy Lindstrom, Jimmy O'Connell, Muddy Ruel, Joe Shaute, George Sisler, Cy Williams, Glenn Wright, and Tom Zachary. The estimate of 25 percent comes from Burk, *Never Just a Game*, 172. Since nationally only about 5 percent of men had had the advantage of a college experience, it is clear that the complement of major leaguers was an unusually well-educated group of men.

5. Quoted in Ritter, *Glory*, 153.
6. Voigt, *American Baseball*, vol. 2, 79. The thirteen survivors were Babe Adams, Max Carey, Ty Cobb, Eddie Collins, Shano Collins, Jake Daubert, Harry Hooper, Walter Johnson, Rube Marquard, Stuffy McInnis, Jack Quinn, Tris Speaker, and Zack Wheat.
7. This line of analysis was advanced by *The Sporting News*, on the editorial page, October 23, 1924.
8. The 1919 entrant was Frankie Frisch. The 1920 season brought Joe Sewell and Pie Traynor to the majors, and 1921 saw the arrival of Goose Goslin and, for one game, Kiki Cuyler. By contrast, 1922 brought three entries, 1923 brought five, 1924 brought six, and 1925 and 1926 brought three each.
9. Forty-nine future Hall of Famers, accounting for almost 20 percent of the year's at-bats, played in 1924. Bill James (*Politics of Glory*, 246–47) notes that typically throughout baseball history the men chosen for the Hall have accounted for 10–12 percent of at-bats. Every team in 1924 contained a future Hall of Famer except the Phillies.
10. Frederick G. Lieb, "The Passing of the Super-Pitcher," *Baseball Magazine* 32 (February 1924): 400.
11. Frederick G. Lieb, "Has Batting Returned to a State of Normalcy?" *Baseball Magazine* 34 (March 1925): 449.
12. Quoted in Maury Allen, *You Could Look It Up: The Life of Casey Stengel* (New York: Times Books, 1979), 78.
13. Quoted in Ritter, *Glory*, 258.
14. Hugh S. Fullerton, "How the Ball Players of the Big Leagues Live and Act When off the Diamond," *American Magazine* (July 1911): 322.
15. Ritter, *Glory*, 123.
16. Ibid., 13.
17. Exhibition games were often spectacles, pure and simple—about the only way in a pretelevision age that fans (except in the deep south) who did not live near major league cities could see the heroes they read about. On July 25, 1924, for example, the Yankees played in Indianapolis. Babe Ruth hit home runs in his first 2 plate appearances, switched around to bat right-handed on his third trip to the plate (and struck out), and pitched one inning.
18. Some clubs traveled more than eleven thousand miles by rail during the 1924 season.
19. Ritter, *Glory*, 279–80.
20. As almost all major leaguers recalled, however, major league travel beat minor league travel. In the minors, teams usually traveled by bus. If they made overnight train trips, the players were expected to sleep in their seats and carry their own uniforms. In opponents' cities, they stayed in fleabag hotels with as many as eight men to a room.
21. Bill Starr, *Clearing the Bases: Baseball Then and Now* (New York: Michael Kesend, 1989), 83.
22. And then there were the injuries sustained off the field. Late in May, Elam

Vangilder, pitcher for the Browns, hurt his pitching hand while winding up his phonograph!

23. The description is Pete Sheehy's. Leo Trachtenberg, "Pete Sheehy: A Last Interview," *Baseball History* 1 (Winter 1986): 31.

24. On Reese, see David W. Anderson, "Bonesetter Reese," *Baseball Research Journal* 30 (2001): 18–19.

25. McGraw, *My Thirty Years*, 53; Ritter, *Glory*, 226, 284.

26. Ritter, *Glory*, 276. The words are Lefty O'Doul's, an attribution that suggests precisely how severely some players want to sanitize history. Bunker Hill was more candid: "We didn't talk baseball much off the field." Carmen Hill, *An Autobiography: The Battles of Bunker Hill: The Life and Times of Carmen P. Hill* (n.p.: Krause, 1985), 34.

27. Rube Marquard said that "there was very little drinking in baseball in those days," explaining that it was difficult to both a carouser and a good ballplayer. Ritter, *Glory*, 15.

28. Cobb, *My Life in Baseball*, 131; Ritter, *Glory*, 192.

29. Dan Gutman, *Baseball Babylon: From the Black Sox to Pete Rose, the Real Stories behind the Scandals That Rocked the Game* (New York: Penguin, 1992).

30. Seymour, *Golden Age*, 431.

31. *Sporting News*, March 6, June 12, August 14, and November 13, 1924.

32. McGraw, *My Thirty Years*, 256–60. The St. Louis Browns, largely at the insistence of Urban Shocker, permitted wives to attend spring training in 1924. Management labeled Shocker a troublemaker for this demand, but manager George Sisler supported his star pitcher.

33. Voigt, *American Baseball*, vol. 2, 71, 221.

34. Donald Honig, *Baseball America: The Heroes of the Game and the Times of Their Glory* (New York: Macmillan, 1985), 138.

Chapter 6. From Independence Day to Labor Day

1. *Sporting News*, July 24, 1924.

2. Ibid.

3. *New York Times*, July 31, 1924.

4. *Sporting News*, August 28, 1924.

5. The major league record (at the time) of 16 strikeouts in a game was held by Rube Waddell.

6. *New York Times*, August 31, 1924.

7. I have relied heavily on C. David Stephan, "Batting Barrages: Streaks, Tears, Booms & Rampages," *Grandstand Baseball Annual 1996*, 12:104–5, for this account of Hornsby's accomplishment. The term "rampage," which I shall use, is one of Stephan's coinages. He defines it as a period—only six batters have managed one—in which a hitter is able to bat at least .450 over the course of at least 90 base hits. I have made a very modest correction to Stephan's calculation of Hornsby's totals.

8. Hornsby was deeply disappointed by the effect of the injury. Sensing that he was in an extraordinary groove, he had recently announced his hope of surpassing George Sisler's (still-standing) record 257 hits in a season, set in 1920. The injury made his goal totally unachievable. In fact, however, it was probably unreachable in any case, for even when he played in as many games as Sisler, Hornsby averaged about 40 fewer at-bats each year owing to pitchers' greater readiness to walk him rather than risk an extra-base hit. Hornsby wound up the 1924 season with 227 base hits.

9. *New York Times*, August 24, 1924.

10. *Washington Evening Star*, July 6, 1924.

11. *Sporting News*, July 24, 1924. Manush was born in Tuscumbia, Alabama.

12. *New York Times*, July 25, 1924.

13. The Browns protested the game when umpire Brick Owens directed a member of the team to bat out of order!

14. The reader might wonder: Where was Walter Johnson? Harris held him out of the series for fear that the midsummer Missouri heat would wilt his star hurler.

15. The acquisition of McNeely caused several stirs. First, one of the terms of the agreement was that Wid Matthews would be lent to Sacramento. Even though Matthews had lost his regular slot in July, he remained popular with Washington fandom. Should McNeely flop, the fans could be expected to remind Griffith of Matthews. Second, when Griffith learned that McNeely had recently dislocated his shoulder—that Sacramento had sold him damaged goods—he refused to pay until he could ascertain whether McNeely could still play. Judge Landis upheld Griffith's decision, McNeely soon demonstrated that his damaged shoulder would not impair his hitting, and Griffith eventually paid the sales price.

16. Strictly speaking, the on-base percentages I give in this discussion are only approximate. They are calculated by a formula of (BH+BB)/PA. They, therefore, do not take into account occasions where batters got on base as a result of defensive errors, catcher interference, or having been hit by a pitch. I couldn't find these data—perhaps because they represent rare events.

17. How does Hornsby's best run of 48 games in this 1924 season stack up against Ruth's 3 storms? It was close but not quite so good. In the games between July 15 and August 29, Hornsby bested Ruth in batting by a slight margin (.488 to .480) but was behind him in each of the other three categories: home runs (14 to 20), slugging average (.856 to .954), and on-base percentage (.562 to .575).

Before the reader explodes in disbelief at this apparent relegation of Bonds, I need to say something about his 2 incredible storms in 2001. Over the first 48-game stretch (April 12–June 7), he hit 30 home runs and slugged 1.041—the highest ever for a 48-game span. But he batted (only?) .361 and thus, despite the 51 walks, compiled an on-base percentage of (only?) .525. Over the second 48-game stretch (July 25–September 24), he hit 25 home runs and slugged .987. But he batted (only?) .380 while recording an on-base percentage of .549. There is no doubt that Bonds's 2001 season is the greatest offensive season any batter has ever achieved, better even than Ruth's accomplishment in 1920. But Ruth's significantly higher batting averages during his storms make my point by showing that he was *hitting* his way on base more often than Bonds. Another way of making the point is to note that Ruth got 45 singles during his storm while Bonds got only 32 in his two storms together. For discussions of other remarkable barrages, see Stephan, "Batting Barrages," 100–14.

18. *New York Times*, August 12, 1924.
19. *Washington Evening Star*, August 26, 1924. To another reporter, Sisler said that the Browns "all regretted that the game could not go nine innings as there seemed little doubt that Johnson would again pitch a no-hit game." Johnson had pitched a 9-inning no-hitter on July 1, 1920. Sisler's remark was a reference to the fact that a shortened no-hitter would not be an official no-hitter. *Sporting News*, September 4, 1924.
20. F. C. Lane, "If I Were Only Young Once More!" *Baseball Magazine* 33 (November 1924): 531.
21. *New York Times*, August 30, 1924.
22. Goslin had recently been deliberately trying to emulate Babe Ruth's stance. Maybe he was mastering the master's technique.

Chapter 7. The Game of Baseball in the 1920s

1. I have relied heavily on Philip J. Lowry, *Green Cathedrals* (Cooperstown, N.Y.: Society for American Baseball Research, 1986), especially 3–4.
2. Even so, Ban Johnson worried that games were becoming protracted. In July 1924, he ordered American League umpires to suspend players who continued to delay games after being warned. *Sporting News*, August 7, 1924.
3. But not always. When a spectator in Washington refused to return a ball on August 18, he was arrested, removed from the stadium, and booked on a charge of petty larceny. *Washington Post*, August 19, 1924.
4. Honig, *Man in the Dugout*, 283.
5. *Sporting News*, July 17, 1924.
6. McGraw, *My Thirty Years*, 83.
7. Rather ingenious makeshift solutions were required when one of the umpires was injured and forced to leave the field. On June 12, 1924, when one arbiter withdrew from a game between the Indians and the Red Sox, he was replaced on the base paths by two men—the trainer for the Red Sox and a sandlot umpire from Cleveland. American League umpires even made a sartorial splash in 1924 when Ban Johnson instructed the crews in August to change from their traditional blue garb to olive drab.
8. Jack Kavanaugh, "Brits in the Baseball Hall of Fame," *National Pastime* 12 (1992): 69.
9. As I write, the last year that saw a playing manager was 1986 (Pete Rose, at Cincinnati). The last year that saw more than one was 1953 (Eddie Stanky, with

the Cardinals, and Phil Cavaretta, with the Cubs). None of these men was a regular player, unlike all five in 1924.

10. Slugging percentages in the 1920s jumped even more sharply than batting averages. The mean league slugging average in the years 1910–19 was .337. The identically derived figure for the years 1920–29 was .397—an increase of 60 points or 18 percent.

   As John McGraw had explained a decade earlier, "Baseball is largely a matter of chance and probability." *How to Play Baseball* (New York: J. J. Little and Ives, 1913), 142.

11. *Sporting News*, February 12, 1924.

12. F. C. Lane, quoted in *Literary Digest* 82 (August 2, 1924): 52.

13. *Sporting News*, December 27, 1923.

14. I do not have statistics for the number of runners caught stealing prior to the 1920 season. I am assuming—but cannot prove—that the ratio of success to nonsuccess was largely the same in the era of more frequent steals. If it differed, I suspect that the difference would strengthen my point, since it is likely that, in an era of more aggressive base running, the proportion of unsuccessful attempts would be higher.

15. The rule changes of 1920 provided a far cleaner definition of a balk than earlier rules had afforded. But balks were often judgment calls, and umpires in the 1920s tended to give pitchers wider latitude than umpires of later generations. I do not know whether umpires in the pre-1920 days were equally obliging to hurlers. If they were not, my argument would need to be adjusted.

16. Ritter, *Glory*, 33.

17. *Sporting News*, May 1, 1924.

18. Ibid., March 20, 1924.

19. The best left-handed pitchers in baseball in 1924 were probably Herb Pennock of the Yankees and Eppa Rixey of the Reds. Both are in the Hall of Fame.

20. *Sporting News*, October 18, 1923.

21. Quoted in *Literary Digest* 79 (October 13, 1923): 72–76.

22. Hornsby, *My Kind of Baseball*, 32.

Chapter 8. From Labor Day to the End of the Season

1. The Brooklyn team had won the pennant in 1900, 1916, and 1920.

2. *Sporting News*, September 4, 1924.

3. This run of doubleheaders was a consequence of the need to make up games that had been lost in the early-season monsoons.

4. The New York Yankees actually won 5 consecutive doubleheaders in 1906 (coincidentally in the middle, as were the 1924 Robins, of a 15-game winning streak). But the New Yorkers had a day off in the middle of their demanding twin-bill schedule, and, for what it's worth, one of their victories was by forfeit.

5. The Dodgers had also won 29 of 35 when they lost the nightcap. During this

remarkable run, Dazzy Vance and Bill Doak had each supplied 7 victories and Burleigh Grimes was just a step behind, with 6.

6. *Sporting News*, September 18, 1924.

7. As a result of the storming of the fence, one estimate put the number who saw the game free at seven thousand. Lee Allen, *The Giants and Dodgers: The Fabulous Story of Baseball's Fiercest Feud* (New York: G. P. Putnam's Sons, 1964), 124.

8. Frisch got hits in his first 6 at-bats, tying the twentieth-century record for hits in a single game. On his seventh plate appearance, he bunted and was thrown out at first.

9. *New York Times*, September 13, 1924.

10. Washington's 5 final home games of the season were all against second division teams; nevertheless, 105,000 fans turned out for the games.

11. The honor was then called the League Award. Ineligible for consideration were previous winners (George Sisler in 1922 and Babe Ruth in 1923) and playing managers (Ty Cobb, Bucky Harris, and Tris Speaker). Had he been eligible, Ruth probably would have won. Eddie Collins finished a somewhat distant second behind Johnson.

12. Gregg had once been a fine pitcher, stringing together 3 consecutive 20-victory seasons for the Cleveland Indians in 1911, 1912, and 1913.

13. *New York Times*, September 4, 1924. It is interesting to note that Babe Ruth said that Beall had "the best curve ball I ever saw." Williams, *Baseball Reader*, 85.

14. It was Nehf's fourth home run of the year. Incredibly, all 4 had been hit off one hurler—the Cardinals' Johnny Stuart.

15. Almost seventy years passed before another major leaguer—Mark Whiten in 1993—managed to bat in 12 runs in a single game. This total has never been surpassed.

16. Joseph Reichler and Ben Olan, *Baseball's Unforgettable Games* (New York: Ronald Press, 1960), 174.

17. *Washington Post*, September 17, 1924, section 2.

18. Lefler had batted .369, in the Eastern League, playing for Worcester. He played in the majors only in 1924, but got 5 hits in 8 at-bats for the Senators. Earlier in the year he had gone 0–for–1 for the Braves. He thus had a lifetime batting average of .556! He later practiced law.

19. *Washington Post*, September 11, 1924.

20. It was a hit he sorely wanted, for with it he reached the 200-hit mark for the ninth time in his career and surpassed Willie Keeler's old major league record of eight 200-hit seasons.

21. Ruth had not hit a home run for over a week. He had three physical problems at this time: a stiff left arm, an aching left shoulder, and a sore ankle. Observers thought that he was swinging his bat with only one arm.

22. Marberry had a chance to institute a 1-2-3 double play to end the tenth with a Washington victory. Instead, he threw to the wrong base—second—and in addition misdirected his throw into center field.

23. *Washington Post*, September 21, 1924, sports section.

24. Only Walter Johnson, Christy Mathewson, and Eddie Plank had previously logged more than 300 major league victories in the twentieth century.

25. *New York Times*, September 22, 1924.

26. Frederick G. Lieb, *The Pittsburgh Pirates* (New York: G. P. Putnam's Sons, 1948), 200.

27. *New York Times*, September 20, 1924.

28. Barnes got this rap early. The quotation comes from *New York Times*, June 6, 1924.

29. Cuyler had a sore shoulder, made worse by the suddenly cool weather.

30. This was the greatest number of strikeouts posted by a pitcher since Walter Johnson's 312 in 1913.

31. *New York Times*, September 29, 1924.

32. Steve Wulf wrote a wonderful piece on Sam Rice: "The Secrets of Sam," *Sports Illustrated* 79 (July 19, 1993): 58–64.

33. Victory 92 not only secured the pennant for Washington, it made the 1924 Nationals the winningest team in the history of the franchise up to that point, as they surpassed the 91 victories garnered in 1912.

34. Having clinched the pennant, Washington could relax. During the final, meaningless game of the season on September 30, Nick Altrock, the forty-seven-year-old pitching coach, pitched 2 innings. Altrock played the clown, "praying" when balls were hit, "pitching" his glove rather than the ball, and provoking laughter even from umpires Tom Connolly and Brick Owens. The Red Sox ran all over the Senators to clinch seventh place, 13–1. Altrock also tripled in his 1 at-bat (because the outfielders were drawn into the infield!), and so ended the year with a batting average of 1.000. Altrock had played his first major league game in 1898 and would make his last plate appearance in 1933. About Altrock, see Jim Blenko, "Nick Altrock: Washington's Coach and Clown," *National Pastime* 18 (1998): 73–77.

35. As defined by the cities supporting major league clubs in 1924, Washington was the last city to win a pennant. Washington teams had been unsuccessful for thirty-nine years—two years in the American Association, one year in the Union Association, thirteen years in the National League, and twenty-three years in the American League. Though St. Louis had not seen a pennant winner in the twentieth century, the old St. Louis Browns had been four-time winners in the American Association in the 1880s.

36. The most elaborate of these boards, constructed in a city theater, used shadowgraphs to assist the spectators in visualizing players racing around the base paths.

37. Will Rogers affords a representative example. In his syndicated column, he wrote, "Today the entire baseball world is not just pulling for Johnson the Pitcher; they are pulling for Johnson the Man." Jack Kavanaugh, *Walter Johnson: A Life* (South Bend, Ind.: Diamond Communications, 1995), 173.

38. *New York Times*, October 1, 1924.

39. Ibid.

40. Ibid., October 3, 1924.

41. Within a few days, O'Connell was attributing to his three teammates direct statements of encouragement for proceeding with the bribe effort. But his clearer memory came suspiciously late and did not hurt them.

42. *New York Times*, October 2, 1924.

43. Graham, *McGraw*, 186.

44. *New York Times*, October 3, 1924.

45. Lee Allen, *The National League Story*, rev. ed. (New York: Hill & Wang, 1961), 176.

46. *New York Times*, October 3, 1924.

47. Eugene Murdock, *Ban Johnson: Czar of Baseball* (Westport, Conn.: Greenwood Press, 1982), 209. More than two decades earlier, Johnson had been instrumental in inducing Griffith to cast his lot with the new American League, and Griffith, in turn, had been one of the stars whose successes lent credibility to Johnson's new circuit. Up until October 1924, each man had regarded the other as a strong friend.

48. Tommy Holmes, *Baseball's Great Teams: The Dodgers* (New York: Macmillan, 1975), 24.

49. Seymour, *Golden Age*, 379. This is the most measured account of the affair. But also see Lowell Blaisdell, "Mystery and Tragedy: The O'Connell–Dolan Scandal," *Baseball Research Journal* 11 (1982): 44–49.

50. *Sporting News*, October 9, 1924.

51. J. G. Taylor Spink, *Judge Landis and Twenty-Five Years of Baseball* (New York: Thomas Y. Crowell, 1947), 138–39.

52. There was also much speculation about motive. After all, why try to bribe an opponent into rolling over when victory is about to be yours, anyway? On September 27, the Giants needed only 1 more win or 1 more Dodger loss to clinch the pennant, and the Giants were playing the feckless Phillies. Neither O'Connell nor Dolan suggested motives, but two hypotheses have been proffered. According to one, the Giants were still fearful of losing the pennant, since Frisch and Groh were still injured. According to the other, gamblers needed the Giants to take the pennant by a 2-game margin in order to win their bets.

53. *New York Times*, October 2, 1924.

Chapter 9. The Season in Review

1. Bentley's is a remarkable story. The "circumstances" he felt victimized by were, first, his loss of two years of play during World War I, and second, the very richness of his talent, which led him to be insufficiently focused. In the minor leagues, he was so good as both a hitter (.349 in the International League in 1922) and pitcher (41–5 over several years in the early 1920s) that he seemed a second Babe Ruth. John McGraw was so eager to get him that he paid $65,000 and three players to Jack Dunn of Baltimore for the rights to Bentley.

But he was never more than good in the majors. F. C. Lane, "Why Jack Bentley is a 'Victim of Circumstances,'" *Baseball Magazine* 32 (February 1924): 395.

2. The Giants played .566 ball after July 4; the Dodgers played .600 ball and the Pirates .605 ball.

3. The Hall of Fame members are Frankie Frisch, Travis Jackson, George Kelly, Freddy Lindstrom, Bill Terry, Hack Wilson, and Ross Youngs. Not all, of course, were playing Hall of Fame ball in 1924.

4. Morris A. Bealle, *The Washington Senators: An 87-Year History of the World's Oldest Baseball Club and Most Incurable Fandom* (Washington, D.C.: Columbia Publishing Company, 1947), 115.

5. The famous exception was the "prince of the Nationals," Walter Johnson. The sharpest words most people heard pass his lips were, "Goodness gracious sakes alive!"

6. This judgment is attributed to veteran Washington sportswriter Sam Lacy. Jim Reisler, *Black Writers/Black Baseball: An Anthology of Articles from Black Sportswriters Who Covered the Negro Leagues* (Jefferson, N.C.: McFarland, 1994), 19.

7. *Washington Post*, August 31, 1924.

8. Honig, *Man in the Dugout*, 261.

9. *Washington Daily News*, October 2, 1924.

10. F. C. Lane, "Our All-American Baseball Club of 1924," *Baseball Magazine* 34 (December 1924): 311–13+.

11. The modern statistic called "fielding runs" does not bear out the judgment of contemporaries. Given the difficulties inherent in quantifying fielding skill, however, I'm inclined to go with the judgments of contemporaries.

12. The average was only the fourth best in the league, but the top four teams were clustered within 4 points of each other.

13. John J. Ward, "The Man Who Gave Washington Their Punch," *Baseball Magazine* 34 (December 1924): 298.

14. Rice and Judge were teammates for so long—1915–17 and 1919–32—that they hold the record for the most hits ever (4,996) by two major league teammates. Biff Brecher and Albey M. Reiner, "Teammates with the Most Combined Hits," *Baseball Research Journal* 23 (1994): 18.

15. Griffith Stadium was a spacious arena. Prior to the 1924 season, Clark Griffith had raised the height of the right field fence to 40 feet. Still, only one other team—the 1916 Red Sox—has managed to win the pennant while hitting only 1 home run at home.

16. The words are Muddy Ruel's. John P. Carmichael, *My Greatest Day in Baseball* (New York: Grossett & Dunlap, 1963; originally published, New York: A. S. Barnes, 1945), 181.

17. Mogridge (16) and Zachary (15) won 31 games between them. Only Cleveland's two southpaws, Joe Shaute (20) and Sherry Smith (12), won more, and they trailed the Washington pair in joint earned run average.

18. The words are Calvin Griffith's, explaining his father's point of view. Bob Cairns, *Penmen: Baseball's Greatest Bullpen Stories Told by the Men Who Brought the Game Relief* (New York: St. Martin's, 1992), 18.

19. It is important to recall that the notion of a "save" had not been formally constructed in 1924. These figures are post facto reconstructions, and I draw the calculations from *Total Baseball*. Because baseball was not so strategically specialized then as now, neither Marberry nor Russell was used exclusively in save situations. Marberry understood that because baseball had not yet translated the basic concept of a "save" into a discrete statistic, the relief pitcher was at a disadvantage in arguing for his worth. "If the relief pitcher," he later complained, "holds the opposing club in check, he gets no credit. The pitcher who preceded him and couldn't stand the pace wins the game." John Thorn, *The Relief Pitcher: Baseball's New Hero* (New York: E. P. Dutton, 1979), 6.

20. This information also comes from Thorn's *Relief Pitcher* (50–52), a truly wonderful book.

21. Ibid., 52.

22. F. C. Lane, "Fred Marberry, King of Relief Hurlers" *Baseball Magazine*, 34 (December 1924): 304.

23. It would not be exceeded until 1933, when another pennant-winning Washington team recorded 26.

24. Lane, "If I Were Only Young," 532.

25. Marberry relieved Johnson 13 times during the year, helping to preserve 5 of his victories. Johnson finished only 53 percent of the games he started in 1924, the lowest percentage of his career to that point.

26. Grimes pitched 310⅔ innings; Vance pitched 308⅓. By way of contrast, Walter Johnson, sometimes asked to go only 7 or so innings in a start, pitched a somewhat less demanding 277⅔ innings. Since 1924 it has been unusual for National League teammates to chalk up 300+–inning seasons. Bucky Walters and Paul Derringer did it for Cincinnati's championship team in 1939, Don Drysdale and Sandy Koufax did it for Los Angeles' championship teams in 1963 and 1965, and in 1969 Claude Osteen and Bill Singer became the last duo of teammates to reach this level of work, hurling for a mediocre Los Angeles team. (It is not a coincidence that three of those four seasons occurred in the low-offense interlude of 1963 to 1969.) The last season in which any pitcher exceeded 300 innings was 1980, when Steve Carlton slipped past that mark.

27. Another way of making the same point is to note that the Dodgers played .636 ball against non–New York City teams, while the Giants played only .603 ball against the same six clubs.

28. Playing in the era of Harry Heilmann, Al Simmons, and George Sisler, Babe Ruth—despite a lifetime batting average of .342—won only this one batting championship. In May 1924, Ruth had predicted that "a mark of about .375" would suffice to lead the league. As was so often the case when it came to batting, Ruth was an authority. *New York Times*, May 1, 1924.

29. Dominant as he was, Ruth never won a triple crown (i.e., leading the league in

batting average, home runs, and runs batted in). By driving in 8 more runs than the Babe in 1924, Goose Goslin blocked him out in his only batting championship year.

30. McGraw, *My Thirty Years*, 184.

31. Honig, *Baseball America*, 145.

32. F. C. Lane, "The Man Who Might Rival 'Babe' Ruth," *Baseball Magazine* 33 (September 1924): 435–37+. The view was not entirely aberrational. In early 1925, Carl Mays, who had pitched in the National League in 1924 after a career in the American League, stated that "Rogers Hornsby, in my own opinion, is the greatest hitter in a baseball uniform today." Mays, "Is Hornsby Baseball's Greatest Hitter?" *Baseball Magazine* 34 (February 1925): 392. After the 1924 season, Hornsby's salary was raised to $22,500, making him the second-highest paid player (behind Ruth's $52,000) in the game.

33. The reader should note that this remark is disputable. Napoleon Lajoie's official average for 1901, the American League's first year as a major league, is .422, but baseball historians believe the recorders of the time erred, and *Total Baseball* gives Lajoie an average of .426. Hugh Duffy, Tip O'Neill, Ross Barnes, and Willie Keeler had all equaled or exceeded .424 in the nineteenth century. It is certain that no one has hit higher than .424 between 1924 and the current day.

34. Hornsby's four-year average was also .402. Ty Cobb had managed that four-year pace from 1910 through 1913, but only Hornsby has a *five*-year average that exceeds .400.

35. Richie Ashburn in 1958, Carl Yastrzemski in 1963, and Lennie Dykstra in 1993.

36. William Curran, *Big Sticks: The Batting Revolution of the Twenties* (New York: William Morrow, 1990), 15.

37. The words are taken from the American League's explanation. *Total Baseball*, 193. The first National League award was made in 1924; the American League award was inaugurated in 1922. It is a sign of the times that batters won these league awards on every other occasion they were conferred in the 1920s. Johnson had won a still-earlier version of the MVP title, receiving the Chalmers Award in 1913. It should be noted that Vance, in edging out Hornsby by three votes, was the beneficiary of the inconceivable decision of one sportswriter, Jack Ryder of the *Cincinnati Enquirer*, to ignore the Cardinal completely in ranking his ten candidates. Since Vance was thirty-three when the season began and Johnson thirty-six, these two provide the highest average age of any pair of most valuable player designees.

38. Triple crowns are unusual. The most any pitcher has achieved in a career is three, a mark reached by both Johnson and Grover Cleveland Alexander. Coincident triple crowns are very unusual. Christy Mathewson and Rube Waddell matched crowns in 1905 (though the earned run average was not yet an official statistic), and Johnson and Hippo Vaughn duplicated the feat in 1918. The 1924 season marks the last time such twin mastery occurred.

39. It is a mark of Marberry's importance to Johnson that the 270⅔ innings he

pitched in 1924 were fewer than he had been credited with in any of the earlier seasons in which he had won 20 or more games. The presence of Marberry allowed Johnson to baby his arm.

40. Because the game did not last nine innings, it is not officially recognized as a no-hitter.

41. That is to say, 13 consecutive decisions were victories. In fact, he started 18 games—and thus had 5 no-decisions—during that 13-victory streak.

42. In recognition of Johnson's stature and contribution to Washington's success, Clark Griffith raised his salary from $12,000 to $20,000 for 1925.

43. Walter Johnson in 1913, Bobby Shantz in 1952, Steve Carlton in 1972, Ron Guidrey in 1978, Roger Clemens in 1986, and Pedro Martinez in 1999.

44. Neal McCabe and Constance McCabe, *Baseball's Golden Age: The Photographs of Charles M. Conlin* (New York: Harry N. Abrams, 1993), 58.

45. The only game that Cobb missed was the final game of the season—a late makeup game that he chose not even to attend.

46. The words, very representative, are Doc Cramer's. Cramer played outfield for four American League teams over a twenty-year career. Donald Honig, *Baseball When the Grass Was Real: Baseball from the Twenties to the Forties Told by the Men Who Played It* (Lincoln: University of Nebraska Press, 1993; reprint ed., New York: Coward, McCann, and Geoghegan, 1975), 196. With their work in 1924, both Tris Speaker and Eddie Collins moved to within about 50 base hits of a 3,000 career total. Only Cap Anson, Ty Cobb, Nap Lajoie, and Honus Wagner had previously reached it. (Anson's claim was undisputed in 1924; not all latter-day historians agree, however.)

47. F. C. Lane, "Growing Better with Age," *Baseball Magazine* 34 (March 1925): 436.

48. "Burleigh Grimes, A Great Pitcher with a Weak Club," *ibid.*, 32 (May 1924): 540.

49. *New York Times*, March 20, 1924. An average of .305 is, of course, creditable, but a contextual setting diminishes its luster: The American League boasted 26 regular batters who hit .300 or more in 1924.

50. James T. Farrell, *My Baseball Diary* (New York: A. S. Barnes, 1957), 275.

51. Frederick G. Lieb discussed the rookies of 1924 in "Baseball's Star Rookies," *Baseball Magazine* 33 (August 1924): 393–95+.

52. "He was as cocky as a little bantam rooster after that," Jimmy Cooney reported. Joseph Lawler, "Jimmy Cooney in Two Unaided Triple Plays," *Baseball Research Journal* 13 (1984): 39.

Chapter 10. The World Series

1. Even before August had ended, more than five thousand applications for Series tickets had arrived at the Nationals' business office. The 1924 World Series was the first "Dixie" World Series, and a number of southerners traveled hundreds of miles to attend a game in the nation's capital. It was a sign of regional affec-

tion that, when the Nationals came out for fielding practice before the final game played in Washington, the band played "Dixie." On Griffith Stadium, see David Gough, "Griffith Stadium," *National Pastime* 16 (1996): 46–50.

2. Connolly and Dinneen had been present at the first modern World Series in 1903, Connolly as an umpire and Dinneen as a player.

3. On Phillips, see Robert Hardy, "The Megaphone Man," *National Pastime* 17 (1997): 131–32.

4. *Washington Post*, September 3, 1924.

5. Ibid., October 3, 1924, section 2.

6. When right-handed pitchers had started against the Giants, the New Yorkers had recorded a winning percentage of .615. When lefties had started, that percentage had dropped to .583.

7. Nick Altrock, the pitching coach who had hurled 2 innings in the final game of the season, was also a veteran of World Series play, having won a game for the "hitless wonder" White Sox in 1906.

8. The Nationals were established as 11:10 favorites on the eve of the Series. Professional gamblers reckoned that the injuries to Groh and Frisch and the demoralization consequent upon the bribery scandal more than counterbalanced the power and experience of the Giants.

9. The special ground rules entailed by the existence of the temporary seats specified that balls that bounced into these seats would be counted as home runs.

10. Art Nehf had much to be pleased about in this game, but he was proudest of all that he had reached Walter Johnson for 3 hits.

11. Johnson had thrown 165 pitches during the game, an astonishingly high number by current standards.

12. William Klem and William J. Slocum, "Umpire Bill Klem's Own Story," *Collier's* 127 (April 14, 1951); 69. The most extraordinary aspect of the matter is that Commissioner Landis publicly declared his disagreement with Klem on the decision: "I have my doubts about his ruling when he called Goslin out at first." *Washington Post*, October 6, 1924, section 2. If Landis felt free to criticize the call of an umpire on an exceedingly close play, it is easy to see why neither Klem nor Ban Johnson—the great upholder of umpires—cared for the authoritarian commissioner.

13. *New York Times*, October 5, 1924.

14. Kavanaugh, *Walter Johnson*, 188.

15. As a mark of how changes in the seating arrangements affected the games, the reader will note that each of the 4 home runs hit thus far landed in a temporary area. Not a single one would have been a home run under ordinary conditions. Since the Nationals were now beneficiaries, rather than victims, of the changed arrangements, Harris could not resist noting that "what's sauce for the goose is sauce for the gander." *Washington Post*, October 6, 1924, section 1.

16. Fred Lieb explained his thinking in "Scoring Plays That Create a World's Champion," *Baseball Magazine* 34 (December 1924): 302.

17. The official announcer, megaphone in hand, even provided an element of humor

throughout the game, not knowing what to do with Ossie Bluege's name. Sometimes it was "Bluejay," sometimes "Blooj," and sometimes a swallowed gulp. John J. Ward, "A World's Champion Who Belongs," *Baseball Magazine* 34 (January 1925): 366.

18. Honig, *Man in the Dugout*, 148.

19. Many of the game's greatest names attended the Series in 1924, among them current heroes such as Ty Cobb, Rogers Hornsby, and George Sisler, and celebrated retirees like Christy Mathewson and Jesse Burkett.

20. *New York Times*, October 8, 1924.

21. *Washington Post*, October 8, 1924, section 1.

22. Harris's 8 assists in the game tied a World Series mark for second basemen.

23. *Time* 4 (October 20, 1924): 24.

24. John McGraw later criticized his third base coach, Hughie Jennings, for waving Meusel home in this situation. I don't know where the ball was when Jennings made his decision, but he knew that Rice and Harris both had strong, quick arms.

25. *Washington Post*, October 8, 1924.

26. *New York Times*, October 8, 1924.

27. Ibid.

28. Having tied the World Series record for assists by a second baseman (8) the previous day, Bucky Harris set a World Series record (again, 8) for putouts in the game on October 8. It was a busy Series for the Washington manager.

29. Many years later, Lindstrom, reflecting on this day, said—and I have trouble believing him—"I was just dumb enough not to be aware of [Johnson's] greatness. To me he was just another pitcher." Glenn Dickey, *The History of the World Series since 1903* (New York: Stein Day, 1984), 84.

30. *New York Times*, October 9, 1924.

31. Carmichael, *My Greatest Day in Baseball*, 119.

32. *New York Times*, October 9, 1924.

33. *Washington Post*, October 9, 1924.

34. *New York Times*, October 10, 1924. I include the story because it's a good one and occurs twice in the *Times*. But the writer for the *Washington Post* reported on October 10, 1924, that Peckinpaugh was assisted from the field to roaring applause from an appreciative throng of spectators. Both stories can't be right.

35. The standard story of Harris's plan is well-known. For the Giants' knowledge of it, see Honig, *Man in Dugout*, 148. For the Nationals' response to the Giants' knowledge, see *Sporting News*, November 6, 1924.

36. The game was sold out, but since people had only two days' notice about where the seventh game would be played, many of the ticket purchasers—that is, the would-be scalpers—couldn't find secondary buyers for their admission passes.

37. *Washington Post*, October 10, 1924, section 2.

38. Henry W. Thomas, *Walter Johnson: Baseball's Big Train* (Washington, D.C.: Phenom Press, 1995), 239.

39. Prior to the game, Ruel had received a telegram of advice from his boyhood

coach John Sheridan, now the eminent St. Louis sportswriter. The advice was puerile—"probably swinging too late; pick only good ones"—but appreciated. Yet Sheridan also added, presciently, "two hits today" and "you will win today's game." *Sporting News*, October 23, 1924.

40. The description is Heinie Groh's. If he had not injured his knee late in the season, Groh would have been playing third base for the Giants. Ritter, *Glory*, 304.

41. Carmichael, *My Greatest Day in Baseball*, 119.

42. The 1924 season was the first in Johnson's career in which he had not made a single relief appearance. In earlier years he had sometimes relieved as frequently as 13 times in a season.

43. "Washington's Big Day in Baseball," *Literary Digest* 83 (October 25, 1924): 58.

44. Kelly swung at all three offerings. It's worth quoting from Grantland Rice's wonderful account of Johnson's feat. The Big Train was "the Johnson of a decade ago—blinding, baffling speed that . . . closed down on the rally with the snap of death." Ibid., 54. Heywood Broun was similarly moved. "When I want to reassure myself that the soul of man is too staunch to die, I will remember that Walter Johnson struck out George Kelly with one out and a runner on third base." Quoted in Thomas, *Johnson*, 250. Ossie Bluege said that when in trouble, Johnson would put his glove down, tighten his belt, pick bits of dirt from around the mound, slowly drop them, and then resume his pitching task. Honig, *Man in Dugout*, 149.

45. McGraw could be fairly confident that Harris would not bat for Miller, since Peckinpaugh was injured and Taylor had already been removed from the game.

46. In his 1913 book, McGraw had written: "With men on first and third, with one out, I prefer to try to retire the side on a double play unless the batter is very fast." *How to Play*, 150.

47. All 5 of the strikeouts Johnson recorded in his relief stint were of future Hall of Famers—Frisch, Jackson, Kelly (2), and Wilson.

48. The words are Muddy Ruel's, relating a conversation he had with Dinneen to Ty Cobb. Ruel added: "I was having trouble following Walter's speed, myself." Cobb, *My Life in Baseball*, 268.

49. Lowell Reidenbaugh, *The Sporting News Selects Baseball's Fifty Greatest Games* (St. Louis: Sporting News Publishing Company, 1986), 105.

50. The cautionary tale of Fred Merkle was in everyone's mind: By failing to touch second when a winning run run apparently scored in 1908, he cost the Giants the game and the pennant. McNeely ran out his hit to first, and, by the logic that gave Peckinpaugh a double in the second game, was credited with a double. More relevantly, Johnson tagged second base before leaving the field.

51. *Washington Post*, October 12, 1924.

52. William Taafe, "Gone . . . and Forgotten?" *Sports Illustrated* 67 (October 26, 1987): 129.

53. Had the play occurred today, we could count on televised instant replays to give us ample opportunity to analyze the character of McNeely's hit. But all we have are the accounts of spectators who had only a fraction of a second to take in the

play. Not surprisingly, their tales are discrepant. That the ball took an errant hop can be taken as established; McNeely himself spoke of the "lucky bounce" that turned an ordinary ground ball into a Series-winning hit. But whereas most accounts say that it leaped over Lindstrom's head (a "humpback grounder" was one term used), a few have him diving for it, and one describes the blow as a line drive between the third baseman and the foul line. *New York Times*, October 12, 1924; *Washington Post*, October 11, 1924, and October 13, 1924.

54. "It wasn't Freddie's fault," Heinie Groh said. "It could have happened to anybody." Ritter, *Glory*, 305.

55. "Washington's Big Day," 56.

56. *Washington Post*, October 11, 1924.

57. Graham, *McGraw of the Giants*, 188.

58. Harrison covered the World Series for *The New York Times*. The quotation is taken from his piece on the seventh game, which was reprinted in Charles Einstein, ed., *The Third Fireside Book of Baseball* (New York: Simon & Schuster, 1968), 195–98. A remembrance of the game by the great Shirley Povich appeared in the *Washington Post* on October 22, 1994. It is reprinted in *Grandstand Baseball Annual 1998*: 62–66.

59. Noel Hynd, "When the Yankees Beat the Giants in the 1923 World Series, A New Era Begins," *Sports Illustrated* 65 (November 3, 1986): 114ff.

60. *New York Times*, October 11, 1924.

61. John Durant, *Highlights of the World Series* (New York: Hastings, 1963), 66. It was reported that, in fact, McGraw had been more disappointed after his 1923 loss to the Yankees. Moreover, he also said in the aftermath of the loss in Washington, "The Senators' victory seems to have pleased the big majority of persons, and that is something, after all." *New York Times*, October 12, 1924. Bucky Harris did not object to people saying that the Nationals had been lucky. He could afford to be generous-spirited: He had won.

62. *New York Times*, October 10, 1924.

63. Harvey Frommer, *Baseball's Greatest Managers* (New York: Franklin Watts, 1985), 82.

64. President Coolidge attended the first, sixth, and seventh games. He listened to the second on his yacht. Reports suggested that his wife was the keener baseball fan of the two.

65. *Reach's Official Baseball Guide, 1925*, 208.

66. *Washington Post*, October 11, 1924.

67. The losers' checks came to $3,820 each.

68. As a hint of the cloud under which the Series began, it is useful to note that, in the first 2 games, National fans shouted at Giant outfielders, "We will give you $500 if you drop it." For the final 2 games, there are no reports of such razzing.

69. Lieb, *Baseball as I Have Known It*, 121.

BIBLIOGRAPHY

General Books

Adair, Robert Kemp. *The Physics of Baseball.* New York: Harper & Row, 1990.

Alexander, Charles. *Our Game: An American Baseball History.* New York: Henry Holt, 1991.

Allen, Lee. *The American League Story.* Revised ed. New York: Hill & Wang, 1965.

———. *The Giants and the Dodgers: The Fabulous Story of Baseball's Fiercest Feud.* New York: G. P. Putnam's Sons, 1964.

———. *The National League Story.* Revised ed. New York: Hill & Wang, 1961.

———. *The World Series: The Story of Baseball's Annual Championship.* New York: G. P. Putnam's Sons, 1969.

Alvarez, Mark, ed. *The Perfect Game.* Dallas: Tatloy Publishing Company, 1993.

Anderson, David W. *More Than Merkle: A History of the Best and Most Exciting Baseball Season in Human History.* Lincoln: University of Nebraska Press, 2000.

Andreano, Ralph. *No Joy in Mudville: The Dilemma of Major League Baseball.* Cambridge, Mass.: Schenkman, 1965.

Asinof, Eliot. *Eight Men Out.* New York: Holt, Rinehart, and Winston, 1963.

Blake, Mike. *Baseball Chronicles: An Oral History of Baseball through the Decades.* Cincinnati: Betterway Books, 1994.

Burk, Robert F. *Much More Than a Game: Players, Owners, and American Baseball since 1921.* Chapel Hill: University of North Carolina Press, 2001.

———. *Never Just a Game: Players, Owners and American Baseball to 1920.* Chapel Hill: University of North Carolina Press, 1994.

Burnett, W. R. *The Roar of the Crowd: Conversations with an Ex-Big-Leaguer.* New York: Clarkson N. Potter, 1964.

Cairns, Bob. *Penmen: Baseball's Greatest Bullpen Stories Told by the Men Who Brought the Game Relief.* New York: St. Martin's, 1992.

Carmichael, John P. *My Greatest Day in Baseball.* New York: Grossett & Dunlap, 1963. Originally published, New York: A. S. Barnes, 1945.

Coffin, Tristram Potter. *The Old Ball Game: Baseball in Folklore and Fiction.* New York: Herder and Herder, 1971.

Cohen, Richard M., and Neft, David S. *The World Series: Complete Play-by-Play of Every Game, 1903–1989, Compiled by the Authors of "The Sports Encyclopedia: Baseball."* New York: St. Martin's, 1990.

Connor, Anthony J. *Baseball for the Love of It: Hall of Famers Tell It Like It Was*. New York: Macmillan, 1982.

Cox, James A. *The Lively Ball: Baseball in the Roaring Twenties*. Alexandria, Va.: Redefinition, 1989.

Crepeau, Richard. *Baseball: America's Diamond Mind, 1919–1941*. Orlando: University Presses of Florida, 1980.

Curran, William. *Big Sticks: The Batting Revolution of the Twenties*. New York: William Morrow, 1990.

Daley, Arthur. *Times at Bat: A Half-Century of Baseball*. New York: Random House, 1950.

Danzig, Allison, and Joe Reichler. *The History of Baseball: Its Great Players, Teams, and Managers*. Englewood Cliffs, N.J.: Prentice-Hall, 1959.

Davenport, John W. *Baseball's Pennant Races: A Graphic View*. Madison, Wis.: First Impressions, 1981.

Devaney, John, and Burt Goldblatt. *The World Series: A Complete Pictorial History*. Chicago: Rand McNally, 1972.

Dickey, Glenn. *The Great No-Hitters*. Radnor, Pa.: Chilton, 1976.

———. *The History of American League Baseball since 1901*. New York: Stein & Day, 1980.

———. *The History of the World Series since 1903*. New York: Stein & Day, 1984.

Durant, John. *Highlights of the World Series*. New York: Hastings, 1963.

Durso, Joseph. *Baseball and the American Dream*. St. Louis: Sporting News Publishing Company, 1986.

Einstein, Charles, ed. *The Third Fireside Book of Baseball*. New York: Simon & Schuster, 1968.

Evers, John, and Hugh Fullerton. *Touching Second: The Science of Baseball*. Chicago: Reilly and Britton, 1910.

Falkner, David. *The Short Season: The Hard Work and High Times of Baseball in the Spring*. New York: Times Books, 1986.

Fleming, G. H. *Murderer's Row*. New York: William Morrow, 1985.

Frommer, Harvey. *Baseball's Greatest Managers*. New York: Franklin Watts, 1985.

Gerlach, Larry R. *The Men in Blue: Conversations with Umpires*. New York: Viking Press, 1980.

Gershman, Michael. *Diamonds: The Evolution of the Ballpark*. Boston: Houghton Mifflin, 1993.

Gies, Joseph, and Robert H. Shoemaker. *Stars of the Series: A Complete History of the World Series*. New York: Crowell, 1964.

Gutman, Dan. *Baseball Babylon: From the Black Sox to Pete Rose, the Real Stories behind the Scandals That Rocked the Game*. New York: Penguin, 1992.

———. *It Ain't Cheatin' If You Don't Get Caught*. New York: Penguin, 1990.

Honig, Donald. *Baseball America: The Heroes of the Game and the Times of Their Glory*. New York: Macmillan, 1985.

———. *Baseball When the Grass Was Real: Baseball from the Twenties to the Forties*

Bibliography

Told by the Men Who Played It. Lincoln: University of Nebraska Press, 1993. Reprint ed., New York: Coward, McCann, and Geoghegan, 1975.

———. *The Man in the Dugout: Fifteen Big League Managers Speak Their Minds.* Chicago: Follett Publishing Company, 1977.

———. *The National League.* New York: Crown, 1987.

———. *October Heroes: Great World Series Games Remembered by the Men Who Played Them.* New York: Simon & Schuster, 1979.

James, Bill. *The Politics of Glory: How Baseball's Hall of Fame REALLY Works.* New York: Macmillan, 1994.

Jennings, Kenneth M. *Balls and Strikes: The Money Game in Professional Baseball.* New York: Praeger, 1990.

Kahn, James M. *The Umpire Story.* New York: G. P. Putnam's Sons, 1953.

Kaiser, David. *Epic Season: The 1948 American League Pennant Race.* Amherst: University of Massachusetts Press, 1998.

Katz, Lawrence S. *Baseball in 1934: The Watershed Season of the National Pastime.* Jefferson, N.C.: McFarland, 1995.

Kerrane, Kevin. *Dollar Sign on the Muscle: The World of Baseball Scouting.* New York: Beaufort Books, 1984.

Koppett, Leonard. *The New Thinking Fan's Guide to Baseball.* New York: Simon & Schuster, 1991.

Lowenfish, Lee, and Tony Lupien. *The Imperfect Diamond: The Story of Baseball's Reserve System and the Men Who Fought to Change It.* New York: Stein & Day, 1980.

Lowry, Philip J. *Green Cathedrals.* Cooperstown, N.Y.: Society for American Baseball Research, 1986.

McCabe, Neal, and Constance McCabe. *Baseball's Golden Age: The Photographs of Charles M. Conlin.* New York: Harry N. Abrams, 1993.

McGraw, John. *How to Play Baseball.* New York: J. J. Little and Ives, 1913.

Meany, Tom. *Baseball's Greatest Teams.* New York: A. S. Barnes, 1949.

Mosedale, John. *The Greatest of All: The 1927 New York Yankees.* New York: Dial Press, 1974.

Oakley, J. Ronald. *Baseball's Last Golden Age, 1946–1960: The National Pastime in a Time of Glory and Change.* Jefferson, N.C.: McFarland, 1994.

Obojski, Robert. *Bush League: A History of Minor League Baseball.* New York: Macmillan, 1975.

Quigley, Martin. *The Crooked Pitch.* Chapel Hill, N.C.: Algonquin, 1984.

Rader, Benjamin G. *Baseball: A History of America's Game.* Chicago: University of Illinois Press, 1992.

Reach's Official Baseball Guide. Philadelphia: A. G. Reach, 1924, 1925.

Reichler, Joseph L., ed. *The World Series: A 75th Anniversary.* New York: Simon & Schuster, 1978.

Reichler, Joseph, and Ben Olan. *Baseball's Unforgettable Games.* New York: Ronald Press, 1960.

Bibliography

Reidenbaugh, Lowell. *The Sporting News Selects Baseball's Fifty Greatest Games.* St. Louis: Sporting News Publishing Company, 1986.

Reisler, Jim. *Black Writers/Black Baseball: An Anthology of Articles from Black Sportswriters Who Covered the Negro Leagues.* Jefferson, N.C.: McFarland, 1994.

Rickey, Branch, and Robert Riger. *The American Diamond: A Documentary of the Game.* New York: Simon & Schuster, 1965.

Riess, Steven. *Touching Base: Professional Baseball and American Culture in the Progressive Era.* Westport, Conn.: Greenwood Press, 1980.

Ritter, Lawrence S. *The Glory of Their Times: The Story of the Early Days of Baseball Told by the Men Who Played It.* New enlarged edition. New York: William Morrow, 1984. Originally published, New York: Macmillan, 1966.

Ritter, Lawrence, and Donald Honig. *The Image of Their Greatness.* New York: Crown Publishers, 1979.

Scully, Gerald W. *The Business of Major League Baseball.* Chicago: University of Chicago Press, 1989.

Seymour, Harold. *Baseball: The Golden Age.* New York: Oxford University Press, 1971.

Smith, Curt. *Voices of the Game: The First Full-Scale Overview of Baseball Broadcasting, 1921 to the Present.* South Bend, Ind.: Diamond Communications, 1987.

Smith, Ira L. *Baseball's Famous First Basemen.* New York: A. S. Barnes, 1956.

Smith, Robert. *Baseball.* Revised ed. New York: Simon & Schuster, 1970.

―――. *World Series: The Games and the Players.* Garden City, N.Y.: Doubleday, 1967.

Sommers, Paul M., ed. *Diamonds Are Forever: The Business of Baseball.* Washington, D.C.: Brookings Institution, 1992.

Sowell, Mike. *The Pitch That Killed.* New York: Collier Books, 1991.

Spalding's Official Base Ball Guide. New York: American Sports Publishing Company, 1924, 1925.

Starr, Bill. *Clearing the Bases: Baseball Then and Now.* New York: Michael Kesend, 1989.

Sullivan, Neil J. *The Minors: The Struggles and the Triumphs of Baseball's Poor Relation from 1876 to the Present.* New York: St. Martin's, 1990.

Thorn, John. *The Relief Pitcher: Baseball's New Hero.* New York: E. P. Dutton, 1979.

Thorn, John, and John B. Holway. *The Pitcher.* New York: Prentice-Hall, 1987.

Turner, Frederick. *When the Boys Came Back: Baseball and 1946.* New York: Henry Holt, 1996.

United States, House of Representatives. *Organized Baseball: Report of the Subcommittee on the Study of Monopoly Power of the Committee on the Judiciary.* House Report 2002, 82d Congress, 2d session. Washington, D.C.: Government Printing Office, 1952.

Voigt, David Quentin. *American Baseball.* Vol. 2: *From the Commissioners to Continental Expansion.* University Park: Pennsylvania State University Press, 1983.

Ward, Geoffrey C., and Ken Burns. *Baseball: 25 Great Moments.* New York: Knopf, 1994.

White, G. Edward. *Creating the National Pastime: Baseball Transforms Itself, 1903– 1953*. Princeton: Princeton University Press, 1996.

Williams, Joe. *The Joe Williams Baseball Reader*. Edited by Peter Williams. Chapel Hill, N.C.: Algonquin Books, 1989.

Woodward, Stanley. *Sports Page*. New York: Simon & Schuster, 1949.

Zinsser, William Knowlton. *Spring Training*. New York: Harper & Row, 1989.

Zoss, Joel, and John Bowman. *Diamonds in the Rough: The Untold History of Baseball*. New York: Macmillan, 1989.

Team Histories

Ahrens, Art, and Eddie Gold. *The Cubs: The Complete Record of Chicago Cubs Baseball*. New York: Collier Books, 1986.

Allen, Lee. *The Cincinnati Reds*. New York: G. P. Putnam's Sons, 1948.

Anderson, Dave, Harold Rosenthal, et al. *The Yankees: The Four Fabulous Eras of Baseball's Most Famous Team*. New York: Random House, 1979.

Bealle, Morris A. *The Washington Senators: An 87-Year History of the World's Oldest Baseball Club and Most Incurable Fandom*. Washington, D.C.: Columbia Publishing Company, 1947.

Berry, Henry, and Harold Berry. *Boston Red Sox: The Complete Record of Red Sox Baseball*. New York: Collier Books, 1984.

Berry, John. *Baseball's Great Teams: Boston Red Sox*. New York: Macmillan, 1975.

Brown, Warren. *The Chicago Cubs*. New York: G. P. Putnam's Sons, 1946.

———. *The Chicago White Sox*. New York: G. P. Putnam's Sons, 1952.

Cohen, Stanley. *Dodgers! The First Hundred Years*. New York: Birch Lane Press, 1990.

Durant, John. *The Dodgers: An Illustrated History of Those Unpredictable Bums*. New York: Hastings, 1948.

Enright, Jim. *Baseball's Great Teams: Chicago Cubs*. New York: Macmillan, 1975.

Falls, Joe. *Baseball's Great Teams: Detroit Tigers*. New York: Macmillan, 1975.

Fitzgerald, Ed, ed. *The Story of the Brooklyn Dodgers*. New York: Bantam, 1948.

Graham, Frank. *The New York Giants: An Informal History*. New York: G. P. Putnam's Sons, 1952.

———. *The New York Yankees: An Informal History*. New York: G. P. Putnam's Sons, 1943.

Holmes, Tommy. *Baseball's Great Teams: The Dodgers*. New York: Macmillan, 1975.

Honig, Donald. *The Boston Red Sox: An Illustrated History*. New York: Prentice-Hall, 1990.

Hynd, Noel. *The Giants of the Polo Grounds: The Glorious Times of Baseball's New York Giants*. New York: Doubleday, 1988.

Kaese, Harold. *The Boston Braves*. New York: G. P. Putnam's Sons, 1948.

Lewis, Franklin. *The Cleveland Indians*. New York: G. P. Putnam's Sons, 1949.

Lieb, Frederick G. *The Boston Red Sox*. New York: G. P. Putnam's Sons, 1946.

———. *The Detroit Tigers*. New York: G. P. Putnam's Sons, 1946.

————. *The Pittsburgh Pirates*. New York: G. P. Putnam's Sons, 1948.

————. *The St. Louis Cardinals: The Story of a Great Baseball Club*. New York: G. P. Putnam's Sons, 1944.

Lieb, Frederick G., and Stan Baumgartner. *The Philadelphia Phillies*. New York: G. P. Putnam's Sons, 1953.

Lindberg, Richard. *Who's on Third? The Chicago White Sox Story*. South Bend, Ind.: Icarus Press, 1983.

Povich, Shirley. *The Washington Senators*. New York: G. P. Putnam's Sons, 1954.

Smizik, Bob. *The Pittsburgh Pirates: An Illustrated History*. New York: Walker, 1990.

Sullivan, George. *The Picture History of the Boston Red Sox*. Indianapolis: Bobbs-Merrill, 1979.

Sullivan, George, and David Cataneo. *Detroit Tigers: The Complete Record of Detroit Tiger Baseball*. New York: Collier Books, 1985.

Sullivan, George, and John Powers. *Yankees: An Illustrated History*. Englewood Cliffs, N.J.: Prentice-Hall, 1982.

Tiemann, Robert L. *Cardinal Classics: Outstanding Games from Each of the St. Louis Baseball Club's 100 Seasons*. St. Louis: Baseball Histories, 1982.

Tullius, John. *I'd Rather Be a Yankee: An Oral History of America's Most Loved and Hated Baseball Team*. New York: Macmillan, 1986.

Autobiographies, Biographies, Memoirs, Reminiscences

Alexander, Charles C. *John McGraw*. New York: Viking Press, 1988.

————. *Rogers Hornsby: A Biography*. New York: Henry Holt, 1995.

————. *Ty Cobb: Baseball's Fierce Immortal*. New York: Oxford University Press, 1984.

Allen, Maury. *You Could Look It Up: The Life of Casey Stengel*. New York: Times Books, 1979.

Barrow, Edward Grant, with James M. Kahn. *My Fifty Years in Baseball*. New York: Coward-McCann, 1951.

Cobb, Tyrus Raymond, and Al Stump. *My Life in Baseball: The True Record*. Lincoln: University of Nebraska Press, 1993. Originally published, New York: Doubleday, 1961.

Cochrane, Mickey. *Baseball: The Fan's Game*. Cleveland: Society for American Baseball Research, 1992. Originally published, New York: Funk and Wagnalls, 1939.

Corum, Bill. *Off and Running*. New York: Henry Holt, 1959.

Creamer, Robert W. *Babe: The Legend Comes to Life*. New York: Simon & Schuster, 1974.

————. *Stengel: His Life and Times*. New York: Simon & Schuster, 1984.

Dawidoff, Nicholas. *The Catcher Was a Spy: The Mysterious Life of Moe Berg*. New York: Pantheon Books, 1994.

Durso, Joseph. *Casey and Mr. McGraw*. St. Louis: Sporting News Publishing Company, 1989.

————. *The Days of Mr. McGraw*. Englewood Cliffs, N.J.: Prentice-Hall, 1969.

Bibliography

Einstein, Charles, ed. *The Third Fireside Book of Baseball*. New York: Simon & Schuster, 1968.

Farrell, James T. *My Baseball Diary*. New York: A. S. Barnes, 1957.

Fountain, Charles. *Sportswriter: The Life and Times of Grantland Rice*. New York: Oxford University Press, 1993.

Frick, Ford C. *Games, Asterisks, and People: Memoirs of a Lucky Fan*. New York: Crown, 1973.

Frommer, Harvey. *Shoeless Joe and Ragtime Baseball*. Dallas: Taylor Publishing Company, 1992.

Graham, Frank. *McGraw of the Giants: An Informal Biography*. New York: G. P. Putnam's Sons, 1944.

Hill, Carmen. *An Autobiography: The Battles of Bunker Hill, The Life and Times of Carmen P. Hill*. N.P.: Krause, 1985.

Hornsby, Rogers. *My Kind of Baseball*. Edited by J. Roy Stockton. New York: David McKay, 1953.

Hornsby, Rogers, and Bill Surface. *My War with Baseball*. New York: Coward-McCann, 1962.

Kavanaugh, Jack. *Ol' Pete: The Grover Cleveland Alexander Story*. South Bend, Ind.: Diamond Communications, 1996.

———. *Walter Johnson: A Life*. South Bend, Ind.: Diamond Communications, 1995.

Kavanaugh, Jack, and Norman Macht. *Uncle Robbie*. Cleveland: Society for American Baseball Research, 1999.

Lieb, Frederick. *Baseball as I Have Known It*. New York: Coward, McCann, and Geoghegan, 1977.

———. *Connie Mack: Grand Old Man of Baseball*. New York: G. P. Putnam's Sons, 1945.

Mack, Connie. *My 66 Years in the Big Leagues: The Great Story of America's National Game*. Philadelphia: John C. Winston, 1950.

Maranville, Walter. *Run, Rabbit, Run: The Hilarious and Mostly True Tales of Rabbit Maranville*. Introduction by Harold Seymour. Cleveland: Society for American Baseball Research, 1991.

McCallum, John. *The Tiger Wore Spikes: An Informal Biography of Ty Cobb*. New York: A. S. Barnes, 1956.

———. *Ty Cobb*. New York: Praeger, 1975.

McGraw, John. *My Thirty Years in Baseball*. New York: Arno Press, 1974. Originally published, New York: Boni and Liveright, 1923.

Murdock, Eugene. *Ban Johnson: Czar of Baseball*. Westport, Conn.: Greenwood Press, 1982.

Pietrusza, David. *Judge and Jury: The Life and Times of Judge Kenesaw Mountain Landis*. South Bend, Ind.: Diamond Communications, 1998.

Rice, Grantland. *The Tumult and the Shouting: My Life in Sport*. New York: A. S. Barnes, 1954.

Robinson, Ray. *Matty: An American Hero: Christy Mathewson of the New York Giants*. New York: Oxford University Press, 1993.

Schacht, Al. *Clowning through Baseball*. New York: A. S. Barnes, 1941.

Smelser, Marshall. *The Life That Ruth Built: A Biography*. New York: Quadrangle, 1975.

Sobol, Ken. *Babe Ruth and the American Dream*. New York: Random House, 1974.

Spink, J. G. Taylor. *Judge Landis and Twenty-Five Years of Baseball*. New York: Thomas Y. Crowell, 1947.

Thomas, Henry W. *Walter Johnson: Baseball's Big Train*. Washington, D.C.: Phenom Press, 1995.

Veeck, Bill, with Ed Linn. *The Hustler's Handbook*. New York: G. P. Putnam's Sons, 1965.

Williams, Peter. *When the Giants Were Giants: Bill Terry and the Golden Age of New York Baseball*. Chapel Hill, N.C.: Algonquin, 1994.

Zingg, Paul J. *Harry Hooper: An American Baseball Life*. Chicago: University of Illinois Press, 1993.

Articles

Ahrens, Arthur. "The Tragic Saga of Charlie Hollocher." *Baseball Research Journal* 15 (1986), 6–8.

Ammon, Larry. "The Clown Prince of Baseball." *Baseball Research Journal* 11 (1982): 119–27.

Anderson, David W. "Bonesetter Reese." *Baseball Research Journal* 30 (2001): 18–19.

"Baseball and the Crooks." *The Outlook* 138 (October 15, 1924): 235–36.

"Baseball Has Changed Some in Thirty Years, Says John J. McGraw." *Literary Digest* 61 (May 10, 1919): 96–101.

"Baseball's Grand Old Man." *Literary Digest* 73 (May 6, 1922): 62–65.

"Base-Stealing's Sensational Decline." *Literary Digest* 73 (April 29, 1922): 41–42.

Beall, Robert W. "A Sensible Way to Rate Fielders." *Baseball Magazine* 33 (June 1924): 305–6.

"Behind the Scenes in a Big League Clubhouse." *Baseball Magazine* 34 (April 1925): 504.

Bergen, Phil. "Wheat in the Chaff." *Baseball Research Journal* 14 (1985): 61–62.

"Bibb Falk, A New Outfield Star." *Baseball Magazine* 34 (March 1925): 439–40.

"Big Leaguers in Training." *Literary Digest* 44 (March 30, 1912): 654–57.

Bjarkman, Peter C. "First Hispanic Star? Dolf Luque, of Course." *Baseball Research Journal* 19 (1990): 28–32.

Blaisdell, Lowell. "Mystery and Tragedy: The O'Connell–Dolan Scandal." *Baseball Research Journal* 11 (1982): 44–49.

Blenko, Jim. "Nick Altrock: Washington's Coach and Clown." *National Pastime* 18 (1998): 73–77.

Bloodgood, Clifford. "Consistency in Baseball Records." *Baseball Magazine* 32 (March 1924): 460.

Boren, Steve. "The Bizarre Career of Rube Benton." *Baseball Research Journal* 12 (1983): 180–83.

Brecher, Biff, and Albey M. Reiner. "Teammates with the Most Combined Hits." *Baseball Research Journal* 23 (1994): 17–18.

Brown, William E., Jr. "Sunday Baseball Comes to Boston." *National Pastime* 14 (1994): 83–85.

Bulger, Bozeman. "The Baseball Business from the Inside." *Collier's* 69 (March 25, 1922): 13 ff.

"Burleigh Grimes, A Great Pitcher with a Weak Club." *Baseball Magazine* 32 (May 1924): 540.

Cardello, Joseph. "Dazzy Vance in 1930." *Baseball Research Journal* 25 (1966): 127–30.

"Christy Mathewson Picks an All-America Team for Collier's." *Collier's* 74 (October 11, 1924): 8–9 ff.

"Confessions of a Big League Club Trainer." *Baseball Magazine* 32 (February 1924): 415–16.

"Country Boys in the Big Leagues." *Literary Digest* 85 (April 18, 1925): 60–62.

Dacy, G. H. "Science Solves the Secrets of Baseballs." *St. Nicholas* 51 (April 1924): 609–11.

"Dead Shot 'Dazzy' Vance of the Brooklyn Club." *Baseball Magazine* 32 (January 1924): 361–62.

Deane, Bill. "The Best Fielders of the Century." *National Pastime* 2 (Fall 1982): 2–4.

Demaree, Al. "Grand-Stand Girls—Women and Baseball Don't Mix." *Collier's* 81 (June 2, 1928): 35–36.

"Doctored Baseballs in the Game." *Literary Digest* 78 (September 22, 1923): 64–69.

Driver, David. "Eppa Rixey." *National Pastime* 15 (1995): 85–87.

Dunlavy, Bruce. "Hitting Power and Good Bat Control, A Rare Combination." *Baseball Digest* (November 1993): 60–61.

Evans, Billy. "How a Baseball Is Made." *St. Nicholas* 47 (June 1920): 745–46.

Farmer, Ted. "Eppa Rixie, Virginia Squire." *Grandstand Baseball Annual 1996*: 57–60.

Fimrite, Ron. "His Own Biggest Fan." *Sports Illustrated* 79 (July 19, 1993): 76–80.

Foreman, Charles J. "The Season's Most Sensational Rookie." *Baseball Magazine* 33 (September 1924): 438+.

Fox, Edward Lyell. "South with the Ball Teams." *Outing* 60 (April 1912): 24–34.

———. "What Is Inside Baseball?" *Outing* 58 (July 1911): 488–97.

Fullerton, Hugh S. "Baseball—The Business and the Sport." *American Review of Reviews* 63 (April 1921): 417–20.

———. "How the Ball Players of the Big Leagues Live and Act When off the Diamond." *American Magazine* (July 1911), 321–31.

Gettelson, Leonard. "The Season of 1924 Finds Many Broken Records." *Baseball Magazine* 34 (April 1925): 509–10+.

Gough, David. "Griffith Stadium." *National Pastime* 16 (1996): 46–50.

Gould, James M. "How Rogers Hornsby Smashed All Modern Records." *Baseball Magazine* 34 (December 1924): 305–6.

————. "Will Rogers Hornsby Ever Hit .500?" *Baseball Magazine* 34 (March 1925): 456+.

Graber, Ralph. "Jack Bentley's Sad Tale: Victim of Circumstances." *Baseball Research Journal* 15 (1986): 23–25.

Guschov, Stephen D. "Baseball's Antitrust Exemption." *Baseball Research Journal* 23 (1994): 69–74.

Hailey, Gary D., and Douglas R. Pappas. "Baseball and the Law." In *Total Baseball*. Edited by John Thorn, Pete Palmer, and Michael Gershman. Fourth ed. New York: Viking, 1995, 600–7.

Hanna, W. B. "The Right-Handed Hitter Comes into His Own." *Baseball Magazine* 33 (October 1924): 495.

"Hans Wagner's Team of Baseball Immortals." *Literary Digest* 80 (January 26, 1924): 60–62.

Hardy, Robert. "The Megaphone Man." *National Pastime* 17 (1997): 131–32.

Hoefer, W. R. "The Return of the Player Manager." *Baseball Magazine* 32 (January 1924): 345–46.

Hoie, Bob. "The Farm System." In *Total Baseball*. Edited by John Thorn and Pete Palmer. Second ed., New York: Warner Books, 1991, 644–47.

————. "The Minor Leagues." In *Total Baseball*. Fourth ed., Edited by John Thorn, Pete Palmer, and Michael Gershman. New York: Viking, 1995, 532–46.

Hornsby, Rogers. "Why Good Pitchers Are Easy to Hit." *Baseball Magazine* 28 (April 1919): 335–36.

"How Baseball's Biggest Pitcher Reached the Top." *Literary Digest* 79 (November 10, 1923): 67–71.

"How News Is Flashed across the Nation." *Popular Mechanics* 42 (October 1924): 567–72.

"How Science Has Aided National Game." *Popular Mechanics* 41 (May 1924): 676–79.

"Humors and Tragedies of Baseball Training-Time in Dixie." *Literary Digest* 59 (April 9, 1921): 63–68.

Hynd, Noel. "When the Yankees Beat the Giants in the 1923 World Series, A New Era Begins." *Sports Illustrated* 65 (November 3, 1986): 114+.

"Is New York Getting Too Many Pennants?" *Literary Digest* 79 (October 13, 1923): 72–76.

Karst, Gene. "The Great Days, the Great Stars." *National Pastime* 3 (1983): 48–51.

Kaufman, Charles. "Bibb Falk: Can You Fill Shoeless Joe's Shoes?" *National Pastime* 19 (1999): 103–6.

Kavanaugh, Jack. "Brits in the Baseball Hall of Fame." *National Pastime* 12 (1992): 67–69.

Keetz, Frank. "The Board." *National Pastime* 12 (1992): 3–4.

Klem, William, and William J. Slocum. "Umpire Bill Klem's Own Story." *Collier's* 127 (March 31, 1951): 30–31+; (April 7, 1951): 30–31+; (April 14, 1951): 30–31+; (April 21, 1951): 30–31+.

Knight, Tom. "Burleigh Grimes: Not Just a Spitballer." *National Pastime* 16 (1996): 72–73.

Koefod, J. C. "The Greatest Pitcher of Modern Times." *Baseball Magazine* 32 (March 1924): 549–50+.

———. "The Star of the World Series." *Baseball Magazine* 33 (December 1924): 291–92.

Kruekeberg, Dan. "Take-Charge Cy." *National Pastime* 4 (Spring 1985): 7–11.

Lane, F. C. "Bill McKechnie, the Pirate Chief." *Baseball Magazine* 32 (April 1924): 487.

———. "Burleigh Grimes, A Pitcher Who Can Go the Distance." *Baseball Magazine* 33 (November 1924): 545+.

———. "Can a Pennant Be Won or Lost in Winter?" *Baseball Magazine* 32 (February 1924): 387–89+.

———. "The Changing Trends in Present-Day Baseball." *Baseball Magazine* 32 (May 1924): 535–36+; 33 (June 1924): 297–98+; (July 1924): 345–46+; (August 1924): 401–2+; (October 1924): 493–94.

———. "A Close-Up of Baseball's Greatest Outfielder." *Baseball Magazine* 33 (October 1924): 497–98+.

———. "An Erratic Batting Champion." *Baseball Magazine* 34 (February 1925): 389–90+.

———. "The Extraordinary Career of 'Muddy' Ruel." *Baseball Magazine* 33 (July 1924): 359–60+.

———. "Fred Marberry, King of Relief Hurlers." *Baseball Magazine* 34 (December 1924): 304.

———. "Growing Better with Age." *Baseball Magazine* 34 (March 1925): 435–37+.

———. "Here's To a Veteran Pitcher." *Baseball Magazine* 34 (April 1925): 383–84.

———. "The Home Run Slugger of the National League." *Baseball Magazine* 33 (August 1924): 390+.

———. "How Max Carey Became a Baseball Star." *Baseball Magazine* 33 (October 1924): 483–84+.

———. "How the Big Leagues Compared in 1924." *Baseball Magazine* 34 (April 1925): 491–92+.

———. "How the National and American Leagues Compared in 1923." *Baseball Magazine* 32 (March 1924): 445–47+.

———. "If I Were Only Young Once More!" *Baseball Magazine* 33 (November 1924): 531–32+.

———. "Kelly's Place in the Greatest Infield." *Baseball Magazine* 32 (March 1924): 452+.

———. "The Man Who Gave Pittsburgh Its Batting Punch." *Baseball Magazine* 33 (November 1924): 536+.

———. "The Man Who Might Rival 'Babe' Ruth." *Baseball Magazine* 33 (September 1924): 435–37+.

———. "Our All American Baseball Club of 1924." *Baseball Magazine* 34 (December 1924): 311–13+.

———. "A Review of the Recent Scandal." *Baseball Magazine* 34 (December 1924): 299–300+.

———. "The Season's Pitching Sensation." *Baseball Magazine* 34 (February 1925): 401+.

———. "What Hornsby's Record Might Have Been." *Baseball Magazine* 34 (January 1925): 347–48.

———. "Why Jack Bentley is a 'Victim of Circumstances.'" *Baseball Magazine* 32 (February 1924): 386–95.

———. "Why Max Carey Should Be a Big Drawing Card." *Baseball Magazine* 33 (August 1924): 405–6.

———. "Why Need Baseball Apologize?" *Baseball Magazine* 34 (January 1925): 353–54+.

———. "Wrecking Baseball's Greatest Infield." *Baseball Magazine* 34 (March 1925): 453+.

Langford, Walter. "An Interview with Glenn Wright." *Baseball Research Journal* 19 (1990): 71–76.

Lawler, Joseph. "Jimmy Cooney in Two Unaided Triple Plays." *Baseball Research Journal* 13 (1984): 39–41.

Lehman, H. S. "Geographic Origins of Professional Baseball Players." *Journal of Education Research* (October 1940), 130–38.

Levy, Jane. "Ossie Bluege: The Quirkless Man." *National Pastime* 6 (Winter 1987): 18–21.

Lieb, Frederick G. "Baseball's Star Rookies." *Baseball Magazine* 33 (August 1924): 393–95+.

———. "Has Batting Returned to a State of Normalcy?" *Baseball Magazine* 34 (March 1925): 449–50+.

———. "The Passing of the Super-Pitcher." *Baseball Magazine* 33 (February 1924): 399–401+.

———. "Scoring Plays That Create a World's Champion." *Baseball Magazine* 34 (December 1924): 301–3+.

———. "The Star of the National League." *Baseball Magazine* 34 (January 1925): 349–50.

———. "What 'Color' Means to a Ball Player." *Baseball Magazine* 32 (January 1924): 349–51.

"Lively Controversy over the Lively Ball." *Literary Digest* 103 (October 5, 1929): 78–81.

MacDonald, Arthur. "The Psychology of Baseball." *Scientific American* 113 (August 28, 1915): 188–89.

———. "Statistics of Baseball." *Scientific American* 112 (May 1, 1915): 418–22.

Marazzi, Rich. "Al Schacht, 'the Clown Prince of Baseball.'" *Baseball History* 1 (Winter 1986): 34–45.

Mays, Carl. "Is Hornsby Baseball's Greatest Hitter?" *Baseball Magazine* 34 (February 1925): 391–92+.

McGeehan, W. O. "Baseball: 'Business as Usual.'" *North American Review* 204 (March 1927): 119–24.

McMartin, Jim. "Two Measures of Fielding Ability." *Baseball Research Journal* 12 (1983): 56–61.

"More Home Runs?" *Popular Mechanics* 45 (June 1926): 986–89.

Okkonen, Marc. "Team Nicknames, 1900–1910." *National Pastime* 6 (1987): 18–21.

Phelon, W. A. "Washington." *Baseball Magazine* 34 (December 1924): 307–9+.

———. "When Baseball Moves South for Spring Training." *Baseball Magazine* 32 (April 1924): 507–8+.

———. "Who Will Win the Big League Pennants?" *Baseball Magazine* 32 (May 1924): 531–33+.

Pietrusza, David. "The Business of Baseball." In *Total Baseball*, Edited by John Thorn, Pete Palmer, and Michael Gershman. Fourth ed. New York: Viking, 1995, 588–99.

Povich, Shirley. "1924: When Senators Were Kings." *Grandstand Baseball Annual* 1998, 14:62–66. Originally published in Washington Post, October 22, 1994.

"A Proposed Cure for the 'Dollar Germ' in the World Series." *Literary Digest* 84 (January 3, 1925): 24.

Puff, Richard A. "Silent George Burns: A Star in the Sunfield." *Baseball Research Journal* 12 (1983): 119–25.

"The Rejuvenation of Eddie Collins—Champion Base-Stealer." *Baseball Magazine* 33 (September 1924): 449–50+.

Rice, Grantland. "The Greatest Thrill of 1924." *Collier's* 75 (January 10, 1925): 16.

———. "The Mightiest Mauler: Hornsby the Great." *Collier's* 77 (March 13, 1926): 24.

———. "What Do They Do besides Eat?" *Collier's* 75 (March 28, 1925): 25.

Richard, Kenneth D. "Remembering Carl Mays." *Baseball Research Journal* 30 (2001): 122–26.

"The Sad Decline of Base-Thievery in Baseball." *Literary Digest* 82 (August 2, 1924): 52.

"The Sad Life of a Losing Manager." *Baseball Magazine* 32 (March 1924): 438+.

Sanborn, Irving. "The Decline of Curve Ball Pitching." *Baseball Magazine* 32 (April 1924): 483–85.

———. "The Problem of the Crumbling Pitching Staff." *Baseball Magazine* 32 (March 1924): 439–41.

———. "The Slimy Trail of the Baseball Pool." *Baseball Magazine* 34 (July 1925): 341–43.

———. "Who Won the Old Ball Game, Anyway?" *Baseball Magazine* 34 (March 1925): 441–43.

Selko, Jamie. "Harry Who? The Story of Harry Heilmann's Four Batting Titles." *National Pastime* 15 (1995): 45–50.

"The Sheet Anchor of the Washington Infield." *Baseball Magazine* 34 (February 1925): 404.

"Sixteen Years as a Big League Star." *Baseball Magazine* 32 (March 1924): 435–37+.

Smith, Chester L. "Barney Dreyfuss Unearths a Player Gold Mine." *Baseball Magazine* 34 (April 1925): 489+.

"Soaking the Old Apple, à la Mr. Hornsby." *Literary Digest* 78 (September 1, 1923): 55–57.

Spatz, Lyle. "The Best NL Rookie Crop? The 1924 Pirates by Far." *Baseball Research Journal* 16 (1987): 57.

———. "SABR's 1900–1948 Rookies of the Year." *Baseball Research Journal* 15 (1986): 2–4.

Steinberg, Steve L. "Free Agency in 1923? A Shocker for Baseball." *National Pastime* 20 (2000): 121–23.

Stephan, C. David. "Batting Barrages: Streaks, Tears, Booms & Rampages." *Grandstand Baseball Annual 1996*, 12: 100–14.

Stoddart, Dayton. "What Baseball Has Taught Ty Cobb." *Collier's* 74 (July 19, 1924): 7+.

Stump, Al. "Dames Are the Biggest Headache." *Baseball Digest* (September 1959), 5–7+.

"The Supreme Athletic Effort of All Time." *Baseball Magazine* 34 (January 1925): 341–42+.

Taafe, William. "Gone . . . and Forgotten?" *Sports Illustrated* 67 (October 26, 1987): 128–29+.

Thornley, Stew. "'Unser Choe' Hauser: Double 60." *Baseball Research Journal* 20 (1991): 20–21.

Trachtenberg, Leo. "Pete Sheehy: A Last Interview." *Baseball History* 1 (Winter 1986): 28–33.

Treadwell, L. S. "The Lively Ball." *Scientific American* 141 (October 1929): 310–12.

Vance, Dazzy, with Furman Bisher. "I'd Hate to Pitch Nowadays." *Saturday Evening Post* 208 (August 20, 1955): 27+.

"A Veteran's Grand Record on the Pitching Mound." *Baseball Magazine* 33 (August 1924): 387–89+.

Vorhees, R. L. "Joseph Kren Is Batmaker to the Kings of Swat: Interview." *American Magazine* 101 (June 1926): 66–67.

Wallace, Francis. "College Men in the Big Leagues." *Scribner's* (October 1927), 490–95.

Warburton, Paul. "George Sisler." *National Pastime* 19 (1999): 93–97.

———. "Rogers Hornsby." *Baseball Research Journal* 28 (1999): 3–7.

Ward, John J. "Baseball's Hardest Hitting Shortstop." *Baseball Magazine* 32 (February 1924): 405.

———. "Hollis Thurston's Great Record." *Baseball Magazine* 33 (October 1924): 488+.

———. "The Kid Who Starred in a World's Series." *Baseball Magazine* 34 (February 1925): 411.

———. "The Man Who Gave Washington Their Punch." *Baseball Magazine* 34 (December 1924): 298.

————. "Tris Speaker, King of the Two-Base Hitters." *Baseball Magazine* 33 (July 1924): 355+.

————. "A Unique Pitching Family." *Baseball Magazine* 33 (September 1924) 457+.

————. "A World's Champion Who Belongs." *Baseball Magazine* 34 (January 1925): 366.

"Washington a Winner." *Baseball Magazine* 33 (September 1924): 439–40.

"Washington Exults." *The Outlook* 138 (October 8, 1924): 195.

"Washington's Big Day in Baseball." *Literary Digest* 83 (October 25, 1924): 50–58.

Wayman, Joseph M. "Roush's Ruled-Out Batting Title." *Baseball Research Journal* 22 (1993): 9–10.

"What Is the Keystone of a Baseball Team?" *Literary Digest* 81 (June 21, 1924): 57–59.

"Why I Bear Down on Every Pitch." *Baseball Magazine* 34 (January 1925): 339–40.

Wooley, Edward Mott. "The Business Side of Baseball." *McClure's Magazine* 39 (July 1912), 241–56.

Wulf, Steve. "The Secrets of Sam." *Sports Illustrated* 79 (July 19, 1993): 58–64.

Yaffa, Lawrence. "An Era Most Have Forgotten." *Baseball Research Journal* 15 (1986): 60–61.

Reference Works

Carter, Craig, ed. *The Complete Baseball Record Book*. St. Louis: Sporting News Publishing Company, 1992.

Neft, David S., and Richard M. Cohen. *The Sports Encyclopedia: Baseball*. Fourth ed. New York: St. Martin's, 1994.

Reichler, Joseph L., ed. *The Baseball Encyclopedia*. Fifth ed. New York: Macmillan, 1982.

Thorn, John, Pete Palmer, and Michael Gershman, eds. *Total Baseball*. Seventh ed. Kingston, N.Y.: Total Sports, 2001.

INDEX

REED BROWNING received his B.A. from Dartmouth College in 1960 and a Ph.D. from Yale University in 1965. Professor Browning has taught in the Department of History at Kenyon College since 1967. He served as Provost from 1986 through 1994 and Acting President in 1989. In 2000, he was awarded the Trustee Teaching Excellence Award.